The
Life and Writings
of
Betsey Chamberlain

JUDITH A. RANTA

The Life and Writings of Betsey Chamberlain

NATIVE AMERICAN MILL WORKER

NORTHEASTERN UNIVERSITY PRESS

BOSTON

Library of Congress Cataloging-in-Publication Data

Ranta, Judith A., 1953–
The life and writings of Betsey Chamberlain : Native American
mill worker / Judith A. Ranta.
p.   cm.
Includes bibliographical references and index.
ISBN 1-55553-564-X (pbk. : alk. paper)—
ISBN 1-55553-565-8 (cloth : alk. paper)
1. Chamberlain, Betsey Guppy, 1797–1886.   2. Textile workers—
United States—Biography.   3. Indians of North America—
Biography.   4. Textile industry in literature.   I. Title.
HD8039.T42 U6636   2003
331.4'877'0092—dc21   2002015423

Designed by Steve Kress

Composed in Garamond #3 by Coghill Composition, Richmond, Viriginia.
Printed and bound by Maple Press, York, Pennsylvania.
The paper is Sebago Antique, an acid-free stock.

MANUFACTURED IN THE UNITED STATES OF AMERICA

07 06 05 04 03   5 4 3 2 1

To the Abenaki People,
Past, Present, and Future

Contents

Contents

Illustrations

Preface

ONE SPRING DAY in 1831, a thirty-three-year-old woman disembarked from a stagecoach in Lowell, Massachusetts, to begin working in the textile mills. Coming from New Hampshire, Betsey Guppy Chamberlain (1797–1886) discovered a town far larger, livelier, and noisier than anything she had previously experienced. Here were cobblestone streets lined with tall brick buildings; shop windows filled with colorful displays of calicoes, books, fruit, bonnets, confections, shoes, and much more; and sidewalks crowded with people of all descriptions. The clatter of whirling spindles and power looms resounded from the mills. When suddenly the bells began to ring, factory women came pouring into the streets, thousands of them—far more than a country girl from New Hampshire had ever seen together. Lowell was a place Chamberlain would come to know well, working there intermittently over the next nineteen years.

As Chamberlain took stock of Lowell, so Lowell observed her. She made a distinctive impression, with her long black hair, erect carriage, and graceful movements. Besides the trunk and bandbox that held her few articles of clothing and other possessions, Chamberlain carried burdens unknown to Lowell's many teenaged working girls. Her youth had been clouded by her father and brother's entanglement in a long series of legal cases and criminal charges. Then in 1823, two years into her first marriage, her husband, Josiah Chamberlain, had suddenly passed away, leaving her the care of two infants. She had struggled long but ultimately in vain to hold onto their small farm in Brookfield, New Hampshire. Finally, like so many other poor women of her time, she sought work in one of New England's flourishing textile mills, probably leaving her children back home with relatives or friends. In the mills a woman could obtain cash wages of two or three dollars per week—more than a seamstress or even a schoolteacher earned.

Chamberlain, knowing that her children depended on her, was fortified to endure the hardships of mill life. Like most factory women, she probably lodged in a corporation boardinghouse. Besides the pleasures of meeting new people and socializing, these accommodations had their hardships, including lack of privacy, poor ventilation, and sometimes inadequate food. Sharing a small room with five to seven other women must have taxed Chamberlain's independent spirit. And then there was the demanding work schedule: twelve to fourteen hours per day, six days a week. The excessive hours were the chief grievance of antebellum mill workers.

For those who could endure the hours and boardinghouse conditions, Lowell offered cultural opportunities that must have seemed almost unbelievable to an early nineteenth-century woman raised in a small northern New England community. The town abounded with libraries, bookstores, lyceum lectures, dancing and singing schools, balls, concerts, evening schools, circuses, and a host of other entertainments. In Lowell the first magazines written entirely by women were published. Chamberlain contributed to two of those, the *Lowell Offering* (1840–45) and *The New England Offering* (1847–50). Her rich and varied sketches reveal that she took full advantage of Lowell's libraries and culture. She became, as her mill companion, Harriet Hanson Robinson (1825–1911), later wrote, the *Lowell Offering's* "most original" and "most noted" writer.[1]

Besides her capacity for hard work, Chamberlain brought a depth of experience and talent to Lowell and to her writings. As her sketches and stories show, she possessed wit and humor; empathy; belief in women's rights; love of ballads and stories; enjoyment of festivities and all kinds of "merry-makings," as she called them; pride in her Native (or American Indian) heritage; as well as a great a hunger for learning. She was of mixed descent, English and possibly Abenaki or Narragansett—or both. In Lowell, as in her New Hampshire hometown, Chamberlain found herself surrounded by a predominantly Euro-American community. At a time when Native and mixed-race people were scorned, she found the courage to claim her heritage proudly and write in defense of Native people.

Although her writings convey her distinctive individuality and support for women's, workers,' and Native people's rights, Chamberlain published under multiple pen names, as did other frequent *Lowell Offering* and *New England Offering* contributors. Thanks to the efforts of Harriet Hanson Robinson, some of the *Lowell Offering's* poems, essays, and fiction can be traced to individual women. In 1902 Robinson published a key to the names and pseudonyms of many *Lowell Offering* writers, including Betsey Chamberlain, whom she knew for at least several years. Chamberlain's four signatures range from the ordinary "B. C." and "Betsey" to the more fanciful "Tabitha" and "Jemima."

Since Chamberlain's writings are scattered among four pen names and because she also assigned pseudonyms for places associated with her New Hampshire childhood (for example, "Salmagundi" for Wolfeboro), her identity and origins have been obscured. Some digging has been required to uncover her life history.[2]

Chamberlain has been as absent from published histories of Wolfeboro and Brookfield, New Hampshire, as from Lowell town histories. Although she published many sketches of Wolfeboro people and events, there is no mention of her in Benjamin F. Parker's massive *History of the Town of Wolfeborough, New Hampshire* (1901) beyond a notation of her first marriage. In Lowell histories only a few of the leading lights among the factory women, such as Lucy Larcom and Harriet Farley, are given any attention. The obscurity created by Chamberlain's pseudonyms, combined with her political writings, mixed-race heritage, and troubled family background, may well account for her erasure from mainstream local histories, which until recently have often neglected non-Euro-American community members.

A different picture of Lowell emerges when one considers the experience of an older, mixed-race woman such as Chamberlain. The standard view of 1830s and 1840s Lowell has been that of a rather bland, homogeneous community of young Euro-American farm girls working a few years before marriage, sheltered by the mill owners' paternalism. Likewise, the *Lowell Offering* has been characterized as a genteel publication, imitative of the era's ladies' magazines and lacking social criticism. A widow, Chamberlain worked as many as nineteen years to support herself, her children, and perhaps other family members. She took advantage of Lowell's cultural opportunities to publish some captivating, humorous pieces and others that challenge persecution of Native people, excessive mill hours, and women's oppression. Then, like so many early working women, Chamberlain disappeared from view. Knowing her life and writings helps restore the multicultural dimension often missing from Lowell and New England history. Her complex life and rich writings add greatly, as well, to our understanding of nineteenth-century American women.

Transcription of the Writings

The text reproduces thirty-four of Chamberlain's thirty-seven known writings, transcribed from the *Lowell Offering* and *The New England*

Offering with as little change as possible. While obvious typographical errors and irregular punctuation have been normalized, I have retained archaic usage and spelling. Endnotes identify obsolete or unfamiliar terms, as well as the numerous quotations and allusions. Chamberlain's sketches and stories have been grouped according to significant thematic or generic concerns, such as women's issues and the local-color sketch. Within chapters, the writings are arranged alphabetically by title, so that they can be easily located. The only exception to this is the placement of "The Whortleberry Excursion" before its sequel, "The Sugar-Making Excursion." Because of considerations of space and quality, three of Chamberlain's pieces ("Our Physician," "A Legend of the Olden Time," and "The Delusion of the Heart") have been omitted from this volume. Some discussion of these, however, can be found in the introduction.

Acknowledgments

WORKING ON THIS PROJECT, I have been blessed to meet many people I otherwise never would have and to receive their gracious assistance. In Lowell, Massachusetts, I was ably assisted by Martha Mayo of the Center for Lowell History and by the church historian Barbara F. Reed. Over the Internet, I received fascinating instruction in Abenaki history and genealogy from Nancy Lecompte of Ne-Do-Ba. I was privileged to meet two of Betsey Guppy's cousin's descendants, Jill Cresey-Gross and Maurie Hill, who generously shared their family files. My New Hampshire benefactors include Louise Gehman, Director of the Wolfeboro Public Library. Thanks also to Donald Erlenkotter for furnishing Boutwell family papers. I owe my greatest research debt to Craig F. Evans, town archivist for Brookfield, New Hampshire, who helped above and beyond the call of duty. Among other feats, he shared his discovery of Chamberlain's third marriage and her move to Illinois. And it was he who located the elusive Harriet Guppy Kelley obituary linking the women to the *Lowell Offering*. For these and other generous acts, as well as for his perceptiveness and good humor, I extend thanks to Craig. My appreciation also to the editors and anonymous reviewers at Northeastern University Press, whose encouragement and suggestions have added greatly to this book.

In terms of libraries, I am deeply indebted to the wonderful staff and superb collections of The New York Public Library, especially their Milstein Division of U.S. History, Local History and Genealogy. I received assistance at the New York Genealogical and Biographical Society Library, the Manhattan Family History Center of the Church of Jesus Christ of Latter-Day Saints, the National Archives and Records Administration's New York Regional Office, the New Hampshire State Library, New Hampshire Historical Society, the Center for Lowell (Massachusetts) History, Boston Public Library, Massachusetts Historical Society, the Library of Congress, Wheaton (Illinois) Public Library, and the Du Page County (Illinois) Historical Museum. The support of my colleagues at White Plains Public Library has been much appreciated. I am grateful to Brenda Goleburn and Pat Haag for sharing the journey. Love and many thanks, as always, to Marc for his encouragement, support, and forbearance with my research trips and countless hours at the computer. Author's proceeds will be contributed toward placing a memorial near the probable location of Betsey Chamberlain's unmarked grave.

Part One

Biographical
and
Critical Introduction

Piecing Together a Portrait

A MIXED-RACE WRITER of English and Algonkian heritage, Betsey Guppy Chamberlain (1797–1886) composed colorful prose pieces that include the earliest known Native women's fiction. She was also one of the first Native women to publish writings protesting Native people's persecution. Aside from her accomplishments as an early local-color writer, she was a feminist and humorist. Although Chamberlain's writings were admired in her own time, her work has since been forgotten, suggesting the extent to which the voices and experience of early American working women of color have been erased. Drawing from Euro-American and Native oral and literary traditions, Chamberlain's writings illuminate the multicultural roots of New England.

Although a portrait of Chamberlain has not yet been found, it is possible to piece together an image of sorts from various nineteenth-century writings. In one of her girlhood sketches, Chamberlain creates an unconventional and spirited self-portrait. Her narrator favorably contrasts her own ruddy hardiness with approved notions of pale, lady-like fragility as personified in a young neighbor, Ruthy: "Now though I in my young days was about as broad as I was long, with a face as round as the full moon, and cheeks as red as peony, and owned a pair of hands which had been lengthened and widened, thickened and roughened, reddened and toughened, by long and intimate acquaintance with the wash-tub, scouring-cloth, and broom-stick; though I was as tough as a squaw, and could not have been persuaded that I had a nerve about me, yet I never looked at Ruthy without blessing my stars that I was not 'a natural born lady.' "[1] This sketch appears in one of thirty-seven brief prose pieces that Chamberlain contributed to the mill women's periodicals, the *Lowell Offering* and *The New England*

Offering. In this and other writings, Chamberlain signifies her difference from the Anglo-American ideal of the delicate, pale lady.

In her mill memoir, *Loom and Spindle* (1898), Harriet Hanson Robinson furnishes an appreciative portrait of her companion, Betsey Chamberlain:

> Mrs. Chamberlain was the most original, the most prolific, and the most noted of all the early story-writers. Her writings were characterized . . . "by humorous incidents and sound common sense," as is shown by her setting forth of certain utopian schemes of right living.
>
> Mrs. Chamberlain was a widow, and came to Lowell with three children from some "community" (probably the Shakers), where she had not been contented. She had inherited Indian blood, and was proud of it. She had long, straight black hair, and walked very erect, with great freedom of movement. One of her sons was afterwards connected with the *New York Tribune*.[2]

Writing fifty years later, Robinson remembered vividly the excellence of Chamberlain's writings and her striking physical appearance.

The physical attributes that Robinson ascribes to Chamberlain evoke descriptions of other northern New England Native women, such as Molly Ockett (Abenaki, d. 1816), also remembered for "walk-[ing] remarkably erect even in old age." In Trudy Ann Parker's *Aunt Sarah*, a historical novel about the author's Abenaki great-grandmother, Sarah is depicted with "hair as black as a crow's wing" and "always carr[ying] her head high and her back very straight." Parker's Abenaki characters also share Chamberlain's desire for freedom and pride in her "Indian blood." Robinson's observation of Chamberlain's "great freedom of movement" suggests the latter's self-possession and vigor.[3]

Elsewhere in her book, Robinson quotes the comments of Abel C. Thomas, the *Lowell Offering*'s first editor. Thomas appreciated Chamberlain's writings and contributions to the factory women's Improvement Circle for writing and discussion, over which he presided. As he wrote: "Mrs. Betsey Chamberlain, a widow who worked in the mills for the support and education of her two children, was a constant Circle helper, and vitalized many pages of *The Offering* by humorous incidents and the wit of sound common sense."[4] Many of her sketches' autobiographical details can be matched to the life experiences of Betsey Guppy, born on 29 December 1797, the daughter of William Guppy and Comfort Meserve of Wolfeboro, New Hampshire.

Recovery of Chamberlain's Life and Writings

Assembling Chamberlain's biography has required much detective work, especially because her writings partially obscure her identity and because she lived a long life, married four times, and relocated from New England to the Midwest. The marginalization of the *Lowell Offering* and its writers, as well as the mill women's literary self-effacement and tendency to obscure their origins, compounds the difficulty of studying individual writers. Besides her four pen names, Chamberlain was known by five different surnames during her lifetime. Most often I have used "Chamberlain" or "Betsey," since she was known to the *Lowell Offering* as "Betsey Chamberlain" or "Mrs. Chamberlain." To reconstruct her life experience, I have consulted numerous sources, including internal evidence from her writings; Native oral traditions maintained by the Guppy family; public records including census, vital, town, probate, land, and court records; published genealogical and historical texts; and periodicals.

I discovered Chamberlain's identity by building from Robinson's and Thomas's biographical sketches. Once I had collected the writings published under Chamberlain's various pen names, I could cull autobiographical details from the texts. Fortunately, these include enough clues to enable discovery of the author and connect the life with the writings. Through Chamberlain, we can reach new insights into the meaning of work for the textile mill women who were the first American women to work in large numbers outside the home. As far as possible, Chamberlain shaped her work experience to her own ends, toiling intermittently to make money needed at home and taking advantage of Lowell's cultural opportunities for creative expression and recognition.

On Chamberlain herself, no comparable books or even articles have been published. Only a few nineteenth-century mill women writers (Harriet Hanson Robinson, Sarah Bagley, and Lucy Larcom) have been studied in depth,[5] and there have been no published compilations since the nineteenth century of the writings of an individual *Lowell Offering* writer. In the nineteenth century, several "mill-girl" authors (Harriet Farley, Harriot F. Curtis, Lucy Larcom, and Abba A. Goddard) published volumes of their own writings, all currently out of print.[6] Benita Eisler's recent anthology, *The Lowell Offering: Writings by New England Mill Women, 1840–1845*, includes three of Chamberlain's pieces but no background on the author or her writings.

When Chamberlain's *Lowell Offering* and *New England Offering* writings are brought together, the magnitude of her achievement becomes apparent. In about four years, while working twelve to fourteen hours a day, six days a week, and with only a few years of common-school education, Chamberlain wrote by hand the equivalent of 170 typed, double-spaced pages. A great need for creative expression and intellectual fulfillment must have impelled so much writing in such a short time and in circumstances so adverse to creativity. Since *Lowell Offering* writers received some payment for their contributions, economic gain may also have been a motive.

In an early sketch, "A Letter about Old Maids," Betsey Guppy Chamberlain's narrator explains her intention to record "recollections of my youthful days . . . chiefly recollections of simple country girls, the companions of my earlier years" (p. 158). Indeed, most of her writings recount incidents or legends associated with her hometown, Wolfeboro, New Hampshire, and environs. Chamberlain's insistence on simplicity is something of a pose, although she imbues many of her pieces with a captivating naïveté. Upon careful reading, one finds her "simple country girls" revealing unexpected depths and complexities. Likewise, study of Chamberlain's life and writings discloses a multifaceted and richly creative person.

Native American Identity: The New England Context

Several factors complicate the discussion of Chamberlain as a Native American writer. The history of Euro-American and Native relations in New England, coupled with a general lack of knowledge about Northeast Native history and culture, has obscured the history of New England Native nations and individuals. Many people's ideas of Indians have been formed around notions of the reservation-based Western tribes. But New England Native people differ significantly from those of the West, not only in their culture but in their history. At the time of European contact, fourteen or more nations that were related linguistically, culturally, and sometimes politically within the Algonkian Confederacy inhabited the area now known as New England. In Massachusetts these nations included the Wampanoag, Nipmuc, and Massachusett, while the Pennacook and Sokoki Abenaki inhabited New Hampshire. Enduring the earliest, most sustained colonial occupation, Northeast Native nations suffered great losses in population and land holdings resulting from disease, war, and settlers' greed. In New England, settlers' efforts to obliterate Native people's culture and existence were more prolonged and thoroughgoing than in other parts of the northern New World. Consequently, Northeast Native history and culture have been more difficult to recover, although many New England Native nations are currently enjoying a revival of membership and cultural recovery.

While there are numerous, sometimes large reservations in other regions, the Northeast possesses only a few tiny reserves. In some states, such as New Hampshire and Vermont, there have never been any reservations. Likewise, virtually nothing comparable to the West's extensive Indian censuses, such as the Dawes and Guion Miller rolls, exists for New England Native people. A report on the "Indians" of Massachusetts published in 1849, when Chamberlain was working in Lowell, lists only the names of those individuals—many racially mixed—living with known tribes, for example, the "Chappequiddic Tribe," the "Marshpee Tribe," and the "Dudley Tribe, Worcester." Cities such as Lowell and Boston, whose inhabitants surely included some Native and mixed-race people, are entirely omitted. In federal censuses, Native and mixed-race New England people were often identified as "white" if they lived in Euro-American communities, as did Betsey Guppy Chamberlain's family. The inadequacy of census and other records is symptomatic of the attempts to erase Native people's history and presence from New England.[7]

This is an appropriate moment to address issues of terminology currently applied to Native people. While the term *Native American* is now favored by many educated non-Natives, most Native people reject this label. They prefer to be identified by their tribal affiliations (Abenaki, Narragansett, etc.), but this is not possible for Chamberlain since hers is unknown. Her Native ancestry almost certainly derives from a tribe of the Algonkian Confederacy, so she could be described

7

as Algonkian-English. Nowadays the term *Native American* has been rejected by many Native people for its imperialist connotations. They regard themselves as natives not of America but rather of their own tribal lands. The Abenaki people, for instance, are natives of "N'Dakinna" or "our land." While some prefer *American Indian* to *Native American,* the term *Indian* is also inadequate, since Native people did not, of course, originate in India. When referring to Chamberlain, I have chosen to use the terms *Native* and *mixed race.* The label *mixed blood,* while still acceptable to some Native people, to others carries connotations of eugenics and racial impurity. The healthy debates surrounding language, as reflected in this manuscript, spring from the renaissance of Native culture, particularly in New England.

Until fairly recently, many Euro-Americans have considered Native people so entirely absent from New England that they are assumed to have left the area centuries ago or never even to have inhabited such states as Vermont. These misconceptions arise from the old ideology of the vanishing Indian. Recent scholars, most notably Colin Calloway and Laurel Thatcher Ulrich, have explored the pervasive early American ideology of the disappearing Indian. By the nineteenth century, many non-Natives believed that Native people were doomed to extinction, as disease and warfare reduced their numbers and the expanding non-Native population claimed their lands. The myth had particular salience for New England. As Calloway asserts, "Nowhere did Indian extinction seem more assured than in New England." Nonetheless, as shown in the essays collected in Calloway's *After King Philip's War: Presence and Persistence in Indian New England,* some New England Native people did manage to survive and adapt, often living quietly on Yankee society's margins.[8]

For Natives who did not conveniently vanish, several forces have worked to obscure their history and culture. Those nineteenth-century New England Native and mixed-race people who survived faced great pressure to abandon their culture and hide their identities. Many intermarried with whites or blacks, as happened with Betsey Guppy Chamberlain's forebears. Those who settled down to the Euro-American life of farming, as did the Guppy family, attempted to assimilate or at least appear to, effacing their Native identities. Calloway explains, "Indian people who did not disappear from view faced racism and persecution." Thus, many mixed-race New England families preserved evidence of Native ancestry only in oral traditions, often kept a carefully

8

guarded family secret. Chamberlain shares the problems of incomplete documentation so common among New England mixed-race people.[9]

Since Chamberlain, like most published Native writers, had a mixed heritage, how can she be characterized as a Native writer of the United States? Building upon the work of other scholars and writers, Kenneth M. Roemer has developed useful criteria for determining who is a Native American writer. Applying his four criteria (which follow), I would characterize Chamberlain as a Native writer, although her identity is partially veiled in mystery. One measure employed by the government and others to determine Native identity is an individual's degree of "Indian blood." Harriet H. Robinson's remark that Chamberlain "had inherited Indian blood," as well as Guppy family oral traditions going back many generations, suggests that she possessed at least one-quarter Native blood. The Guppy family today maintains that their eighteenth-century forebears in Wolfeboro and Brookfield, New Hampshire, derived their ancestry in part from local Abenaki. According to family correspondence and other documents, Joshua Guppy (Betsey's paternal grandfather) married an Indian woman in Wolfeboro.[10]

Another of Roemer's measures is community opinion. We know that among Chamberlain's contemporaries at least Robinson considered her Native, and she has been accepted as such by some current Native people. Several of Chamberlain's writings and part of my research on her have been included on an Abenaki Web site, *Ne-Do-Ba*. Commitment to Native causes, the third criterion, is at least as important as the foregoing ones. Chamberlain's publication of two pieces, "A Fire-Side Scene" and "The Indian Pledge," strongly criticizing Euro-American persecution of Native people, demonstrates that she was deeply committed to Native causes for at least the period of her residence in Lowell. Moreover, Robinson recalled that Chamberlain "was proud of" her "Indian blood." In order to face the reaction of her Euro-American Lowell neighbors to her writings, she must have been sustained by a strong commitment.[11]

Roemer's final criterion, self-concept, is probably the most difficult to apply to Chamberlain. Since none of her correspondence, diaries, or other personal writings have been found, little is definitely known about how she viewed herself. The autobiographical details of her writings suggest that she did indeed consider herself Native or mixed-race, and that she was proud of this heritage. The narrator of "Recollections of an Old Maid. Number 1" boldly describes herself in girlhood as

having "a face as round as the full moon, and cheeks as red as peony."
Hard work has rendered her "as tough as a squaw" (p. 164). It is
unlikely that a nineteenth-century Euro-American woman would have
compared herself to a "squaw." In the considerable Native features
and content of her writings, Chamberlain virtually acknowledges her
lineage.[12]

Chamberlain's Achievement as an Early Native Writer

Chamberlain's writings appeared contemporaneously with the earliest
known published Native women's writings. These include correspondence transcribed in such Euro-American-authored tractate texts as
The Little Osage Captive (1821) and *Memoir of Catharine Brown, a Christian Indian of the Cherokee Nation* (1825), as well as the part-Algonkian
Ann Plato's *Essays Including Biographies and Miscellaneous Pieces, in Prose
and Poetry* (1841). Chamberlain's writings, appearing from 1840 to
1850, comprise the fullest and most varied known corpus published
by an early Native woman. Her pieces "The Indian Pledge" (1842)
and "A Fire-Side Scene" (1842) feature some of the earliest known
Native women's published protests against Indian persecution, the
first being Ann Plato's "The Natives of America" (1841). Moreover,
Chamberlain's "A Legend of the Olden Time," "The Indian Pledge,"
and "The Delusion of the Heart" are the earliest recovered published
fiction by a Native writer. ("A Legend of the Olden Time" and "The
Delusion of the Heart" are not reproduced in this volume.)

In speaking of Chamberlain's literary achievement, it is important
to remember that a vast body of Native women's oral literature preceded, coexisted with, and followed her written efforts. The novelty of
Chamberlain's creative achievement is deeply rooted in Native oral
culture. Written literature, imposed on North American Native cultures by Euro-American settlers, has never been embraced by all Native people. To some traditional Algonkian, as Evan T. Pritchard
(Micmac) explains in *No Word for Time: The Way of the Algonquin People,*
"writing in the English way is an unnatural thing to do and causes
confusion." The traditional Wabanaki (Native people inhabiting Abenaki homelands) he knew neither owned nor read books and had no
interest in them. Their interests lay in maintaining and contributing
to their own oral literatures and cultures.[13]

Fig. *1*. Woman weaver, Lowell banknote, circa 1860. *Courtesy of the Lowell Historical Society*

Chamberlain's writings constitute a hybrid product of Euro-American and Native cultures, attesting to New England Natives' "presence and persistence." Although her family managed to remain in New England into the nineteenth century, during Chamberlain's lifetime they lost their foothold in the Wolfeboro, New Hampshire, area. Like many other nineteenth-century New England Native and mixed-race women, Chamberlain was gradually dispossessed of the property once enjoyed by her family. She and her sister traveled to work in the textile mills of Newmarket, New Hampshire, and Lowell, Massachusetts—an experience shared by other New England Native women (see Figure 1).[14]

Loom and Spindle's brief comments distinguish Chamberlain as someone unusual among *Lowell Offering* writers, most of whom seem to have been young, single Euro-American women. But Chamberlain, a widow and mother, openly claimed (at least to Robinson) her "Indian blood"—a courageous act given the era's anti-Native racism. Robinson's identification of Chamberlain's pseudonyms enables one to trace thirty-three prose pieces written by her and published in the *Lowell Offering* between October 1840 and January 1843. From December 1848 to February 1850, four additional brief prose texts appearing in *The New England Offering*, a Lowell periodical continuing the *Lowell Offering,* can be attributed to her. According to Harriet H. Robinson's unpublished papers, Chamberlain's writings appear in *The New England Offering* under the signature "Betsey."[15]

Chamberlain's prolific *Lowell Offering* and *New England Offering* contributions constitute an unusually full body of work that suggests much about her views and experience. Woman-centered, her many engaging local-color sketches offer original portraits of ordinary—and sometimes extraordinary—rural women. Perceptive, strong, and unconventional, Chamberlain infuses her best writings with vitality and humor. The sketches also represent many facets of rural life in the early republic, conveying as well the strain of bridging two antagonistic cultures: that of the persecuted and suppressed Northeast Algonkian and that of the dominant Anglo-Protestant society.

Several of Chamberlain's writings reflect knowledge of the Algonkian, specifically Narragansett or Wampanoag, language and religious beliefs, indicating that she was of Northeast Native stock, possibly Narragansett. Although the Narragansett are usually associated with the Rhode Island area, because of extensive migrations of Northeast Native people Chamberlain could have been part Narragansett. Several New Hampshire histories, including Frank B. Sanborn's *New Hampshire,* trace the migration of Narragansett and other southern New England Algonkian to New Hampshire and elsewhere after the death of Metacomet (known as "King Philip") and the defeat of the New England Indians in King Philip's War in 1676. Chamberlain's ancestors could have been among the Narragansett migrating north into New Hampshire, where several generations of her Euro-American forebears lived.[16]

Her ambivalent treatment of Euro-American and Native cultures correlates with her bicultural identity. While two of her pieces express anger at persecution of Native people, several others reflect identification with Euro-American culture and even some stereotypical representation of Native "savages." This ambivalence can be seen in the work of other nineteenth-century mixed-race writers of New England, such as William Apess (Pequot) and Ann Plato (Algonkian?/African American). Like Chamberlain, they were living and writing in an era of intense persecution of Native people, and their writings embody the clash of cultures.

Critical Approaches

A work of feminist recovery, this text employs feminist and new historicist approaches to illuminate the historical and oral and written literary traditions informing Chamberlain's richly varied writings. It would not even be possible to recover a mixed-race mill worker's writings if not for recent scholarship opening up the field of noncanonical American writing. Since the 1980s, literary studies such as Cathy N. Davidson's *Revolution and the Word* (1986) and David S. Reynolds's *Beneath the American Renaissance* (1988) have turned attention to the breadth and hitherto-unacknowledged interest of nineteenth-century "popular" literature. Chamberlain epitomizes the undeservedly dismissed nineteenth-century popular author.

Aside from gauging Chamberlain's achievement as a Native writer, I have included a survey of early American writings by and about Native people, many of which are little known. Chamberlain's writings are examined against the backdrop of others anticipating hers, such as the tractate *Poor Sarah; or, The Indian Woman* (1820), *The Little Osage Captive* (1821) by Elias Cornelius, and *Memoir of Catharine Brown* (1825) by Rufus B. Anderson; the work of the Ojibwa Jane Johnston Schoolcraft (Bame-wa-was-ge-zhik-a-quay); Lydia Maria Child's pro-Native "Adventure in the Woods" (1826) and *The First Settlers of New-England* (1829); William Apess's writings; Frances H. Whipple's *Memoirs of Elleanor Eldridge* (1838); Ann Plato's *Essays Including Biographies and Miscellaneous Pieces* (1841); and other writings about Natives appearing in the *Lowell Offering*.

Given her woman-centered and feminist qualities, Chamberlain also makes a significant contribution to women's culture. Since humor represents one dimension of her feminism, I will discuss Chamberlain's writings in the context of such early American female humorists as Tabitha Tenney and Caroline Kirkland. Taken together, Chamberlain's writings make a stronger feminist statement than can be found in the work of not only other *Lowell Offering* writers, but even many other antebellum female literary writers. One of her dream visions, "A New Society," advocates fair wages for laborers, equal pay and educational opportunities for men and women, and an eight-hour workday—a radical concept at a time when workers were struggling for the ten-hour day. Chamberlain also expresses her feminism in her village sketches of rural New Hampshire women, examining the quality of women's lives and often recommending changes in societal views and treatment of them. She promotes women's education and improved treatment of old women.

Of her thirty-seven periodical pieces, twenty-eight are autobiographically based local-color sketches reflecting influences of Washington Irving, Mary Russell Mitford, Sarah J. Hale, and Catharine Sedgwick. The texts also reveal oral literary influences, including Native ones. Examination of the autobiographical qualities of Chamberlain's writings shows that she altered and shaped occurrences, especially those connected with family troubles, to suit her rhetorical purposes, revealing the truth while protecting her family's privacy. Thus she shielded her children and other family members from public scrutiny, while preserving her opportunity to publish. A discussion of the elements of oral literary traditions informing Chamberlain's sketches will show how she participated in storytelling traditions that were a vital feature of her culture. It is my hope that this study will contribute to illuminating common people's oral and written culture in the post-Revolutionary period.

Chamberlain's Life and Family

THE BIOGRAPHICAL FRAGMENTS gathered from Chamberlain's writings and various secondary sources enable a partial reconstruction of her personal and family history, allowing a rare glimpse into the life of an early American long marginalized because of her gender, race, and class. While this biography inevitably includes some gaps, it is possible to outline Chamberlain's life into old age, revealing that she lived a full and long life until the age of eighty-eight, moving from New Hampshire to Massachusetts to Illinois and marrying four times. Although her oftentimes naïve writings project the self-image of a simple, contented country woman, Chamberlain's life circumstances as revealed in public records and the occasional authorial aside suggest considerable family and personal hardship. Chamberlain emerges as a complex woman who faced grave loss and disappointment in personal relationships, including the early deaths of her mother and first husband and her father's serious legal troubles. She also struggled with her own "turbulent" emotions and tendency to "gloomy sadness," probably exacerbated by the discrimination and racism she encountered.[17]

The biography traces Chamberlain's ancestors back four or more generations, and considers the familial and historical heritage that shaped her character and writings. While some documentation links her Native ancestry to her paternal line, she could also have inherited "Indian blood" from yet undiscovered sources on her mother's side, since mixed-race people tended to intermarry. Guppy family oral tradition and Nicholas Guppy's "Genealogy of the Guppy Family" maintain that Chamberlain's paternal grandmother, Sarah Loud Guppy, was an Abenaki woman. Heritage aside, Chamberlain's other life experience can also be discussed, including her four known marriages and

Fig. 2. William H. Bartlett engraving, "Lake Winnipisseogee from Red Hill" (1836). *Courtesy of the New York Public Library*

two children. The rather meager evidence of her later life suggests that she continued to struggle with family troubles and financial difficulties into old age. Widowed twice, Chamberlain exercised considerable independence and strength in supporting herself, her children, and sometimes other family members for many years.

Roots in the Wolfeboro, New Hampshire, Area

Although Chamberlain assigns pseudonyms for most geographic and personal names associated with her hometown, close reading reveals that she was raised in the beautiful town of Wolfeboro, New Hampshire, on the southeastern shore of Lake Winnipesaukee (Figure 2). The location of her early life is confirmed by several sketches in which the narrator refers to her hometown as "Salmagundi." In "The First Wedding in Salmagundi," the narrator explains that the country estate of New Hampshire's Governor John Wentworth—an actual person—

"was in Salmagundi" (p. 187), and local histories reveal that Wentworth's house was in Wolfeboro. Several other pieces concern occurrences in the vicinity of Lake Winipisiogee (as Lake Winnipesaukee was called in the nineteenth century; there is some variation in spelling). In "Sabbath Morning," Chamberlain's factory-girl narrator longs to return to her "own loved Winipisiogee . . . [where she] could discern the islands of Varney and Barndoor . . . also Rattlesnake Island" (p. 132). These Lake Winnipesaukee islands are all visible from the southern part of Wolfeboro, where Chamberlain lived as a child and young woman.

Two of her local-color sketches, "The Black Glove" and "The First Wedding in Salmagundi," recount incidents of Wolfeboro history that would have been known only to someone closely connected with the town. "The Black Glove" tells of a Quaker woman, Hannah B., knitting a glove for Mr. A., soon to be ordained to the town ministry. In his *History of the Town of Wolfeborough*, Benjamin F. Parker relates the late-eighteenth-century occurrence of Mrs. Bassett, "the wife of John Bassett, the Quaker," knitting a black glove for Ebenezer Allen prior to his ordination. Parker explains that the glove was needed to cover "the stump" of Allen's arm, severed in an accident.[18] Chamberlain's narrator discreetly notes that Mr. A. had "but one hand" (p. 180).

Wolfeboro's first wedding was remembered by the townspeople as a great event. Chamberlain devoted a story to it, and Benjamin F. Parker and another historian also remarked on the occurrence. As a child, Chamberlain's narrator heard about "The First Wedding in Salmagundi" from "Johnny O'Lara, an old man, who used to chop wood at [her] father's door" (p. 187). The first couple were wed under an oak tree on Lake Winnipesaukee's shore. According to Parker's *History*, they were Reuben and Sarah Libby, married "under the branches of a large oak tree." In *The Libby Family in America*, Charles T. Libby recounts the wedding of Reuben and Sarah Libby at "Wolfborough Neck" in 1766: "They were married under an oak tree on the shore of the lake." To her own wedding sketch, Chamberlain adds such gay details as "three musicians, with a bagpipe, fife, and a Scotch fiddle," and a dinner of "plum puddings, baked lamb, and green peas" (p. 189).[19]

These prose pieces and several others in which Chamberlain's narrator recounts childhood memories confirm that she lived most of her early life in Wolfeboro. Located in Carroll (originally Strafford) County,

Wolfeboro prior to Euro-American settlement had been the home of the Abenaki Native people of the Northeastern Algonkian Confederacy. Q. David Bowers explains in his recent Wolfeboro history that when English settlers took possession of the land in 1759, few Native people remained in the area. Many had died from disease, war, and starvation. When the French and Indian War ended in 1760, most of the remaining Natives migrated north "to the French settlements on the St. Lawrence River." In the Lake Winnipesaukee region, Native peoples' activities had included hunting, fishing, and growing corn, beans, and squash. The Abenaki scholar Henry Lorne Masta traces the name *Winnipesaukee* to the Abenaki words *Wiwninbes aki*, meaning "lake between and around land or islands" (*wiwni* meaning "around," *nbes* denoting "lake," and *aki* for "land" or "island"). Native relics found in or near Wolfeboro and currently housed at the Libby Museum include a stone hearth, tools, arrowheads, and dugout canoes. Intriguingly, Benjamin F. Parker explains, "Within the limits of Pine Hill cemetery there was, when Wolfeborough was first settled, a cleared spot of ground called the 'Indian Dance.'"[20]

Although the number of Wabanaki people dwelling near Lake Winnipesaukee had dwindled by 1760, previously there had been much mixing of Indians and Euro-Americans in New Hampshire settlements. In his history of King Philip's War, George M. Bodge describes the close intermingling of Native people and settlers in seventeenth-century Dover: "Dover was a frontier town. . . . Large numbers of Indians were coming and going among the settlers, were received and entertained in their houses, were well acquainted with the habits and peculiarities of their home-life and ways of business and worship, and it is probable that there was no place in the Colony where the relations of settlers and Indians were more free and kindly than in this settlement at Dover." Apparently, the close association of Natives and Euro-American settlers continued into the mid-eighteenth century. In his work on New England Native people, Colin G. Calloway cites Susanna Johnson's observations of Indians' and settlers' free mixing in 1750s New Hampshire.[21]

Several of Chamberlain's male Guppy and Meserve ancestors were living in the Dover and Winnipesaukee areas in the early eighteenth century. One "Jeames Gupy" resided in Dover circa 1715 to 1718. In 1733 in Dover, New Hampshire, James and Joshua Guppy were among the signers of a petition to Governor Belcher, and in 1732 Mr.

James Guppy dwelled in Somersworth, New Hampshire. According to another source, in 1736 James Guppy sold some of the Dover land on which he had been living. It is not known whether or how this James Guppy was related to Betsey's grandfather, Joshua Guppy, but given the Guppy name's rarity he probably was kin. According to "Walter Bryent's Winnipesaukee Journal, 1747," both "Sergant Guppy" and "Colonel Miserve" had traveled to "winipesockee pond." Northern New England's frontier conditions and the scarcity of Euro-American women sometimes resulted in cohabitation or marriage between Euro-American men and Native women.[22]

In the late eighteenth century when Betsey Guppy Chamberlain was born, about nine hundred people, many of them Euro-American settlers from Portsmouth, New Hampshire, lived in Wolfeboro. Most subsisted upon farming, an arduous occupation given New Hampshire's rocky soil and harsh climate. The settlers raised Indian corn, rye, flax, potatoes, and turnips. Fish and meat supplemented their diet. Among a myriad of child-care responsibilities and household chores, women made cloth and prepared the family's clothing. They spun wool, cotton, and flax, and from the cloth woven at home sewed their families' clothing. Betsey Chamberlain's *Lowell Offering* pieces represent many facets of everyday life in early Wolfeboro, particularly women's activities such as spinning, sewing, knitting, cooking, and child care. For some of her female characters, as for Chamberlain herself, reading and study formed as much a part of daily life.[23]

In 1853 while attending a Free Soil Convention in Wolfeboro, John Greenleaf Whittier described the beautiful town and its surroundings for the *National Era:*

> Ten miles from Alton Bay, gliding between a long projecting headland and a small island, we enter a broad and beautiful bay, at the head of which lies the village of Wolfeboro,' its dwellings brilliant in white and green, scattered in picturesque irregularity along the fertile slopes of the southward trending hills, looking out over crystal clear waters upon long broken ranges of misty mountains on the opposite shore. Nothing finer than its site can be found in New England. It has two large hotels, a flourishing academy, an orthodox [i.e., Congregational] and Friends' meeting house. . . . The lake itself, some twenty-four miles in length by ten in its widest

part, is about 500 feet above tide water, and is walled around by mountains from 800 to 2,000 feet higher. Back of these still loftier summits lean hard and blue against the northern sky—Ossipee, White Face, Chocorua's Peak, Moorehillock; and, misty and dim beyond all, the great Notch mountains.[24]

Wolfeboro must have looked much the same—minus the hotels—in the earlier decades of Betsey Chamberlain's youth. As her sketches "The First Wedding in Salmagundi" and "Sabbath Morning" show, she too appreciated Winnipesaukee's beautiful, "limpid" waters and the view of the distant mountains.

Finding Betsey Chamberlain in Wolfeboro

In searching for Betsey Chamberlain in Wolfeboro, it was necessary first to determine whether she was a single or married woman. While both Abel Thomas and Harriet Robinson describe her as a widow and mother, in her writings Chamberlain's narratorial persona often characterizes herself as an "old maid." I think, however, that her assumption of this persona was an element of the fanciful, a mask assumed for various reasons, including protecting her children from anti-Native racism and expressing her sense of marginality. Her sister Harriet Guppy, who also worked in Lowell mills and may have collaborated in some writings attributed to Betsey, was in her late thirties and never married when the old maid writings were published. The old maid persona may, therefore, represent Harriet more than Betsey. Also, though Betsey was not herself an old maid, she, like Harriet, was middle-aged. At the time of her factory writings, she was considerably older than her typical young coworker. One autobiographical sketch suggests her age. In "Old Maids and Old Bachelors" (1840), Chamberlain's narrator describes herself as a spinster whose age is about "'twice six, twice seven, twice twenty and eleven,' abating one of the twenty's and the eleven" (p. 159). This would make her forty-six, born about 1794.

While there were not any unmarried women named Betsey Chamberlain born in or near Wolfeboro in the 1790s, there were several Betseys born then who married Chamberlains. At the time, Betsey was a popular girls' name, and a few Chamberlain families lived in the

Wolfeboro area. One Betsey Adams Horne (b. 1793), married to William Chamberlain in 1811, died in 1835, so she could not have been the Betsey Chamberlain writing for the *Lowell Offering* and *New England Offering* between 1840 and 1850. Another Betsey, born in 1796, married Ira Chamberlain, but she died in 1840, according to a Wolfeboro cemetery inscription. Betsey Allen Rust, born 13 December 1790 in Wolfeboro, married James Chamberlain Jr., of Brookfield, in 1807 and died in 1816.[25]

Born several years later than is suggested in "Old Maids and Old Bachelors," one Betsey Guppy (or Betsy Guppey) born in or near Wolfeboro on 29 December 1797 emerges as the sole candidate for the *Lowell Offering*'s Betsey Chamberlain. Although no birth record has survived, she was likely born in Brookfield, New Hampshire, since her parents lived there until June 1798. The Brookfield town records note that her father, William, served as the constable and tax collector from March until June 1798, when "the removal of William Guppy out of town" transpired. Subsequently the family moved to the adjacent town of Wolfeboro, where Betsey spent her childhood. On 25 June 1820, in Wolfeboro, Betsey Guppy married "Colonel" Josiah Chamberlain of Brookfield, becoming another Betsey Chamberlain. Wolfeboro town records, as well as land and probate records, concerning Betsey Guppy and her family confirm many autobiographical details of the *Lowell Offering* and *New England Offering* sketches.[26]

In three autobiographical essays, the narrator remarks on her mother's early death and on a stepmother's presence. The narrator of "Old Maids and Old Bachelors" remembers "the good old maid who kept house for my father after my mother's death" (p. 159). In "Fortune-Telling," the narrator recalls a woman who provided her mother with domestic assistance and was very kind to her following her mother's death (p. 150). "Fortune-Telling" also reveals that this was a known fallen woman, suggesting that the Guppy family was quite tolerant and/or did not occupy the kind of elevated social position from which they could discriminate against others. In "The First Wedding in Salmagundi," the narrator remembers sitting at home knitting as a child with her "step-mother" nearby (p. 187). Wolfeboro town records confirm that Betsey Guppy's mother, Comfort, died on 14 February 1802, when Betsey was four years old. Her father remained single for nearly two years, until his marriage on 7 November 1803 to "Miss Sally Marden" of Wolfeboro.[27]

Fig. 3. New Hampshire farmer, early nineteenth century. *Courtesy of the New Hampshire Historical Society*

Forebears

On the identity of her parents and other forebears, Chamberlain's writings offer some clues connecting her with the Dame and Loud surnames (a pedigree chart tracing these and other ancestral lines is included in Appendix A). "The First Dish of Tea" concerns her great-great-grandmother, Abigail Van Dame, orphaned as a child in Portsmouth, New Hampshire. The sketch concludes with intimations of Abigail's later marriage to Captain Lowd of Portsmouth. Chamberlain's family's connection to Portsmouth is fitting, since many of Wolfeboro's early Euro-American settlers arrived in the 1760s from Portsmouth.[28] One mid-eighteenth-century Guppy ancestor was Sarah Loud (a variant spelling of *Lowd*) of Portsmouth, who, according to Howard P. Moore's *A Genealogy of the First Five Generations in America of the Lang Family*, married Joshua Guppy (1739?–1806).[29] Sarah Loud was the daughter of Solomon Loud and Abigail Dame, who married in Portsmouth on 7 March 1735.[30] In "The First Dish of Tea," Chamberlain's naming her character Van Dame and making her a great-great-grandmother rather than a great-grandmother—as she presumably was—accords with her other efforts to obscure her family's identity. On the other hand, Abigail Van Dame's identification as a great-great-grandmother may have been a *Lowell Offering* editor's or printer's error.

While Chamberlain's writings reveal little about her mother, stepmother, and siblings, they do indicate that her father was a farmer, as were most Wolfeboro residents (see Figure 3). "Recollections of My

Childhood" and "Cousin Mary" include reminiscences of the narrator's youth in a farming community. Like many early nineteenth-century men, William Guppy worked at several occupations to support his family. Many records show that he was also a joiner, a carpenter skilled in fine and ornamental work such as furniture-making. For several years he may also have run a tavern, having been issued a license in 1797. In their history of New Hampshire taverns and turnpikes, Donna-Belle Garvin and James L. Garvin contend that most early tavernkeepers enjoyed an "eminent social position." Chamberlain omits this facet of her father's occupations, although some of her sketches, such as "A Winter Evening," represent alcohol-related problems. Chamberlain's failure to mention her father's work as a taverner (an occupation pursued by several other male relatives, as well) probably derives from tavernkeeping's growing disrepute as the nineteenth-century temperance movement spread.[31]

According to Parker's *History of the Town of Wolfeborough*, the first William Guppy house was one of many two-story houses built in the late eighteenth and early nineteenth centuries. Harrison Moore of the Wolfeboro Historical Society, however, contends that the original Guppy house was probably quite small, perhaps one or one and a half stories high. The family's extensive land holdings reached down to Lake Winnipesaukee's shore, supporting Chamberlain's narrator's childhood memories of playing by the lakeside recounted in "Sabbath Morning." The original Guppy house burned and was replaced with a larger one built in 1842, currently standing at 295 South Main Street. The small dwelling where Betsey Guppy was raised may well have resembled the Clark house, built in 1778, about one-quarter mile north on South Main Street (Figure 4).[32]

Although Chamberlain's narrator relates growing up in humble circumstances, town and court records and local histories suggest that William Guppy was a notable and prosperous—albeit a troubled— Wolfeboro resident. In October 1798, not long after moving from Brookfield, William Guppy owned one hundred acres of Wolfeboro land and a dwelling valued at ten dollars. For several years including 1804, he held the position of constable. In town affairs, according to Benjamin F. Parker, the constable was second in importance only to the selectman, serving as "executive of the statue [*sic*] law" and "collector of taxes." William Guppy also participated in founding both a town library and the Wolfeborough-Tuftonborough Academy. De-

Fig. 4. The Clark House (built 1778), Wolfeboro, New Hampshire. *Photograph by Judith Ranta*

spite, or in conjunction with, his legal struggles, William was shrewd and striving enough to accrue considerable real estate in the Winnipesaukee region. Land and probate records reveal that he amassed several hundred acres in towns including Wolfeboro, Brookfield, Tuftonboro, and Sandwich.[33]

On the "Guppey" family, the *Genealogical and Family History of the State of New Hampshire* notes that they were "of Flemish origin and were weavers." They emigrated from Flanders to England in the sixteenth century, and in about 1700 Joshua Guppey settled in New England.[34] William Guppy was the son of Joshua Guppy Jr., and probably of Sarah Loud, who married about 1766 in Portsmouth, New Hampshire. They settled in Brookfield, a New Hampshire farming village adjacent to Wolfeboro, and had at least six children.[35]

Several records suggest that Sarah Loud Guppy may have been an adopted or illegitimate daughter of the presumably Euro-American Louds. Possibly born in Portsmouth, she, like many eighteenth-century women, was illiterate, but her presumed mother and sister were not. A 1779 deed selling a parcel of Barrington, New Hampshire, land owned by the widow Abigail Lowd, as well as by "Joshua Guppy

Yeoman and Sarah his Wife of Middleton" and other family members, virtually confirms that Joshua's wife was indeed Sarah Loud, the daughter of Solomon and Abigail Loud. That she could not sign her name betrays Sarah Loud Guppy's illiteracy. This deed also reveals that Sarah's sister, Ann Loud Guppy, and mother, the widow Abigail Dame Loud, who signed their names, had acquired some literacy. Since a legitimate daughter was unlikely to be less literate than her mother, Sarah may not have been the natural or legitimate daughter of Abigail Dame Loud but was perhaps adopted or illegitimate.[36]

On Sarah Guppy's husband, Howard P. Moore notes that Joshua was a "husbandman and mariner." From 1764 to 1769, he paid taxes—and thus probably resided—in Portsmouth, New Hampshire. According to Chase's history of Brookfield, Joshua also served as coachman for John Wentworth, New Hampshire's governor from 1767 to 1775. He later became a taverner and constable. Following his death in 1806, the "Widdow Sarah Guppy" appears as a taxpayer in the Brookfield, New Hampshire, town records. Her modest property included one acre mowing and tillage, four acres of pasture, and two cows. She continued to pay taxes through 1822, probably dying near then. Her death record has not been found. Although the Guppy family had once owned considerable land in Middleton and Brookfield, they fell upon hard times. By the 1820s Joshua's son Samuel and his family, as well as his nephew Joshua (b. 1754), had become town paupers, dependent upon the Brookfield selectmen for their support. While Samuel Guppy and his wife and children were vendued in a pauper auction, Joshua was cared for by a townsman, Moses White-house, whose expenses the town reimbursed.[37]

Betsey Chamberlain's relatives' struggles shed some light on her entrance into the mills and prolonged employment of some nineteen years. The Guppy family's financial and other difficulties reveal that, although at times the family owned abundant land, their property's value was not substantial enough to prevent a slide into poverty. These difficulties must have contributed to the sense of personal hardship conveyed in Chamberlain's writings. They also illuminate some of the autobiographical features. In one local-color sketch of her hometown, "Tribute to Salmagundi," Chamberlain's narrator objects to the "inhuman practice" of pauper auctions, conducted "in neighboring townships" (p. 225). She thereby advances some social criticism and cautiously discloses some of her family history.

In town records and published sources, one finds—not unexpectedly—much less information about Betsey Chamberlain's mother, Comfort. Women's lives, of course, were not documented in the way many men's were. Town records indicate that Comfort and William Guppy had three children: Benjamin Franklin, born 20 August 1795; Betsey, born 29 December 1797; and Maria Antonnette, born 20 June 1800. A gravestone in the Lakeview Cemetery on North Main Street, Wolfeboro, furnishes several more crucial details. The stone marks another sister's grave, "Harriet Byron, dau. of William Guppy and Comfort Meserve," born 19 January 1802 and deceased December 1877. Harriet's gravestone supplies her mother's maiden name: Meserve. Since Comfort died on 14 February 1802, within several weeks of Harriet's birth, she may have died from childbirth complications.[38]

No town records were located under Comfort's married name, although some traces of her parents, grandparents, and earlier ancestors have been found. Genealogical records for Comfort Meserve appear in the *Family Search* database and in the *Boston Transcript Genealogical Columns. Family Search* identifies Comfort Meserve, born on 10 September 1772 in Dover, New Hampshire, to Stephen Meserve and Mary Yeaton. The *Boston Transcript* corroborates this record, adding Mary Yeaton Meserve's dates: 1753–1849. Born in Dover, New Hampshire, Mary (Molly) Yeaton Meserve was the daughter of Samuel Yeaton (1726?–1763?) and Patience (1730?–1760?; maiden surname unknown). A mariner and husbandman, Samuel was born in New Castle, Isles of Shoals, New Hampshire, and died in Rochester, New Hampshire.[39]

Having emigrated from England, the early Meserves included George, who settled in Wolfeboro in the eighteenth century. Comfort Meserve Guppy, however, was probably not born in Wolfeboro. Guppy family land records reveal that as a widow, Comfort's mother, Mary (Molly) Meserve, who married Enoch Wingate in 1794, left some land in Milton, New Hampshire, to her Guppy children. Thus, Comfort may have come to Wolfeboro from Milton, on the New Hampshire–Maine border. Her father, a yeoman, died in nearby Rochester, New Hampshire. Although Comfort died in Wolfeboro, her grave site has not been found. Like many area residents of that era, she was probably buried in an unmarked grave on family property.[40]

Stephen Meserve (1750?–1792), was the son of Lieutenant Clement Meserve (1716–1800), a Dover, New Hampshire, husbandman and

Revolutionary War veteran, and of Abigail Ham. In her last will and testament, dated 6 October 1801, Clement's wife identifies her own mother as "Abigail Ham" (Betsey's great-great-grandmother). It is not known whether Ham was a maiden or married name. Numerous Ham family members lived in Dover, back to the mid-seventeenth century. Betsey Guppy Chamberlain's great-great-grandmother may have been Abigail (maiden surname Ham or Hodgdon?; d. 4 January 1797), who married John Ham (1699?–1763?) about 1725 and gave birth to a daughter, also Abigail, before 1728. This relation would make Chamberlain a direct descendant of Elizabeth Hull Heard, whose daughter Mary married John Ham. She was spared during an Indian attack at Dover because of her prior kindness to an Native boy. The incident anticipates Chamberlain's representation in "The Indian Pledge" of a Native man's loyalty to a kindly Euro-American woman.[41]

The gaps in genealogical records for Clement Meserve's wife and others of Chamberlain's ancestors remain unexplained, perhaps because eighteenth- and nineteenth-century Americans tended to hide or deny evidence of Native ancestry. There is less ambiguity in tracing the ancestry of Clement, whose parents were Daniel Meserve (b. 1678) and Deborah Otis (b. 1683). The dearth of vital records on Clement's wife and children, however, may be significant. He lived most of his life in Dover, but few of his records have been preserved. In one comprehensive source of Dover vital records, Clement's marriage and his children's baptisms do not even appear. Only his death in 1800 is noted. On the other hand, the births of seven of his brother Daniel Meserve's children are recorded, as is the baptism of Daniel's wife, Abigail. Clement's family may have been omitted from the public record because there was something to hide, such as Native family members. In any event, it is possible that Betsey Guppy also had Native ancestry among her maternal ancestors.[42]

Childhood and Youth

How was Betsey Guppy Chamberlain's early life shaped by her family and their experience? Her autobiographical *Lowell Offering* and *New England Offering* writings, as well as public records, suggest some of her youthful experience and character. As a girl, she was accustomed to playing and roaming outdoors and working hard indoors. The narrator of "Recollections of an Old Maid. Number 1" recalls that in girlhood her hands were "lengthened and widened, thickened and roughened, reddened and toughened, by long and intimate acquaintance with the wash-tub, scouring-cloth, and broom-stick" (p. 164). As this sketch also reveals, Chamberlain knew that she did not fit the ideal of the "natural born lady" (p. 164). Proud of her vitality and capacity for hard physical work, she embraced her rank as a common woman.

Hardships in her youth strengthened her but also clearly burdened her with inner turmoil and sadness. Evidence of strife between the Guppy family and their neighbors elucidates some of the anger at Natives' persecution expressed in "The Indian Pledge" and "A Fire-Side Scene." Her mother's death when Betsey was four must have made a deep impact upon her and left her with an enduring sense of loss. The narrator of "Old Maids and Old Bachelors" recalls "the good old maid who kept house for my father after my mother's death" (p. 159). In "Fortune-Telling," the narrator remembers a neighbor woman who treated her compassionately following her mother's death, suggesting that Chamberlain recalled needing such kindness (p. 150). She honored her mother's memory by giving her daughter her name, Comfort.

Chamberlain's youth was also overshadowed by her father's legal troubles, which must have brought upon her the scorn of some— perhaps many—neighbors, as well as considerable emotional stress. Court records reveal that William Guppy had a difficult time getting along in Wolfeboro, having moved there under dubious circumstances. After being elected Brookfield constable and tax collector in March 1798, he and his family moved to Wolfeboro just three months later. Citing "the removal of William Guppy out of town," Brookfield town records suggest that he was pressured to leave. In Wolfeboro, as New Hampshire Superior Court records show, William's fortunes fluctuated between intervals of ostensibly peaceful residence and strife. From 1799 until his death in 1828, he was involved as either the plaintiff or defendant in twenty-nine Superior Court cases. Some of the charges brought against him, including theft and assault, were quite serious and probably caused Betsey and other family members much duress.[43]

Although neighbors' bias against the Guppys' Native heritage probably played a role in the family's legal troubles, the court records do not show clearly how or to what degree, since William Guppy won a fair number of the cases brought by or against him. His successes are qualified, however, by the fact that he usually won by default, that is, because his opponent failed to appear in court. Since several lawsuits were brought against William by his own children, including Betsey, his legal troubles cannot be construed only as neighbors' harassment. Still, the court records' evidence, viewed in conjunction with the removal of most Guppy family members from the Winnipesaukee area between 1830 and 1850, strongly suggests a pattern of harassment against the family. William was not the only Wolfeboro-area Guppy embroiled in legal troubles. Two "pleas of ejectment" were brought against his brother Samuel Guppy, a Brookfield resident, and nine lawsuits against his oldest son, Benjamin F., in just three years (1825–28). If intended to drive them off their land and out of the area, their neighbors' harassment succeeded, since William died in 1828 at the fairly early age of fifty-eight and both Benjamin and Samuel, as well as many other family members including Betsey, soon relocated.

Between 1799 and 1803, William Guppy brought one lawsuit to recover monies allegedly owed him. That the defendants were two Brookfield men—Reuben Hanson and Moses Whitehouse, a selectman—suggests enmity behind William's removal from Brookfield. After losing the case, Guppy appealed and won modest damages.[44] The years 1804 to 1807 were a quiet period, with no lawsuits brought by or against Guppy family members. During this time, William served as town constable and acquired more land in Wolfeboro and surrounding towns.

From 1808 to 1814, William got entangled in some serious troubles, including a burglary charge. In this period, six cases involving William as plaintiff or defendant were tried in the Superior Court of Judicature. Evidence of intense conflict with neighbors first surfaced in an 1808 case in which William accused Richard Rust of assaulting him in a Wolfeboro store. According to the court records, Rust "with force and arms assaulted the plaintiff [William Guppy] and then and there with force as aforesaid the said Rust did seize with his right hand the plaintiff by the collar and clothes and being so seized did violently push and shove the plaintiff out of the store in which he was then and there standing which greatly injured and bruised the plaintiff in many parts of his body." Against Rust, Guppy won damages and costs of court.[45]

Later in 1808, William Guppy was apprehended, briefly imprisoned, and tried by the state for allegedly breaking into a Wolfeboro
store and stealing merchandise. Samuel Mason claimed that William

> with force and arms did break and enter a certain store of one
> Samuel Mason . . . and six yard of black cotton cambrick of
> the value of six dollars one peice [*sic*] of durant of the value of
> two dollars one peice of purple striped calimanco of the value
> of two dollars one peice of vesting of the value of two dollars
> one shawl of the value of one dollar twenty five cents four pair
> of hose of the value of Five dollars one pinch beck watch of
> the value of seventeen dollars one small trunk of the value of
> one dollar seventy five cents . . . the goods and chattels of the
> said Samuel Mason then and there being found feloniously
> did steal take and carry away.

Besides the shawl, watch, trunk, hose, and textiles (cambrick, durant,
calimanco, and vesting), valuable at a time when cloth was still hand-
woven, Guppy was accused of stealing promissory notes signed by
Mason's debtors for 150 dollars' worth of goods and cash.[46]
  That the jury found William Guppy not guilty of the theft raises
the question of why he was accused in the first place, a question that
gains weight as Guppy's legal troubles, including another theft charge,
unfold. His neighbors' accusations may have derived from the rampant
nineteenth-century typecasting of Indians as savages and thieves.
Thus, when a theft or other crime occurred, a local person known to
be Native or mixed-race was likely to be charged. Despite the verdict
of innocence, William found Mason's charges so injurious that in 1811
and again in 1813 he sued him for defamation of character. Stating
that he, "William Guppy now is a good faithful and honest citizen of
this State and such from the time of his birth hitherto hath conducted
and behaved himself," he alleged that out of envy Samuel Mason had
attacked his character by charging him with theft. Describing himself
as "damnified" by the charges, William declared that he was "not only
greatly scandalized and injured in his good name credit & reputation
but also hath been compelled and under a necessity to lay out and
expend divers great sums of money in this behalf and also to undergo
great and arduous labours and troubles as well in body as mind." After
losing the first defamation case, William was fined the large sum of

157 dollars. Not long after, he again sued Mason for defamation and won very sizable damages and costs amounting to 553 dollars. This case is one of many in which initial verdicts were reversed upon retrial or appeal.[47]

The mutable verdicts notwithstanding, William's family must also have suffered scandal and injury resulting from the criminal charges brought against him. The financial burdens of his imprisonment and court costs, not to mention the insecurity caused the children by their father's detention, harmed his family as well. Charges against him must have hurt William's business prospects as a joiner, farmer, and taverner. In half—fifteen—of the twenty-nine cases in which he was involved, William Guppy sued neighbors for money owed him. Usually he was trying to recover payment "for value received," perhaps for crops or for his services as a joiner. The failure to pay may have represented his neighbors' disdain for him or another form of harassment.

In 1808 when her father was apprehended and imprisoned for theft, Betsey, aged ten, was still quite young and dependent. Although she likely suffered scorn and abuse from other children and neighbors, her writings omit direct reference to this painful subject. Some details, however, seem to link to her family's legal troubles. Chamberlain's familiarity with Superior Court proceedings is reflected by the narrator-self's remarking in "Witchcraft": "Some nineteen or twenty years since, two men, with whom I was well acquainted, had an action pending in the Superior Court" (p. 177). In "Recollections of My Childhood," the narrator's most vivid school memories are of punishments, including being whipped for failing to "courtesy" to the teacher on the street (p. 212). The teacher's knowledge of the criminal charges against Betsey's father, as well as of the family's "Indian blood," may well have contributed to her perception of the child's badness. In other writings, when Betsey's narrator recalls youthful socializing with Wolfeboro neighbors, they are nearly always Quakers. Given the Quakers' tolerance and inclination to defend the oppressed, Betsey and her family may have found in them acceptance and kindliness withheld by other neighbors. As Superior Court, probate, and land records reveal, William Guppy made great efforts to acquire land in Brookfield, New Hampshire, his probable birthplace and the town from which he suddenly removed in 1798. The desire to regain homelands appears as well in Betsey's "Sabbath Morning," when the Lowell factory-girl narrator longs to return to her "own loved Winipisiogee" (p. 132).

In terms of Superior Court records, 1815 to 1819 was another quiet period for William Guppy, when no lawsuits brought by or against him were recorded. The eight years before his death, however, comprised the period of his most intense legal troubles. From 1820 to 1828, William was involved in twenty-one cases, some quite serious. In 1820 he was again charged with theft. Moses Seavey of Wolfeboro accused him of trespassing on his property and stealing a mare, cow, saddle, and bridle, and perpetrating "many other injuries" against him. After Seavey won the case, William apppealed and the verdict was overturned. Although the court eventually pronounced him not guilty, this case again raises the question of why William was accused of theft in the first place. Exactly what provoked his neighbors' hostility, and why did they perceive him as a thief? Except for the likelihood of anti-Native bias, this question must go largely unanswered. Consisting of case summaries, the court records only hint at personal problems and community tensions and conflicts left undocumented.[48]

Most of the cases tried between 1820 and 1828 involve William's attempts to recover money or property, often Brookfield land, owed him. Several other more troubling cases involve his being charged with assaults committed against women. In 1823 the state tried William for an 1821 assault against Mrs. Susannah Drew of Brookfield. The court records report that he "did then and there with force and arms, beat, wound, bruise, and illtreat, and other wrongs to the said Susanna Drew." He was found not guilty (but was later retried for the same assault).[49]

As previously mentioned, Betsey's brother Benjamin also endured his share of legal trouble during this period. In 1826, both he and his father were particularly beset by one neighbor, Ichabod Richards, "Esquire," of Wakefield. The class implications of the battles are significant, as the lower-class Guppys took on the aristocratic Richards. Always identified as an esquire, Richards enjoyed his community's highest honorific, while Benjamin was labeled a husbandman or yeoman and William a joiner or husbandman. In 1826 Richards first successfully sued Benjamin for debt, imposing heavy fines upon him. Shortly after, Richards brought and won another lawsuit against Benjamin for allegedly assaulting him twice in Brookfield, burdening Benjamin with more large fines.[50]

Sometime later in 1826, Richards sued William Guppy for defaming and scandalizing him in 1824. The court records offer a glimpse of William's character, suggesting a source for Betsey's forthrightness and vitality, as seen in the passage characterizing herself "as tough as a squaw" (p. 164). In Dover, before their neighbors, William allegedly declared that Richards had "committed perjury" and "sworn to a lie," calling him "a damn'd rascal" and "a damn'd scoundrel." The jury found William guilty and imposed the stiff fine of 102 dollars. In his 1826 will, William apparently acknowledged his son Benjamin's need for defenses against their enemies. He bequeathed to him little more than an assortment of weapons: "my hand Sword, one pair of pocket pistols, one Coopers axe, one butcher knife, [and] one horse whip." Benjamin would continue to need such weapons. In a note dated 20 February 1830 found in an old Wolfeboro house, he challenged a neighbor to a duel to expiate a terrible insult made against him.[51]

From 1827 to 1828, Superior Court records represent Guppy family members turning against one another. If it is difficult to discover the reasons behind their neighbors' lawsuits, it is even harder to understand why the family began fighting internally. The pressures from neighbors may have finally caused them to begin collapsing from within. Again, the court records offer only case summaries. In 1827, Benjamin F. Guppy and his wife, Martha, filed suit against William Guppy for allegedly assaulting Martha on 7 November 1825. As in the case involving Susannah Drew, William was accused of trespassing "at said Brookfield with force and arms in and upon the said Martha made an assault and her then and there beat bruised and wounded and evil entreated and other enormities to the said Martha." Pregnant at the time, Martha was allegedly so injured that she lost her child, and her life "was greatly despaired of." The court ruled in favor of William, exacting a 14-dollar fine from Benjamin and Martha. Not long after, in an apparently retaliatory action, William sued Benjamin for debt. The court ordered Benjamin to pay William 174 dollars.[52]

In 1828, William lost several cases brought against him because he failed to appear in court. Since he died in August of that year, he was likely ailing in preceding months when the cases were tried. Joseph and Susannah Drew again sued him for his alleged 1821 assault against Susannah. This time the Drews won damages and court costs of 124 dollars. Infighting among Guppy family members continued when Betsey Chamberlain sued her father to recover the dower portion of her Brookfield farm. Simultaneously, Sally Langley successfully sued William to recover her own dower of Brookfield land.[53] Clearly, Chamberlain's father was a difficult man, whose legal troubles and antagonism must have caused her considerable anxiety and distress. On the other hand, he emerges as an individual of much energy, fortitude, and shrewdness, who fought hard against his neighbors' hostilities in an era of virulent anti-Native racism and Indian removals. Publishing her daring pro-Native writings in the midst of another predominantly white community (Lowell), Betsey must have drawn upon William's courageous example. She inherited as well his capacity for hard work and survival in trying circumstances.

Other than the court records and scattered clues in her writings, little is definitely known of Betsey Chamberlain's childhood and young adulthood before she married at age twenty-two. Her writings show that she belonged to the Congregational Church occupying the meetinghouse at Wolfeboro Center. Details of "Our Town. Number 2. Our Meeting-House" reveal her close familiarity with the church and its members, so she must have been a regular churchgoer. Moreover, her writings' numerous Biblical echoes and allusions show that she knew the Bible quite well, as did many factory women of her time. Besides religious worship, in her youth Chamberlain participated in community entertainments such as huskings, quiltings, singing-schools, balls, and debates (see illustration of the village, Figure 5).

Chamberlain's sketches also suggest that she actively joined in such women's collective activities as preparing trousseaus, attending weddings, and nursing the sick. Like many nineteenth-century women, she valued close ties with other women, treasuring their regard. In "Fortune-Telling," the narrator recalls that of a group of local girls invited to Aunt Nancy's house for storytelling and tea, she was one of two invited to spend the night. Her narrator also carefully notes instances when female relatives and neighbors called upon her for assistance. In "Recollections of an Old Maid. Number 2," she recalls being "sent for in haste to assist at the bridal preparations" of a neighbor, Caroline B., and later attending her through a "long nervous fever" (p. 167). Likewise, in "Cousin Mary," the narrator remembers being summoned by her aunt to tend her gravely ill cousin (p. 145). Besides showing that she possessed notable sewing and nursing skills, these remarks suggest that her father's troubles and the bias against her Native heritage did not always prevent neighbors from appreciating her qualities and talents.

Wolf boro'.

Fig. 5. Village at Wolfeboro, New Hampshire, 1859. *Courtesy of the New Hampshire Historical Society*

Teaching School

Several of Chamberlain's sketches reveal that she attended the district school in Wolfeboro for at least a few years. Her harsh schoolgirl experiences, as described in "Recollections of My Childhood," did not deter her, however, from briefly teaching school herself at age twenty-one. Local records show that she worked as a schoolteacher one summer in Brookfield, New Hampshire. Among the town records are found her signed receipts for wages earned from teaching "three months in the middle district in the sumer season" of 1819. She received a total of twenty-four dollars (probably two dollars per week for twelve weeks), not paid until 26 November and 6 December 1819.[54]

Chamberlain's experience was shared by the many New England women who became schoolteachers in the post-Revolutionary decades. In this early era, women were allowed to teach only during summer sessions, when girls attended school along with young children of both sexes who could be spared from farm work. Curiously, Chamberlain's

Fig. 6. Pleasant Valley School House (built circa 1805), Wolfeboro, New Hampshire. *Photograph by Judith Ranta*

schoolteaching experience is not represented in her *Lowell Offering* and *New England Offering* writings. She may have shared the unfavorable view of the profession held by other factory women writers, among whom some teaching experience was common. In a *Lowell Offering* editorial, Harriet Farley reflected upon her own brief stint, "To teach a country school was to have a paltry pittance a few months in the year, and be destitute of employment the remainder of it." Since factory work actually paid better than teaching and allowed for more personal freedom, Farley and other mill women writers found that they preferred it.[55]

In accepting Betsey as their children's teacher, if only briefly, her Brookfield neighbors must have regarded her as a sufficiently responsible and learned young woman. Certainly she was sociable and widely read, and she made no secret of admiring intellect in women. Significantly, no records could be found of her teaching in her hometown, Wolfeboro (see Figure 6). Her father's legal troubles and the family's consequent bad reputation may have prevented her from teaching there. But Brookfield, a smaller town with fewer eligible teachers, may have been less aware of the Guppy family troubles or less able to discriminate in their choice of teachers. Nonetheless, the difficulties may have blocked her path, since there are records of her teaching no more than one term in Brookfield.

First Marriage and Widowhood

Although her *Lowell Offering* sketches characterize Chamberlain's narrator-self as an old maid, Wolfeboro town records report that Betsey Guppy of Wolfeboro and Colonel Josiah Chamberlain (b. 28 August 1787) of Brookfield obtained a marriage certificate on 23 June 1820. They were married by the Rev. Asa Piper of Wakefield, New Hampshire, on 25 June 1820. Reverend Piper served as the pastor of the First Congregational Church in Wakefield from 1785 to 1835. A widower, Josiah Chamberlain had first married Bethiah Lowd of Shapleigh, Maine, in 1810. Bethiah died in 1818, leaving behind three children. It is not known to what extent Betsey assumed the care of these children. Other relatives may have cared for them, since the 1830 Brookfield census records that Betsey's household included only two children born after 1820. Nonetheless, for an interval after her marriage she may have helped care for Bethiah and Josiah's children. Some details of Josiah's life are known. He served as a lieutenant colonel in the New Hampshire State Militia. In the town records of Brookfield, New Hampshire, several items concern him, including his boarding a local schoolteacher.[56]

Within seven months of his marriage to Betsey, Josiah purchased a farm in Brookfield, becoming a husbandman. According to both Strafford County probate records and Chase's town history, Josiah purchased this farm (the property of his brother, the late Captain Ivory Chamberlain, d. 1818) from his mother, Judith Chamberlain, for 959 dollars on 30 January 1821. Judith had been appointed the administratrix of her son Ivory's estate. To pay off debts, she was forced to sell the property, agreeing in probate court to offer it in a way that "will be of the greatest advantage to the heirs of said estate." Josiah was one heir, and the "highest bidder and purchaser" for this land. The 200-acre farm included a "clothing mill," grist mill, and "dwelling house" already mortgaged for 260 dollars. The clothing mill building housed "one machine for carding wool and dressing cloth." The mill's operations must have helped prepare Betsey Chamberlain for textile factory work in Newmarket, New Hampshire, and Lowell, Massachusetts.[57]

On their Brookfield farm, Josiah and Betsey Chamberlain struggled to provide for themselves and their children. By 2 July 1822, Josiah had mortgaged the farm to Betsey's father for one thousand dollars. Even greater hardships were to follow. Records reveal that Josiah died intestate on 19 July 1823. On 5 September 1823, "Betsy Chamberlain of Brookfield was named Administratrix of the estate of Josiah Chamberlain, late of Brookfield, deceased." By June 1824, she had obtained a license to sell Josiah's estate at public auction. Brookfield town records report that on 1 April 1825, the "Widow Betsy Chamberlain" was "in possession" of "the farm formerly owned by Josiah Chamberlain," by then reduced to twenty-four acres. Betsey was able to hold onto some portion of the farm until 1837, although she began selling parcels of it in 1828.[58]

The inventory of Josiah's estate taken on 13 October 1823 offers some glimpses into the life of a poor farmer's wife. Betsey was kept busy with spinning and other textile work, since her belongings included "1 linnen wheel, 1 woolen wheel, 1 clock reel, and 1 pr cotton cards." She and Josiah owned six bed quilts, two coverlets, and a "Calico counterpane," probably made by Betsey herself. They did not, however, own a loom, so she may have shared a neighbor's. Writing must have been a regular activity, since their furniture included two writing desks. She and Josiah owned ten books: "1 lg. bible lettered on the back, 1 lg. bible not lettered, 1 v. 76 Statutes old Edition, 1 vol. Bartletts aphorisms, 1 testament, 1 vol. Robbins Journal, 2 Watts hymns, 1 vol. Watts logic, 1 vol. hapless orphan." The books are all of the serious, edifying variety, except for *The Hapless Orphan; or, Innocent Victim of Revenge* (1793), a popular sentimental romance by "an American Lady." A pair of gold earrings were Betsey's only jewelry.

Josiah's farm implements and militia uniform are counted among their belongings. Their livestock included "2 Cows, 1 Swine, 2 Calves, 2 Sheep, 3 lambs." Besides a modest amount of furniture and clothing, they owned a pair of snowshoes and implements for making maple syrup and sugar. The entire estate, including land and buildings, was valued at $343.33. A subsequent Administration Account reveals that Betsey paid out $255.61 to settle bills, leaving her with only $87.72.[59]

Brookfield town records indicate that William Guppy paid the taxes on his daughter's farm for 1824 and 1825, not surprisingly since he owned the property. By this time, William and his second wife (Sally) had had four children: Thomas Jefferson (b. about 1807), Frances (d. 12 August 1830 at age eighteen), William Penn (b. 1813 or 1814), and Comfort (d. 24 February 1829, aged nine). In 1826, two years before his own death, William Guppy wrote his last will and testament. Generous in his bequests to his other children, he severely shortchanged his eldest two, Benjamin and Betsey, for reasons unspecified in the will or elsewhere. Since in 1827 and 1828 both Betsey and Benjamin sued their father in Superior Court, they may well have challenged his authority in earlier years, angering him and provoking him to retaliate in his will.

William Guppy's final bequests deal especially harshly with Betsey, leaving her much less than his other children. To her he gave only "one cow which I lent her last Spring, and which she now has or has disposed of and one Dollar in money to be paid her by my said Executor." This bequest is particularly meager considering his gifts to his other children, and Betsey's plight as a widow supporting two small children. Her unmarried sister Harriet, for instance, received "sixty acres of land lying and being in said Brookfield, . . . [and] two hundred Dollars of furniture . . . [and] two hundred Dollars in money." The bulk of his property was left to his second wife and his sons by her. Her father's shortchanging of Betsey must have contributed to her becoming a mill worker, although to what extent is not clear, since Harriet also entered the mills in the 1830s. Again to Betsey's detriment, William's will directs that much of his holdings in farmland, including "the Farm formerly owned by Colonel Josiah Chamberlin," be sold and the proceeds donated to the Wolfborough-Tuftonborough Academy.[60]

Court records, specifically Betsey's suit against her father, suggest that she had learned about the will's contents prior to her father's death. She must have been greatly troubled by it. In February 1828, several months before he died and at a time when he may have been ailing, Betsey sued her father to recover her dower. In the early nineteenth century, the law of many states, including New Hampshire, stipulated that a widow receive one-third of lands owned by her husband. In ordering the sale of Josiah Chamberlain's farm, William had not provided for Betsey's dower. Since William did not appear in court, Betsey succeeded in recovering—at least on paper—one-third of Josiah's land. After William's death in July 1828, his inventory left to her the "Reversion of Land set off to the Widow Betsy Chamberlin as her Dower 50.00 [dollars]," certainly a minimal allowance but better than nothing.[61]

In *Women and the Law of Property in Early America,* Marylynn Salmon explains that nineteenth-century dower laws, generally closely followed, were intended primarily to provide immediate support for needy widows and dependent children, such as Chamberlain and her children. If a widow was not granted her dower, she could sue for it. It would have required at least as much courage as desperation for an early nineteenth-century woman to challenge her father in court. Apparently Chamberlain was aided by a woman friend's support, underscoring the importance of female friendship to her. On the same day that Chamberlain's case was heard in court, the dower case of Sally Langley against William Guppy was also tried. Since Langley lived in Maine in 1828, Chamberlain must have maintained a long-standing friendship with her. According to the court records, Langley sought to recover one-third of the Brookfield, New Hampshire, farmland that she and her deceased husband, William Langley, had owned before its purchase by William Guppy. According to local marriage records, Sally Langley had been Sarah H. Dearborn of Wakefield, New Hampshire, likely the intellectual "Sarah D." whom Chamberlain honored in "Recollections of an Old Maid. Number 3." Langley also won her case against William, who failed to appear. Betsey Chamberlain's and Sally Langley's simultaneous successful dower cases exemplify female solidarity triumphing against a male-dominated legal system. These events suggest the importance of women's friendship and support in Chamberlain's life.[62]

William Guppy's gravestone reveals that he died on 20 August 1828, at the age of fifty-eight. Although he owned extensive lands, their worth was to evaporate quickly. From an estate initially valued at $8,492.92, nearly all ($8,250) was expended to cover legacies, bills, and debts, leaving only 242 dollars. In an ostensibly last-ditch effort to restore his reputation among his Wolfeboro neighbors, William had bequeathed nearly one-quarter of his estate to the Wolfeborough-Tuftonborough Academy, for "the promotion of learning and science" and for the hiring of a "preceptor or preceptress." He had also bequeathed funds to the New Hampshire Missionary Society, "for the purpose exclusively of disseminating the Gospel in distitute parts of this County." These magnanimous gestures, nearly impoverishing his widow and children, must have contributed to sending two of his daughters into the mills. By 1833, after 67 dollars had been paid out of William Guppy's estate to the Missionary Society, only 92 remained.[63]

Betsey Chamberlain remained in Brookfield with her children until shortly after 1830. In that year's census, she is recorded as a Brookfield, New Hampshire, "free white" female head of a family, aged thirty to forty, with a boy and girl, each between five and ten years old.[64] In all censuses through 1880, Chamberlain is labeled "free white," as are many of her relatives. Notoriously imprecise, federal censuses before 1860 distinguished only "white" persons by color or race. Otherwise, people were divided into three broad categories: free white; all other free persons (sometimes designated "free colored") except Indians, not taxed; and slaves. With the 1860 census, it became possible to identify a person's color as white, black, or mulatto. Although the 1870 census included "Indian" among the color categories, most genealogists of Native people have found that they are more often identified as white if they lived in a white community, or black if they lived in a black community.[65] Since Betsy Chamberlain and her family seemed to be trying to assimilate in predominantly Euro-American communities—or at least appear to assimilate—they were viewed by census takers as closer to white than to Indian or colored.

The 1830 census supports Abel Thomas's and Harriet Robinson's contention that Chamberlain was the mother of two or three children. In the years immediately following William Guppy's death, Betsey Chamberlain and Sally Guppy sold off piece after piece of their farms. Chamberlain seems to have lost all of Josiah's estate by the late 1830s.[66] Life for nineteenth-century widows, especially those with young children, was agonizingly difficult, since there were few means for women to earn money and, of course, no public assistance. A sense of personal hardship and suffering is reflected in Chamberlain's *Lowell Offering* piece "A Reverie," in which a character remarks that the factory-girl narrator's "earthly pilgrimage" has been one of "losses, crosses and disappointments" (p. 131).

Besides disclosing her origin in Wolfeboro, Chamberlain's local-color writings reveal a close acquaintance with Brookfield people and life. Her familiarity with the town's history, seen in such sketches as "The Whortleberry Excursion," provides further evidence for her ten-year residence there as a young wife and mother. "The Whortleberry

Excursion" recounts the experience of friend Tobias H., a Quaker. As a bachelor first settling in the area, he was obliged to make his home "between two huge rocks," with a front wall of logs. His rustic way of life earned him the nickname of "the bear" (p. 218). In their Brookfield town history, Chase, Bowker, and Pinkham relate the story of Tobias "Bear" (or B'ar) Hanson, a Quaker who moved to Brookfield in the early 1790s and for a time lived alone in a cave fronted by a wooden lean-to.[67]

Mill Work

March 1832 is the last date that Betsey Chamberlain is listed as a resident in the Brookfield tax assessment books, where her property is recorded as three and one-half acres mowing and tillage, nine acres pasture, and buildings worth forty dollars. In March 1833, she is not cited as a Brookfield resident or nonresident.[68] Sometime during the early 1830s, Chamberlain left Brookfield to become a mill worker, no doubt to earn money desperately needed to support her children and herself. The nation's deepening economic woes, which rendered property worthless, ruined many people overnight and culminated in the Panic of 1837. Numerous rural women such as Chamberlain were driven into the mills.

Her autobiographically based writings indicate that she dwelled in a small factory village before moving to Lowell. The narrator of "Christmas" explains that in "by-gone days" she lived "in a small manufacturing village, where there was quite a number of English and Scotch families" (p. 181). Strafford County, New Hampshire, land records supply the manufacturing village's probable location. One deed records that on 16 December 1831, "Betsy Chamberlin of New Market in the County of Rockingham," sold seventeen and one-half acres of her Brookfield property. Newmarket, New Hampshire, possessed several flourishing cotton mills belonging to the Newmarket Manufacturing Company, incorporated in 1822. By 1827 the company had erected three granite mills beside the Lamprey River (see Figure 7). Newmarket even produced its own factory women's periodical, *The Factory Girl,* in the 1840s. Two additional deeds cite Chamberlain's residence in Newmarket. On 14 March 1835, "Betsey Chamberlain, Widow [and] Harriet B. Guppy, single woman, both of

Fig. 7. One of the old granite mills, Newmarket, New Hampshire. *Courtesy of the New Hampshire Historical Society*

New Market" are numbered among the grantors. Again on 4 September 1837, "Betsy Chamberlin widow and Harriet B. Guppy, single woman, both of New Market, Rockingham" are cited as grantors.[69]

The narrator of Chamberlain's "Christmas" explains that she dwelled in "a cottage of two tenements," sharing one with "two young ladies who boarded with me, and slept in an adjoining room" (pp. 181, 184). That Chamberlain may have worked as a seamstress (perhaps in addition to mill work, as did some factory women) is suggested by the narrator's remark that she "had engaged to finish a piece of needlework that evening," toiling until nearly midnight (p. 182). Newmarket, with its opportunities for both mill work and sewing, provided Chamberlain and her sister with a ready livelihood, as did textile mill towns for thousands of poor women.

According to Nellie P. George's historical sketches of Newmarket, working conditions were far from easy, since the average workday spanned some twelve hours and wages were low. Weavers earned from $1.80 to $2.29 per week. In winter, the partially heated mills were sometimes so cold that the women could not work. George's memoirs corroborate Chamberlain's narrator's memory of her English and Scottish immigrant neighbors. George wrote that the antebellum workers included New England natives, as well as "English or Celtic" immigrants. Her text also supports Chamberlain's narrator's recollection of dwelling in "a cottage of two tenements" (p. 181). The Newmarket Manufacturing Company built many "double tenement houses" for workers. The harshness of Newmarket workers' lives prompted an anonymous poet to contribute a verse, "Lines for Newmarket" (1845), to a local paper. The poem's speaker protests against laborers' oppression:

> Thy laborers are driven forth
> To unrequited toil—
> Crime revels unrebuked in *church*,
> In *Mill* and on the soil.

These adverse conditions may well have contributed to Chamberlain's factory girl's "losses, crosses and disappointments."[70]

As noted in *Loom and Spindle,* Harriet Robinson thought that Chamberlain may have come to Lowell from a Shaker community where she had been discontented.[71] Her name is not included among the membership records for the two nineteenth-century New Hampshire Shaker communities at Enfield and Canterbury. Since the membership records are incomplete, it is possible that her name was simply not recorded or that she lived in a Shaker community in another state. Since Robinson was uncertain whether Chamberlain had lived with the Shakers, Newmarket or some other community may have served to provoke the discontent. If Chamberlain did spend time in a Shaker community, their insistence upon men's and women's equality, as well as the feminism derived from her Native culture, may have contributed to her feminist writings, particularly "Origin of Small Talk" and "A New Society." The latter is notable for its early advocacy of equal pay and educational opportunities for men and women.

Fig. 8. View of Lowell from Dracut, Massachusetts, 1840s to 1850s. *Courtesy of the Lowell Historical Society*

Working in Lowell

Lowell, Massachusetts, was a lively and burgeoning mill town in the 1830s and 1840s when Chamberlain worked there. A *Lowell Offering* story recounts a woman's impressions of Lowell upon arriving from New Hampshire in search of work: "It was morning when I arrived . . . the sun poured forth his golden beams . . . and seemed to give new life to the animate creation. The streets were crowded with people of all descriptions, hurrying to and fro. . . . Many things were new to me. I had a prospect of the printing establishment, and factory buildings; I could distinctly hear the din and hum of the machinery. Thus pleasantly the hours of the forenoon passed. Presently the bells began to ring in every direction, and the girls came flocking from the mills in crowds."[72] Also coming to Lowell from New Hampshire, Betsey Chamberlain may have experienced similar sensations of novelty and wonder (see Figure 8).

The community she encountered in Lowell included a distinct Native presence, which must have supported Chamberlain in her efforts to write and publish.[73] Three of Chamberlain's Lowell contemporaries noted Native people's presence in their memoirs. Recording her youthful experience in the 1830s and 1840s, Lucy Larcom wrote: "Some time every summer a fleet of canoes would glide noiselessly up the [Merrimack] river, and a company of Penobscot Indians would land at a green point almost in sight from our windows. Pawtucket Falls had always been one of their favorite camping-places." Concerning the same time period, Harriet Farley recalled:

> I remember also the first time I ever saw the aborigines of our country. They were Penobscots, and then, I believe, upon their way to this city [Lowell]. They encamped among the woods of the Newbury shore, and crossed the river (there about a mile in width) in their little canoes, whenever they wished to beg or trade. . . . They appeared so strange, with their birch-bark canoes and wooden paddles, their women with men's hats and such *outre* dresses, their little boys with their unfailing bows and arrows. . . . Their curious, bright-stained baskets, too, which they sold or gave away. I have one of them now, but it has lost its bright tints. It was given me in return for a slight favor.

In *Loom and Spindle,* Harriet Robinson remembered Native people camping along the Merrimack.[74] Besides the Penobscot, there were probably other Native and mixed-race people working in the mills with Chamberlain. Evidence survives of several "Indian doctors" in 1850s Lowell, so they may well have resided there earlier. The presence of a Native community could have been one of the factors that drew Chamberlain to Lowell.

As the Lowell corporations developed, the town's population grew from 4,085 in 1830 to 25,163 in 1844, female operatives accounting for a large portion. By the mid-1840s, the operative workforce included some 9,000 women and 4,000 men working for eleven corporations producing cotton and woolen cloth and carpets.[75] Like most workers, Chamberlain probably roomed in one of the brick corporation boardinghouses lining the side streets (see Figure 9). The small boardinghouse rooms were shared by six to eight women sleeping two or three to a bed. The typical workday lasted twelve to fourteen hours, beginning about 5:00 A.M. and ending about 7:00 P.M. Despite fac-

Fig. 9. Dutton Street boardinghouses, Lowell, Massachusetts, 1846. *Courtesy of Lowell Historical Society*

tory life's hardships, Lowell was a place where early nineteenth-century women came into their own, founding the first women's periodicals, forming organizations, and enjoying such cultural advantages as lyceums, libraries, and evening schools. It is no wonder that Chamberlain, with her intellectual and feminist interests—not to mention her need to earn a living—gravitated to Lowell.

Betsey Chamberlain apparently lived in Lowell as early as March 1831, moving back and forth between there and Newmarket with the reputed restlessness of factory people. According to the records of Lowell's First Congregational Church, "Mrs. Betsy Chamberlin" was among those who joined the church on 6 March 1831.[76] In 1834 a marriage notice appearing in the Boston *Columbian Centinel* on 18 April announces the marriage "In Lowell, [of] Mr. Thomas Wright to Mrs. Betsey Chamberlain." Another notice published in the *Lowell Mercury* states that "Mr. Thomas Wright" and "Miss Betsey Chamberlain" were married "By the Rev. Mr. [Amos] Blanchard," pastor of the First Congregational Church from 1829 to 1845.[77]

This marriage is puzzling on several counts. By 1840, when she began writing for the *Lowell Offering,* Betsey Chamberlain Wright had reverted to using her former name, "Betsey Chamberlain" or "Mrs. Chamberlain," as she was known to Harriet Hanson Robinson and Abel Thomas.[78] Moreover, one of her pseudonyms was "B. C." and not "B. W." Despite both marriages, she adopted the writing persona of an old maid! Chamberlain's second marriage seems not to have lasted, for undiscovered reasons. Curiously, no Thomas Wright is found in Lowell city directories from 1832 to 1844. Betsey's casual use of her married names follows a family pattern. Her sister Harriet B. Guppy was also later married briefly, from 1847 to 1851, when her husband died.[79] Nonetheless, her 1877 gravestone inscription omits any mention of her marriage, identifying her only as "Harriet Byron, Dau. of William Guppy and Comfort Meserve"—even though her husband, John Kelley, is buried beside her. Apparently, at least for this family, a woman's marital status was not regarded with as much immutability or sacredness as one might expect for nineteenth-century women. This tendency to downplay the significance of marriage can also be seen in Chamberlain's old maid persona.

In "A Vision of Truth," published in early 1841, Chamberlain's factory-girl narrator recalls the visit of a male friend, someone she knew in Lowell almost three years before. This supports Chamberlain's arrival in Lowell in the 1830s. Although there is some evidence that Harriet Guppy also worked in Lowell, her name is not recorded in the 1836 *Lowell Directory,* the only early one to include female operatives' names. A "Betsey Wright," however, appears in the 1836 directory as a worker on the Suffolk Mills and boarding at 4 Suffolk (Figure 10). Since Betsey Wright was, of course, a quite common name, the Suffolk Mills worker may not have been Betsey Guppy Chamberlain Wright. While a "Mrs. Wright," a boardinghouse keeper, is found in the 1840 Lowell census, Harriet Guppy's name is again not found.[80]

Nonetheless, her obituary reports that Harriet Guppy also worked in Lowell, Massachusetts, and wrote for a workers' periodical. From 1847 to 1851, she was married to John Kelley (1791–1851) of Wolfeboro, New Hampshire. When she died in 1877, the following obituary appeared in the *Boston Morning Journal*: "Mrs. Harriet Kelley, widow of John Kelley of Mill Village, in Wolfeboro' [N.H.], was recently found dead in bed in her home. For a year or more past she had been partially deranged and lived alone, but had ample means. Mrs. Kelley was about 77 years of age and was a woman of considerable literary ability. In her younger days, while at work in one of the mills at Lowell, she was a frequent contributor to the magazine that was pro-

Fig. 10. Suffolk Mills, Lowell, Massachusetts, 1850. *Courtesy of the Lowell Historical Society*

jected and published by the operatives of that place." Unless the obituary writer confused Harriet with Betsey, Harriet Guppy not only worked in Lowell but also wrote for the *Lowell Offering*. Although no additional writings have been linked to Harriet, she may have written some of the pieces attributed to her sister. This could help account for Betsey's prolific written output while meeting a demanding mill schedule of nearly eighty-two hours per week. The obituary notwithstanding, Harriet was by no means affluent. Her probate records indicate that her "ample means" amounted to under four hundred dollars. In widowhood, she apparently had supported herself working as a domestic. The 1860 Wolfeboro census identifies Harriet B. Kelley's occupation as "Housework."[81]

Since only one of Chamberlain's *Lowell Offering* writings makes reference to factory work, it is not easy to determine the kinds of mill work done by her or her sister. The factory-girl narrator of "A Reverie" recounts working at a "cloth-frame . . . picking cloth." She awakens from a daydream when her overseer tells her, "The cloth has come in" (p. 131). From these details, it seems likely that Chamberlain worked in the cloth room. According to the *Hand-book for the Visiter to Lowell* (1848), after weaving, cloth was "sent to the cloth-room to be looked over, picked and measured." Both cotton and woolen cloth were picked after weaving. This involved examining cloth under bright light and removing imperfections with tweezers. Any undyed spots were retouched with a brush and dye.

Lucy Larcom, another nineteenth-century factory-girl writer, de-scribes the cloth room as a particularly desirable place to work, being less crowded, quieter, and cleaner than the spinning, weaving, and dressing rooms. The slower pace and shorter workday allowed time for reading and writing. Books, forbidden in the mill's other departments, were allowed in the cloth room. Work there was less physically taxing, but it also paid less. Since Chamberlain was middle-aged and perhaps less hardy than the younger workers, she may have chosen or been assigned a position in the cloth room.[82]

During some of her time in Lowell, Betsey Chamberlain may also have worked as a boardinghouse keeper, a position usually held by middle-aged widows and widowers. The 1840 Lowell census records a "Mrs. Wright," aged forty to fifty, presiding over a household of twenty-eight people, including ten females aged fifteen to twenty and fifteen females aged twenty to thirty, all the young people employed in "manufactures and trade." A scan of this census finds Mrs. Wright's household resembling those of other middle-aged neighbors residing with large groups of young people—probably boardinghouses. The age of the only male in Mrs. Wright's household is identified as fifteen to twenty, the age that Betsey's son would have been. Since the census records no male of the age to be Chamberlain's husband, she may have been separated from Thomas Wright or widowed. As corporation employees, boardinghouse keepers were granted an often-insufficient budget with which to furnish three meals a day for boarders. In addi-tion, they were required to keep the building clean and neat and moni-tor workers' conduct. Although keeping a boardinghouse was hard work, it would have allowed Chamberlain some daytime leisure in which to write.[83]

Chamberlain's Children

While Robinson contends that Chamberlain "came to Lowell with three children," evidence of only a son and daughter by Josiah Chamberlain has been found. No birth records survive, since early Brookfield vital records were destroyed by an 1877 fire. However, some information exists that possibly identifies the children. Betsey's daughter was Comfort Chamberlain (born ca. 1823), who married Austin Barnum on 28 November 1850 in Kane County, Illinois. In *Loom and Spindle,* Robinson comments, "One of [Chamberlain's] sons was afterwards connected with the *New York Tribune.*" Georgia Merrill's *History of Carroll County, New Hampshire* (1889) discusses the "Chamberlin" family's prominence in Brookfield. One became a New York journalist: "Ivory Chamberlin, born in Brookfield about seventy years ago, was a prominent journalist in New York City, where he died a few years since." He may well have been Betsey's son, since her and Josiah's Brookfield farm had belonged to Josiah's deceased brother, Ivory Chamberlain (d. 1818). They could have named their son Ivory to memorialize him.[84]

Several newspapers published Ivory Chamberlain's obituary following his death on 9 March 1881. Since most record that he was born on 13 March 1821, he could indeed have been Betsey Guppy Chamberlain's son, if he was conceived shortly before or after Betsey and Josiah's marriage on 30 June 1820. The *New York Times* reported that Ivory "was born near the village of Wolfsboro, N.H." The *New York Herald,* for which he worked as an editorial writer, also noted: "He was born near the village of Wolfboro', N.H." Although Ivory Chamberlain did not work for the *New York Tribune*—contrary to Harriet H. Robinson's statement—he was a neighbor, friend, and political supporter of Horace Greeley, founder and editor of the paper. Writing in 1898, some seventeen years after Ivory Chamberlain's death, Robinson may have simply confused the *New York Herald* with its rival, the *Tribune.*[85]

Ivory Chamberlain's parents are not identified in any of the obituaries or other records examined. His death certificate filed with New York City's Health Department, however, notes that his parents' birthplace was New Hampshire. Both the *New York Times* and the *New York Herald* trace his ancestry to the Revolution stock: "His ancestors had been patriots in the Revolutionary war, and more than one of the family served as officers in the Continental army." On his father's side, as Strafford County probate records reveal, two of these patriotic ancestors were Captain Ivory Chamberlain and Captain Thomas Chamberlain.[86] Two of his maternal ancestors fought on the colonists' side. Ivory's great-grandfather, Joshua Guppy (1739?–1806), served as a corporal in Captain David Copp's Minute Men Company, Peirce Island, 1775. Ivory's great-great-grandfather, Lieutenant Clement Meserve (1716–1800), served in the New Hampshire militia to reinforce the Continental Army in New York. According to Ivory Chamberlain's obituaries, he spent his boyhood in the Wolfeboro area, which coincides with Betsey Chamberlain's residence in Brookfield until shortly after 1830.[87]

While we cannot yet account for the puzzling or missing genealogical records, some possibilities suggest themselves based upon what is known of Betsey Chamberlain's life. The gaps in the record may reflect racism's impact upon families considered to have Native ancestry. Ivory perhaps wished to hide his parentage to avoid being stigmatized as the son of not only a lowly factory girl but one of Indian blood. Out of a corresponding move to protect her children, Betsey may have adopted her *Lowell Offering* identity of a childless "old maid." Nonetheless, her involvement with the *Lowell Offering* and *The New England Offering* perhaps sowed the seeds for Ivory's journalism career as well as that of his son, Samuel Selwyn Chamberlain, an even more prominent journalist.[88]

As with so many mill women supporting needy families, Chamberlain and her sister Harriet probably also helped to sustain their stepmother, Sally Guppy, and her children back in Wolfeboro. In "Aunt 'Dear Soul,'" Chamberlain's narrator returns to her hometown from working in Lowell, bringing her "ma'am" many "nice things" (p. 139). With her wages, Chamberlain must have bought her stepmother needed supplies and gifts from Lowell. When the original Guppy house was destroyed by fire around 1840, the sisters' mill wages may well have contributed to building the new house in 1842.

Third Marriage and Move to Illinois

A third marriage interrupted Betsey Chamberlain's mill employment, when in 1843 she wed Charles Boutwell, a widowed farmer with as many as six children. One can only speculate about how they met. Prior to this, Charles seems to have lived for at least several years in Niagara County, New York, so she may have met him through Ivory, who resided for a some years in various upstate New York towns. Born in Vermont near 1790, Boutwell served as a private in the Vermont Militia during the War of 1812.[89]

Charles Boutwell may have been among the men writing to the *Lowell Offering* or visiting Lowell looking for a wife. In 1845 an *Offering* editor wrote, "We have received some curious letters from gentlemen at the West, who wish to enter into a correspondence with some one of our contributors; and with the avowed intention of making of such a correspondent their 'lawful wedded wife.'" Harriet Hanson Robinson also observed that "the fame of the *The Lowell Offering* caused the mill-girls to be considered very desirable for wives; and that young men came from near and far to pick and choose for themselves, and generally with good success." In the 1840s the western states, including Illinois and Kansas, became a mecca for Lowell mill women. Besides Betsey Chamberlain, *Lowell Offering* writers migrating west included Lucy Larcom, Emmeline Larcom Spaulding, Elizabeth E. Turner Sawyer, Lydia S. Hall, and Sarah Holbrook.[90]

According to the court records of Du Page County, Illinois, Betsey Chamberlain and Charles Boutwell were married on 26 March 1843 by Ezra Gilbert, a justice of the peace. That Betsey Guppy Chamberlain was the bride is confirmed by Harriet Guppy Kelley's 1878–1885 probate records, in which Betsey C. Boutwell of Wayne, Du Page County, Illinois, is identified as her sister. Soon after their marriage, Charles began buying land in newly established Wayne Township. On 12 July 1844, he purchased eighty acres of public land for 125 dollars. This land, combined with other parcels of adjoining land purchased in 1843, 1845, and 1849, gave Charles and Betsey a farm of some 150 acres.[91]

Since there is no record of Betsey's residing or working in Lowell from 1843 to 1847, she was probably living then in Illinois. However, she returned to work in Lowell from 1848 to 1850, when her writings appear in *The New England Offering*. In the December 1848 issue, "Our Town: How It Looked" is attributed to "Betsey" of "Lowell." "Our Town. Number 3," published in September 1849, again identifies the author's residence as Lowell. Her final piece was published in the February 1850 issue. Although it is not known whether Charles Boutwell accompanied Betsey to Lowell, it is unlikely that he would have, since his large farm must have needed attention.

Why would Betsey Boutwell have returned to Lowell? Foremost may have been the need to earn some quick cash for her new home.

According to one Wayne historian, the early settlers struggled to make a living at farming.[92] Betsey may also have been homesick for New England. Adjusting to an isolated farm must have been difficult. No doubt she missed her life as a single working woman in Lowell, with its libraries, Improvement Circles, lectures, and social opportunities. By 1850, however, she would have been nearing fifty-three and perhaps finding it harder to withstand the rigors of mill work. Lowell was changing, too, as working conditions deteriorated and poorer immigrants replaced the Yankee workforce.

Chamberlain's final *New England Offering* piece, published in February 1850, is the last of her writings that has been found. After 1850, she must have also lost touch with her Lowell companions. Harriet H. Robinson's brief biography of Chamberlain published in *Loom and Spindle* (1898) is much briefer and less informative than the text's "life-stories" of other mill women. Chamberlain's sketch consists essentially of Robinson's and Thomas's reminiscences of her in the 1840s. In *Loom and Spindle's* fuller "life-stories," Robinson quotes from correspondence solicited from the aged former mill women. Chamberlain's brief biography, on the other hand, includes no quoted correspondence, presumably because Robinson was unable to contact her after the 1840s. No correspondence from Chamberlain could be found among Robinson's unpublished papers. Volume 29 of Robinson's papers records the whereabouts and activities of some twenty *Lowell Offering* writers in 1886, including those who had died, but Chamberlain is not mentioned. Her age and racial difference from the other *Lowell Offering* writers may have contributed to isolating her from them.[93]

Betsey had definitely returned to her home with Charles Boutwell in Illinois by 15 October 1850, when the federal census notes her residence there. Before the transcontinental railroad's completion, westward journeys were arduous ones, requiring multiple transfers among water and land conveyances. Another Lowell mill worker, Lucy Larcom, made a similar journey from Massachusetts to Illinois in 1846, as described in her journals. After traveling by stagecoach from Massachusetts to Connecticut, Larcom and her companions boarded a steamboat to New York City. From New York they rode by train to Philadelphia, where they boarded a boat to Baltimore. From there they journeyed by train to Virginia, where they boarded a stagecoach. After sailing in several boats along the Monongahela and Ohio Rivers into Illinois, Larcom and her companions finally reached their destination, Looking-Glass Prairie, St. Clair County.[94] It is a further measure of

Chamberlain's hardiness that between 1843 and 1850 she undertook at least two such journeys from New England to Illinois.

Betsey Chamberlain Boutwell would reside more than forty years in Illinois, longer than her youthful years in New Hampshire. A relatively new site for Euro-American settlement, Du Page County, Illinois, had been created in 1839. The first Euro-Americans settled in Wayne, some thirty miles west of Chicago, in 1834. In a sad coincidence, Chamberlain spent her later life in a town named, according to one Wayne history, "to honor General 'Mad' Anthony Wayne, who had originally opened the area to settlement."[95] This was the General Wayne who led the 1794 massacre of the Miami bitterly denounced in Chamberlain's 1842 piece, "A Fire-Side Scene." While her experience typifies the shocks and insults endured by nineteenth-century Native people, it also shows that General Wayne's and other attacks against Native people could not eliminate them. After all, Chamberlain, with her pride in her Native lineage, settled in the area.

In certain ways, Wayne resembled the New Hampshire villages of her youth. A small community of farmers and laborers, Wayne had a population of 1,030 in 1860. Like Charles and Betsey Chamberlain Boutwell, most heads of families had been born in such eastern states as New York, New Jersey, Connecticut, Massachusetts, and Vermont, or overseas in Ireland and England. Her neighbors even included another former mill worker, Abraham Kershaw, who had worked in the Fall River, Massachusetts, mills beginning at age seven. Although surrounded in Wayne by fellow Easterners, at least until the great German immigration later in the century, Betsey and Charles seem to have involved themselves little in town affairs. Town historians do not record their names among those remembered or active in local affairs.[96]

Evidence suggests that in Wayne, Betsey moved away from the church to which she had belonged as a child and young woman. Although a Congregational Church had been early established in nearby St. Charles, Illinois, Betsey and Charles Boutwell were married in 1843 by a justice of the peace. Betsey C. Boutwell's name does not appear among the 1871 founders of a Congregational Church near her home in Wayne Station, and her fourth marriage in 1866 was solemnized by William Kimball, a Methodist preacher. She may have been drawn away from Congregationalism toward such evangelical sects as Methodism because of their greater social egalitarianism and appeal to racial minorities.[97]

Wayne's natural beauty must have appealed to Betsey. Bounded by the Fox and Du Page Rivers and crossed by streams, the rolling land produced prairie grass and beautiful elms, maples, Scotch pines, and catalpas. Formerly home to the Sauk, Illiniwek, and Potawatomi peoples, the area abounded with such wildlife as beavers, deer, foxes, elk, rabbits, and owls. According to published Wayne histories, all the original Native people had been "removed" from the area prior to Euro-American settlement. Still, some Native people may have managed to survive quietly on the community's margins. As in New Hampshire, people tapped the maple trees to make syrup and sugar. They gathered hickory nuts, raspberries, and wild strawberries. Most of Wayne's early settlers were, like Betsey and Charles Boutwell, transplanted New Englanders, and they created a community similar to what they had known. According to Glos and Weiser's town history, even in 1953 "Wayne retain[ed] the demure air of a New England village."[98] In such a setting, one can imagine Betsey as happy as she might be outside of her beloved Winnipesaukee region.

The area's peacefulness and natural beauty were soon compromised by railroad construction. Completed in December 1848, the Galena and Chicago Union Railway tracks passed through Wayne's western section, renamed Wayne Station, where the Boutwell farm was located. The train tracks bisected Charles and Betsey Boutwell's farm, and land records reveal that they sold property to the railroad (see Figure 11). Some Wayne farmers welcomed the railroad because it would provide an easier means of transporting their wheat, oats, and corn to Chicago. Of such crops, Charles and Betsey must have cultivated at least corn, since Charles's 1864 estate inventory includes a "Grind Stone" and a "Corn Sheller." In the 1850s, like many other Wayne residents, they invested their resources in raising sheep, for Charles's inventory also includes sixty-two sheep. The wool produced from fine wool sheep became an important Wayne farm product.[99]

Betsey's early years in Wayne Station again found her caring for children. The 1850 census reflects that two of Charles Boutwell's children lived with them: George, aged seventeen and identified as a farmer born in New York, and Charles Mortimer, aged thirteen and born in Illinois. Nearby lived Lafayette Boutwell, a twenty-three-year-old married farmer, born in New York, another of Charles's sons. The 1860 Wayne census indicates that Charles Boutwell's age was seventy and Betsey's sixty-two. Charles is identified as a farmer—and a rather prosperous one—owning real estate worth 3,400 dollars and a personal estate of 600 dollars. Their assets placed them among the upper-

Fig. 11. Wayne Station, Illinois. *Photograph by Judith Ranta*

middle rank of Wayne residents. The census does not identify Betsey's occupation. The household includes a young man aged twenty-four, born in New York and employed as a laborer. Mostly farmers and laborers, all 1,030 Wayne residents, including the Boutwells, are labeled "white."[100]

Old Age

Betsey was again compelled to shift for herself, when Charles Boutwell Sr. died 30 October 1863. Since he died intestate, Betsey became the estate's administratrix. Despite her role, the probate records show that she was shortchanged, receiving no land or house but only household items and provisions. Apparently her allotment was one-sixth of the estate, or some six hundred dollars' worth of household goods. Charles and Betsey's 156 acres of land and the buildings thereon were inherited by Charles's grown children from his first marriage. Betsey's inheritance included various articles of furniture and apparel, as well as a stove, provisions for one year, fuel for three months, and one horse, cow, and calf. She also received a spinning wheel, a loom and appendages, and one pair of cards, showing that she remained involved with the textile work that had occupied her in Lowell and earlier in her life. She requested and received fifty dollars to be paid to her daughter, Comfort, for nursing Charles Boutwell during his last sickness.[101]

By January 1866, Charles's sons had sold all the family property to a wealthy neighbor, Daniel Dunham. No further records could be found to explain why the Boutwell children treated Betsey Boutwell and Comfort Barnum with such apparent callousness. Left without any land, the aging women possessed little means of support and no other home. The loss of her farm prompted Betsey Boutwell to take Dunham to court, signing an indenture (contract) with him in March 1866. Just as she had so many years earlier taken the bold step of suing her father to secure her widow's dower, she again asserted herself in court against a more prosperous and powerful man. Filed with the Du Page County Recorder's Office, this Deed and Agreement allots to Betsey the dower to which she "was and is entitled."

Daniel Dunham probably understood that without any land the women had no livelihood and so would have needed public support. The contract was a means of obviating their need for charitable assistance. It allocated to Betsey all of Charles's and her former farm lying west of the railroad tracks that run through Wayne Station. She also received one-third of Charles's nineteen acres of Kane County timberland. Dunham granted her partial use of a barn and barnyard and "exclusive use & occupancy of the Garden enclosed with a picket fence." She was also "entitled to share one third of the Apples that shall grow in the orchard upon said farm." Dunham reserved for himself the right of way from his farm, lying west of Betsey's land, through her property to the railroad.[102] With the land, garden, and barnyard, Betsey Boutwell and her daughter would have the means to support themselves at least in part. The agreement suggests that the women must have been fairly poor in old age, dependent upon the Dunhams' largesse and compelled to work for their subsistence by growing vegetables, raising chickens, picking apples, and whatever else they could do, and selling what they could to support themselves. In her old age, Betsey's life came to resemble that of the hardworking, elderly "Aunt 'Dear Soul'" whom she had appreciatively described in the 1840s.

Dunham's relinquishing some of his land and signing the contract with Betsey may have been less an act of charity than one of expediency. He could certainly afford to be generous, since he and his brothers were some of the wealthiest people in Wayne. In the 1870 census,

Daniel Dunham claimed 25,000 dollars' worth of real estate and a personal estate of 5,500. Although Dunham may have been motivated less by charity than by practicality, his signing the contract with Betsey indicates that he held her in some esteem. Although her stepchildren absconded with her dower, her neighbors must have appreciated her, since Dunham executed the contract with her and other neighbors, the Dolphs, cared for her before her death, as her obituary reveals.[103]

Several months later, at age sixty-eight, Betsey married a fourth time. On 21 November 1866, Mr. I. A. Horn of Kentucky and Mrs. Betsey Boutwell of Du Page County were married by William Kimball, a Methodist "Minister of the Gospel." Like her 1834 marriage to Thomas Wright, however, this union seems to have soon ended for reasons unknown. As in her parting with Wright, no record of a divorce between Betsey and Mr. Horn was found, although subsequent censuses reveal that they did separate. In the 1870 Wayne census, Betsey is identified as "Betsey Boutwell," aged seventy-three. The only person sharing her household was "Comfort Chamberlain," her forty-seven-year-old daughter. Though Comfort had been married to Austin Barnum, she too had reverted to using her former surname. Betsey and Comfort were continuing their family pattern of women's casual use of married names, suggesting a female autonomy unusual for the nineteenth century. In the census, both women's occupation is reported as "Keeps house" and their birthplace as "N.H."[104]

A deeper look at the censuses reveals some harsh realities. The 1860 Illinois census shows Comfort Barnum, aged thirty-seven and born in New Hampshire, sharing a household with her husband, Austin Barnum, and three children aged nine months to eight years. Ten years later, the 1870 census represents Comfort Chamberlain—without husband and children—living with Betsey Boutwell, and in 1880 Comfort, identified as Betsey's widowed daughter, was still sharing her mother's home. But in 1870, two of Comfort's children—if they were alive—would have been young enough still to need their mother's care. Some difficult circumstances, whether of illness, divorce, or death, must have disrupted Comfort's marriage and motherhood.[105]

In the 1870 census, Betsey Boutwell reportedly owned three thousand dollars' worth of real estate, probably the estimated value of the property received as her widow's dower. Comparing the census's enumeration of her neighbors with the 1874 Wayne plat map shows that she and Comfort continued to live in Wayne Station. In fact, they may have occupied a small plat labeled only "A.B.," if this land was purchased for them by Austin Barnum ("A.B.") or by Comfort using an inheritance from Austin. The A.B. plat is located on the southeastern corner of Betsey and Charles Boutwell's former farmland and may have included their farmhouse. Betsey Boutwell's obituary suggests that until her death she continued to occupy the farmhouse she had shared with her husband Charles.[106]

Since in 1870 Betsey's real estate was valued at three thousand dollars and her personal estate two hundred dollars, her old age must have been reasonably secure. The census also discloses that many Wayne residents owned much more property than did Betsey and Comfort. Since Charles's death, their fortunes had declined somewhat. In 1870 a number of Wayne households claimed between twelve and twenty thousand dollars' worth of real estate, so Betsey's three thousand placed her within the lower-middle rank of Wayne residents. Both the 1870 and 1880 censuses show many Wayne households including one or several servants and farm laborers. That no servants or laborers were noted in Betsey and Comfort's household further confirms that their means were modest. In the 1880 census, the value of real estate was not recorded, so it is not known how much property the women owned that year.[107]

It is hard to know how Betsey and Comfort occupied themselves during their long years in Wayne Station. The quiet hamlet offered only two general stores, two blacksmith shops, a railroad depot, and few other business enterprises. Some twentieth-century written sketches of early Wayne settlers have been preserved at the Town Building and reveal something of nineteenth-century life there. According to several, Wayne was strongly abolitionist, supporting a branch of the Underground Railroad. With her deeply held beliefs in multicultural tolerance and social equality, Betsey must have shared her neighbors' antislavery sentiments and perhaps participated in related activities. The descriptions of early Wayne residents show as well that evangelical Christianity and temperance were potent social forces there.[108]

Local newspapers offer further insights on community life, although few nineteenth-century Du Page County newspapers have been preserved. The earliest surviving issues of a local paper covering Wayne, the *Wheaton Illinoian,* begin in January 1885. Published in the nearby town of Wheaton, the county seat, the paper ran regular columns on northern Du Page towns, including Wayne. In 1885 the anonymous Wayne columnist reported that a Literary and Debating Society was meeting regularly and raising funds to establish a public library. While it is not known whether Betsey Boutwell participated in this, it is significant that Wayne had no public library throughout her lifetime. Her reading material must have been limited, surely a hardship for a woman so bright and intellectually curious, whose writings reveal how greatly she enjoyed reading. Other Wayne columns again reflect citizens' keen interests in evangelical Christianity and in temperance or prohibition. In spring 1885, local young people produced the temperance play "Ten Nights in a Barroom," based upon the T. S. Arthur text. Other community activities included county fairs, strawberry festivals, huskings, and other kinds of shared-farmwork socials familiar to Betsey from her rural New Hampshire youth.[109]

Until sometime after 1880, Betsey Boutwell and Comfort Chamberlain Barnum continued to share a home. The census of that year reveals that they still lived in Wayne Station, where Betsey remained until her death. On 1 October 1886, her obituary appeared in the *Wheaton Illinoian:* "Died—Friday afternoon, Sept. 24, '86. Mrs. Betsy Boutwell, aged about 89 years. Mrs. B. was an old resident, living on a farm adjoining the village, which her husband purchased of the Government in July, 1844, and who died some 24 years ago. During her last sickness she lived with Mr. Dolph's family. Funeral services were held at the Congregational church, Rev. Mr. Harbough, of St. Charles, officiating. Her remains were interred in the Little Woods Cemetery."

Since the Dolph family cared for her during her last illness, Comfort probably no longer shared her home. No further traces of Comfort Chamberlain Barnum have been found, so it is not known whether after 1880 she moved away, died, or perhaps remarried. "Mr. Dolph" is probably Edwin Dolph, the owner of a small farm adjacent to the A.B. plat in Wayne Station. New York State natives, Edwin A. and Nancy Dolph had lived in Wayne since at least 1870. In 1886 Edwin would have been about fifty-five years of age and Nancy forty-nine. The Dolph family was active in Wayne Station's Congregational church, Little Home Church by the Wayside, which is probably why Betsey Boutwell's funeral services were held there. Her name is not found among the church's membership lists.[110]

Fig. 12. The Boutwell plot, Little Woods Cemetery, St. Charles, Illinois. *Photograph by Judith Ranta*

Little Woods Cemetery in St. Charles, Kane County, Illinois, lies just west of Wayne Station on Dunham Road, about one and a half miles from the Boutwell farm. Near the intersection of Dunham and Stearns Roads lies this small, wooded cemetery surrounded by horse farms. Since other Boutwell family members and many of her Wayne Station neighbors are buried here, it is indeed the likeliest place for Betsey Boutwell's burial. No gravestone or other marker for her grave has survived, however, if indeed there was one in the first place. Little Woods Cemetery records prior to 1955 were long ago destroyed. She is probably buried in or near the Boutwell plot, which includes graves for her husband Charles, his first wife, and several of their children and grandchildren (Figure 12).[111]

Beyond the evidence of census records, deeds, and her obituary, little is presently known about Betsey Chamberlain Boutwell's and her daughter's life in Wayne after 1863. With much less documentation for the later years than for her earlier life, one gains the impression of a silence falling over Betsey Chamberlain's mature years, perhaps resulting from the combined pressures of hard labor, dislocation, and the struggle against prejudice. Since in her early life she wrote so prolifically and with so much spirit, it seems she would have continued. Yet no other writings have surfaced, and we can only hope that further material on this intriguing woman will someday come to light.

Chamberlain's Writings

ABOUNDING WITH ALLUSIONS, influences, and borrowings from other literature, both oral and written, Chamberlain's richly varied writings offer rare insights into the culture enjoyed by ordinary early Americans. Although scholarship on early nineteenth-century women continues to expand, not enough is yet known about early laboring and mixed-race women. Betsey Chamberlain was someone steeped in her era's popular and high culture, from both Euro-American and Native sources. Her writings draw from a richer well of source material than do those of most other mill women. This chapter examines the multiple sources informing Chamberlain's work, in an attempt to deepen understanding of both her achievement and the culture of common early nineteenth-century Americans. It also considers the ways in which Chamberlain molded and blended her sources to create her own distinctive representations of early U.S. women's lives and of laboring people's experience.

Chamberlain's stories draw together and sometimes merge Euro-American and Northeast Native elements. Her writings can be situated among other early Native texts, underscoring Chamberlain's importance as a mixed-race female writer. Although tribal affiliation is crucial to understanding Native writings, Chamberlain's has not yet been discovered. Therefore, her Native features can only be related rather loosely to other nineteenth-century Northeast Algonkian literature. Still, Chamberlain's pieces help to fill the gap in our knowledge of Northeast Native experience and may suggest new directions for research on these people's literatures.

Chamberlain's thirty-seven *Lowell Offering* and *New England Offering* prose writings fall into several categories: Native pieces protesting Euro-American prejudice and persecution; dream visions, sometimes employing Native conventions and often expressing some critique of the factory; village tales and sketches of life in and near her hometown, Wolfeboro, New Hampshire, embodying oral elements; and miscellaneous pieces, including a seduction tale and an Oriental story. In the latter efforts, Chamberlain tried her hand at imitating some of the popular forms she herself enjoyed. As seen in her household inventory discussed previously, she was familiar with her era's standard religious and didactic literature, as well as with women's popular sentimental fiction.

Chamberlain's varied compositions reflect influences from a range of highbrow and popular literature. The richness of her sources attests to the breadth and strength of the literary culture and oral traditions available to her in Wolfeboro and Lowell. Offering a great range of materials, Lowell's numerous libraries included those founded by its churches, mechanics' associations, and book dealers' circulating libraries. Chamberlain also draws from folk sources. Her numerous local-color sketches belong also to a tradition of New England folk tales, as seen in John Greenleaf Whittier's collection *Legends of New England* (1831) and in the volumes of old legends collected in the 1930s by Eva A. Speare, *New Hampshire Folk Tales* and *More New Hampshire Folk Tales*. In Chamberlain's time, common people appreciated literature now considered highbrow—Shakespeare, Burns, Byron—as well as they knew the many folk ballads and sensational tales in circulation. In her abundant quotations and allusions, she borrowed almost as readily from the Bible and Shakespeare as from ballads, Northeast Native oral traditions, and popular fiction.

Although Chamberlain's writings often reflect her community's lingering Puritanism and didacticism, they also reveal that she knew and admired U.S. women's fiction by such authors as Lydia Maria Child. Chamberlain's Native writings are anticipated by Child's sympathetic Indian writings, particularly "Adventure in the Woods" (1826) and *The First Settlers of New-England: or, Conquest of the Pequods, Narragansets and Pokanokets* (1829). Child's humanitarian writings and activism on behalf of slaves and Native people must have greatly appealed to Chamberlain, in view of her idealism and Native heritage.

Chamberlain's output must also be considered in the context of other *Lowell Offering* and *New England Offering* writings, since a periodical is, of course, a collective genre. She wrote from within a community who met together in Improvement Circles to share their writings and so were closely aware of each other's contributions. Thus, while she reacted to currents of thought and writing in the larger culture and must be considered an American pioneer especially in Native writing, she also responded to a circle of peers and neighbors in Lowell. Some of Chamberlain's periodical contributions, especially the pro-Native pieces, respond directly to Indian texts preceding them in the *Lowell Offering,* often revising her coworkers' limited or bigoted treatment of Native people. Nonetheless her submissions seem to have been much admired by other *Offering* contributors. Later volumes reveal numerous imitations of her local-color tales and sketches.

Early Native American Writings

The first known published writings by Native American women appeared in evangelical tractate literature. In their conversion efforts among the poor, racial minorities, and other newly literate groups, tract societies created literature appealing to these people and their missionaries. In narratives and biographies, Native letters and diary writings are reproduced—often without the authors' permission—to demonstrate, as one Euro-American missionary explains, "that the natives are not only capable of improvement, but that they are, to a high degree, desirous of possessing the means of instruction." Likewise, Chamberlain and other factory workers writing for the *Lowell Offering* felt compelled to demonstrate their capacity for self-betterment. Workers attended Improvement Circles to better their writing and speaking skills, publishing their compositions "to prove to others that [they] could understand, reason, reflect and communicate." Tractate writings were readily available to Chamberlain in Lowell's many church libraries. In her reminiscences of 1830s Lowell, Harriet Robinson recalled that among the religious reading available to workers were "Sunday-school books."[112]

In 1821 *The Little Osage Captive, an Authentic Narrative,* by Elias Cornelius, a Euro-American missionary to Native people in the southeastern United States, was published. Cornelius recounts Christians' "rescue" of an Osage girl, renamed Lydia Carter, from Cherokee captives. The tract's narrative is followed by an appendix of nine Native-authored letters, supposedly edited by Cornelius only for punctuation or to change "one or two words." The letter-writers express Christian religious sentiments, especially gratitude for their conversions. Among them is an unidentified Native woman who composed three letters. A later tract, *Memoir of Catharine Brown* (1825), reveals that these were written by the Cherokee Catharine Brown. Since *The Little Osage Captive* was published in at least five editions between 1821 and 1841, Chamberlain may well have been acquainted with it. This small pamphlet demonstrated that an Indian woman's writings could be published.[113]

Memoir of Catharine Brown, a Christian Indian of the Cherokee Nation, written by Rufus B. Anderson, a Euro-American, and published by the American Sunday School Union in 1832, reproduces many of Brown's letters and diary writings. Issued from 1825 to 1832 in at least six editions, this popular book was held by the Lowell Circulating Library in 1834. Brown's writings—reproduced without her permission—may have been edited by Anderson and/or the publisher, although Anderson claims not to have altered them. As he states: "The greater part of [the letters] have never before been published. . . . Alterations in the sense, are never made; and corrections in the grammar, but rarely." Nonetheless, Brown reputedly objected to the publication of so many of her private writings. One missionary-friend explains that Brown was "much distressed, that so many of her letters had been published" and believed that although "the object at *first* was, to show that an Indian could improve . . . two or three letters would have answered this purpose." To the missionaries, as Anderson reports, Brown's objections merely exemplified her Christian "humility." Chamberlain's writings are not free from the problems surrounding Euro-American mediation of Native writing, although she apparently exercised more autonomy in crafting them for publication. Nonetheless, Brown furnished another writing model, showing that a Native woman's thoughts and experience might be published.[114]

Another evangelical text, *Poor Sarah; or, The Indian Woman* (1820), is noteworthy for its early representation of a Native woman's voice, derived from the narrator/author's actual meetings with the woman. This brief tract has often been attributed to Elias Boudinot (Cherokee) and is sometimes considered the first fiction by a Native writer. The text itself, however, strongly suggests that it was written by a Euro-American woman. Apparently Boudinot only translated *Poor Sarah* into Cherokee, as Theda Perdue's study of Boudinot contends. First published serially in the *Religious Intelligencer* (New Haven, Connecticut) in 1820, *Poor Sarah* was later reprinted serially and issued as a tract, appearing in at least eight editions, variously titled, between 1820 and 1843.[115]

Poor Sarah's unnamed narrator indicates that she first met the Native woman, Sarah, a Connecticut neighbor, in 1814. While Elias Boudinot did spend several years in Connecticut, he did not arrive there until 1817. Sarah addresses the narrator as "Misse," acknowledging her as one of "you white folks"; it seems unlikely that Boudinot would have adopted a Euro-American female writing persona. The text indicates that Sarah died in the summer of 1817, the year that Boudinot arrived, again making it unlikely that he was the tract's author.[116]

Since *Poor Sarah* was so well known and often republished, Chamberlain could easily have been familiar with it. The text's extended representation of a Native woman's voice anticipates Chamberlain's first-person voice, although Chamberlain replaces Sarah's abasement with a more spirited, dignified persona. Sarah describes her conversion experience in a broken English at times obsequious to "God's dear white people." In a characteristic passage, Sarah expresses her growing religious devotion: "So after a great while, God make all my mind peace. I love Jesus; love pray to him, love tell him all my sorrows: He take away my sorrow, make all my soul joy; only sorry because can't read Bible, and learn how to be like Jesus." Although Chamberlain avoided such religious texts' insistence upon Native people's Christian conversion, *Poor Sarah*'s extended representation of a Native woman's voice showed that such a voice might be published. Another evangelical text, William Apess's (Pequot) *The Experiences of Five Christian Indians of the Pequot Tribe* (1833), includes the conversion narratives of four Native women: Mary Apess, Hannah Caleb, Sally George, and Anne Wampy. Although edited by William Apess, the stories are presumably narrated in the women's own words. Their stories constitute another model of Native women recounting their experiences and views for publication.[117]

The first known Native woman to produce a body of work for public distribution was Jane Johnston Schoolcraft (Bame-wa-wa-ge-zhik-a-quay; b. 1800 in Sault Ste. Marie, Michigan; Ojibwa and Scotch-Irish; d. 1841). Under the pen names "Rosa" and "Leelinau," Schoolcraft contributed poetry, Ojibwa legends and tales, and essays to a magazine, *The Literary Voyager; or, Muzzeniegun* (Sault Ste. Marie, 1826–27), edited and cowritten by her husband, Henry Rowe Schoolcraft. This periodical was not conventionally published; it was tran-scribed and circulated in such places as Sault Ste. Marie, Detroit, and New York. *The Literary Voyager* was apparently not available in Lowell, but Henry R. Schoolcraft's *Algic Researches* (1839) and other writings on Native peoples were held by early Lowell libraries. Jane School-craft's and Chamberlain's experiences resonate in certain ways. They both published through the medium of small, unconventional periodi-cals, an avenue more accessible to mixed-race and poor women. And the publication of both women's writings was facilitated by the interest of unconventional men. Like Chamberlain, Schoolcraft blended Euro-American and Native literary sources and strove through some of her writings to create greater understanding of Native peoples among non-Natives.[118]

Yet another influential text must have been Frances H. Whipple's semifictionalized biography of a Narragansett and African-American Rhode Island woman, *Memoirs of Elleanor Eldridge,* first published in 1838 and reprinted five times before 1847, when a sequel, *Elleanor's Second Book,* was published. Although some have presumed that *Mem-oirs* was written by Elleanor Eldridge herself (b. 1785), the narrator identifies the text as "biography." Other passages strongly suggest that the Euro-American Frances H. Whipple, and not Eldridge, was the author. As a well-known, full-length representation of a mixed-race, laboring woman's experience, *Memoirs of Elleanor Eldridge* proba-bly exerted significant influence on Chamberlain. Her near-contempo-rary, Whipple's character also supported herself as a hand spinner and weaver, as well as by other occupations such as domestic service. Ap-parently, for Whipple the interests of nonwhite and laboring women intersected in certain ways, for in 1842 she directed her energies toward founding and editing *The Wampanoag, and Operatives' Journal,* a periodical for mill workers in the Fall River, Massachusetts, area.[119]

Oral and Written Literary Culture in Rural New Hampshire

Chamberlain's writings reflect the richness of oral and written literary sources available to her from childhood. Although raised in a rural community far from a large city, she had access to a range of texts, as well as community storytelling traditions. Her pieces attest to the vibrant oral traditions shared by women, men, and children. Her sketches also reveal that she, like many of her friends, was an avid reader. According to William J. Gilmore's study of reading in a comparable rural Vermont community from 1780 to 1835, the rapid spread of schooling, as well as the mushrooming of the press, created a surprisingly literate citizenry, both male and female.[120]

Chamberlain's output represents her own contributions to oral tradition and other community members' participation in creating local oral literature. Several sketches convey her narrator's childhood pleasure in community storytelling, to which both women and men contributed. In "Recollections of My Childhood," the narrator recalls her early life on a farm. Besides fairy tales shared among the children, she remembers warmly the stories told by "Old Bill," a former sailor who worked occasionally as a day laborer helping out with chores: "But it was a great treat to me to listen to the queer stories of Old Bill, who had once been a sailor, and seen many different countries. . . . I listened with gaping mouth and eyes to his marvellous tales of Spaniards, Frenchmen, Indians, and Negroes; and though I presume they were mostly true, they appeared as wonderful to me as so many fairy tales" (pp. 211–12). This passage suggests the vibrancy of early-nineteenth-century rural storytelling among poor farming people and laborers.

In "Fortune-Telling," Chamberlain depicts women's lively participation in oral literary culture. This sketch suggests as well the existence of a distinct women's oral tradition. With her girlfriends, the narrator visits an elderly female neighbor beloved for her warmth and stories:

> The girls all truly loved the old lady, and were never more happy than when, seated in her neat little parlour, they listened to some legend of olden time, which Aunt Nancy (as we girls familiarly called her) would cull from the well-supplied storehouse of her cranium, for our amusement.
>
> One autumn, Aunt Nancy made a quilting, to which all the girls were invited. We had promised ourselves much merriment at this quilting; for we thought that Aunt Nancy, agreeably to her usual practice, would tell us some of the choicest and rarest of her stories. (p. 149)

Like Aunt Nancy's stories, Chamberlain's sketches share the legends and lore she has heard and carefully remembered.

As William Gilmore observes, means for distributing books, journals, and newspapers in New England became increasingly sophisti-
cated and efficient in the late eighteenth and early nineteenth
centuries. General stores in northern New England towns offered a
variety of printed matter, such as almanacs, the Bible, hymnals, devotional texts, schoolbooks, travel narratives, histories, and novels.
English books fairly flew across the Atlantic.[121] Chamberlain's reminiscences accord with Gilmore's observations. The narrator of "Recollections of an Old Maid. Number 3" recalls the library of her childhood
friend, Nancy E., which included "a Bible, Hymn Book, Assembly's
Catechism, English Reader, and Webster's Spelling Book. . . . also a
singing book, called Village Harmony . . . [and] 'Thomas's Almanac'"
(p. 174). Nancy owned copies of the three popular American novels of
the day, *The Coquette,* by Hannah Foster; *Charlotte. A Tale of Truth,* by
Susanna Rowson; and *Female Quixotism,* by Tabitha Tenney, as well
as the British Elizabeth Helme's *Louisa; or, the Cottage on the Moor.*
Chamberlain's sketches reveal that women shared books and reading
experiences, especially fiction. Her narrator recalls lending Nancy *Arabian Nights' Entertainments* and *The Asylum; or, Alonzo and Melissa,* by
Isaac Mitchell. She notes Nancy's reactions to several books, illustrating that Wolfeboro women shared not only oral traditions but also
private reading reactions.

Betsey Guppy's access to books and journals was enhanced by her
father's involvement in founding a library in Wolfeboro. In 1804 he
helped draft the constitution for a "social" (or lending) library in
Wolfeboro. Members purchased library shares for two dollars each and
then paid thirty-four cents annually to borrow books. Her father's
membership in the library, located on Main Street adjacent to the
Guppy house, must have given Betsey even greater access to reading
material. The contents of her father's small personal library enumer-
ated in his estate inventory suggest the kinds of material available to
Betsey in Wolfeboro. His literary holdings included James Hurdis's
The Village Curate, Johann Wolfgang von Goethe's *Sorrows of Young
Werther,* the anonymous *Letters of an Italian Nun and an English Gentle-
man,* Anne Burke's *Ela, or the Delusions of the Heart,* John McGowan's
French Convert, Isaac Watts's *Hymns and Spiritual Songs,* and Alain R. Le
Sage's *Devil upon Two Sticks.*[122] Such romantic and sensational British
and continental literature as Goethe's, Burke's, and McGowan's texts

contributed to the sensational and exotic elements of Betsey's "La Brainard" and "The Delusion of the Heart."

Literary and Other Culture in Lowell

Already deeply rooted from childhood in a shared culture of oral and written literature, Chamberlain traveled to work in Lowell, a place known for even greater cultural advantages. Attractions there included lyceums, evening schools, concerts and other performances, and plentiful libraries. A great allurement for her contemporaries, Lowell's libraries were likely equally appealing to Chamberlain. As Harriet Robinson observed on the rural women coming to Lowell in the 1830s, "[T]he fame of the circulating libraries, that were soon opened, drew them and kept them there, when no other inducement would have been sufficient." Chamberlain's sketches reflect the richness of her reading in Lowell, echoing such writers as Cowper, Byron, Burns, and Shakespeare. Her writings were enriched by the various kinds of libraries that flourished in Lowell in the 1830s and 1840s, some of which excluded women and most of which charged for use. These included libraries for mechanics associations and churches, circulating libraries, and a city library opened in 1844.[123]

In Chamberlain's time, twenty or more such organizations could be found in Lowell. By studying several published catalogs, as well as Larcom's and Robinson's autobiographies, one can draw a fairly full picture of the books and periodicals available to Chamberlain in Lowell. Since many library catalogs have not survived and because a text's presence in a given library does not, of course, mean that she patronized that library or read that particular book, the presence of various titles in Lowell can be linked loosely to Chamberlain's writings in terms of creating a climate for her artistic choices.

Although the various kinds of libraries differ in some significant ways, certain writers and texts appear in all the catalogs. These include British and American writers, with women quite well represented. Among the popular British authors are Charles Dickens, Mary Russell Mitford, Maria Edgeworth, Hannah More, Sir Walter Scott, William Shakespeare, Jane Austen, Harriet Martineau, Lord Byron, Felicia Hemans, Fanny Burney, Charlotte Elizabeth Tonna, and Robert Southey. Prevalent American writers include James Fenimore Cooper, Lydia

Maria Child, Benjamin Franklin, Catharine Maria Sedgwick, Samuel G. Goodrich (Peter Parley), T. S. Arthur, Jacob Abbott, and Nathaniel P. Willis. Echoes and direct quotations from many of these appear in Chamberlain's work. Other texts that she cites, such as *The Arabian Nights' Entertainments,* Percy's *Reliques of Ancient English Poetry,* and Watts's *Poetical Works,* also appear in many libraries. Books on North American Native people, such as Benjamin Thatcher's *Indian Biography,* Henry R. Schoolcraft's *Algic Researches,* and Samuel Drake's *Biography and History of the Indians of North America,* are quite common as well.

In the 1830s and 1840s, several corporations established libraries for workers, open to both men and women, but none of their catalogs is known to have survived. Similar libraries often enjoying corporation support were those of the mechanics' associations. According to Elfrieda McCauley's study of Lowell's early libraries, from 1825 to 1898 the Mechanics and Laborers' Reading Room at Central and Hurd Streets admitted both men and women. Although no catalogs are apparently extant for this library, several have been preserved for another such library. The Middlesex Mechanic Association Library, founded in 1825, did not admit women until 1856. Still, a perusal of its catalog suggests the kinds of books available at such institutions, as well as the kinds of written material circulating in Lowell during Chamberlain's residence.[124]

The Middlesex Mechanic Association Library catalog is arranged by subjects—science, history, literature, and government and politics. Subjects are construed quite broadly. Science, for one, includes natural history, mathematics, rhetoric, theology, and gazetteers. Although the library did not admit women, its catalog lists a surprising number of titles by and about women, perhaps in deference to Lowell's large female population. Hannah More's *Strictures on the Modern System of Female Education* is found alongside Mrs. Farrar's *Young Ladies' Friend* and Anna B. Jameson's *Memoirs of Celebrated Female Sovereigns.* Women's novels are also well represented, including Fanny Burney's *Cecilia,* four novels by Maria Edgeworth, several titles by Catharine Sedgwick, and Germaine De Stael's *Corinna.* Male friends or coworkers could have lent Chamberlain books from this or other libraries that excluded women. In her autobiography, Lucy Larcom recalls a male coworker's loaning her a book of poetry. And the narrator of Chamberlain's "A

Vision of Truth" mentions socializing with a close male friend in Lowell, so perhaps books were shared as well.[125]

Lowell churches commonly offered libraries for their members. These socially sanctioned collections were the only ones open to women without cost in the 1830s and 1840s. Unfortunately only one Lowell church library catalog is known to have survived, that of the First Unitarian Society. Still, it is important, since a similar church, the Second Universalist, hosted the Improvement Circle attended by Chamberlain and other *Lowell Offering* writers. The First Unitarian Society's catalog likely resembled that of the Second Universalist Church.

The holdings encompass a broad range of subjects—history, travel, philosophy, classics, technology, health, natural history, geology, and sermons. Literary authors are well represented, including Cooper, Scott, Irving, Martineau, Bremer, Edgeworth, Hemans, T. S. Arthur, Shakespeare, Spenser, Sedgwick, Sigourney, and More. Books by and about women are plentiful. These include conduct books, such as Lydia Sigourney's *Letters to Young Ladies* and J. Whitman's *Young Lady's Aid,* and historical studies, such as Lydia M. Child's *History of the Condition of Women in Various Ages and Nations.* The progressive stance of the Unitarians can be seen in this library's holding a copy of Child's *An Appeal in Favor of That Class of Americans Called Africans.* The library lacks the Sunday school books so prevalent in the early nineteenth century, which were probably more common in the libraries of evangelical sects. Harriet H. Robinson recalled that the factory women's "religious reading" included "Sunday-school books," so tractate literature was definitely available in Lowell. Several such titles were held by the Lowell Circulating Library. The broad-ranging and more cerebral subjects of the First Unitarian Society library reflect that sect's liberal rationalism.[126]

As Harriet H. Robinson and other sources indicate, factory women found circulating libraries extremely appealing. These were commonly offered by booksellers. In Chamberlain's time, Lowell supported about nine bookstores, many of which offered circulating libraries of two or three thousand volumes. To borrow materials, subscribers paid an annual fee of five to six dollars. The one extant catalog, that of the Lowell Circulating Library, lists two thousand books held in 1834, ranging from scholarly works to romances and farcical plays.

Circulating libraries roused the most controversy of Lowell's libraries. Carrying many romances and popular dramas, they were considered somewhat indecent, especially for female readers. As a writer for Lowell's *Lady's Pearl* warned in 1840, "[T]he world is flooded with *novels*, which contaminate the mind of their readers, and forever give them a distaste for solid reading. Let the young lady beware of the froth of our circulating libraries—the *very scum of literature.*" With less disapproval, Harriet H. Robinson remembered factory women borrowing and sharing circulating library books with such titles as *Abellino, the Bravo of Venice; Maria Monk; The Castle of Otranto; Eliza Wharton;* and *The Arabian Nights.* Many such texts are found in the Lowell Circulating Library catalog, as well as even more suggestive-sounding ones, for example, *Argal; or The Silver Devil, Being the Adventures of an Evil Spirit; The Book of the Boudoir; The Gamesters; or, Ruins of Innocence;* and *Tales of the Wild and Wonderful.* Plays and humorous writings not found in the mechanics', church, and public libraries were supplied in abundance by the Lowell Circulating Library. Representative titles include *American Comic Annual for 1831; Endless Amusement; Gaities and Gravities, a Series of Essays, Comic Tales, and Fugitive Vagaries; Is She Jealous? An Opera;* and *New Ways to Keep a Wife at Home, a Farce.* Chamberlain's earthy humor could well have been influenced by such writings.[127]

The Circulating Library also offered an ample share of more sober reading, such as the historical and travel books of the other libraries. Perhaps to counter criticism, the library also stocked such religious titles as *Universal Damnation and Salvation* and Cotton Mather's *Essays To Do Good.* The library offered as well some of the fictional titles anticipating aspects of Chamberlain's writings. These include Sigourney's *Traits of the Aborigines of America,* Anderson's *Memoir of Catharine Brown,* Child's *Hobomok,* Sedgwick's *Hope Leslie,* and Hale's *Northwood.* Since circulating libraries were those most readily available to Lowell factory women before the public library opened in 1844, it is likely that Chamberlain patronized them and incorporated their influences into her writings.

Although Lowell's City School Library opened its doors to women in the mid-1840s, it was not available without cost. Nonetheless, its fifty-cent annual fee was a bargain compared with those of the circulating libraries. By the late 1840s, the City School Library comprised more than seven thousand volumes. Lucy Larcom recollected borrowing some of the books that influenced Chamberlain's writings, such as Percy's *Reliques of Ancient English Poetry,* Shakespeare's plays, and "the songs of Burns." The library included a great range of material, including novels. Some of the fiction may have come from Bixby and Whiting's circulating library, a portion of which was contributed to the new public library. In terms of influencing Betsey Chamberlain, noteworthy titles found in the City School Library include Mary Russell Mitford's *Our Village,* Henry Schoolcraft's *Algic Researches,* Caroline Kirkland's *A New Home—Who'll Follow?,* Hannah F. Gould's *Poems,* Lydia Maria Child's *Hobomok,* Catharine Sedgwick's *Hope Leslie,* Cotton Mather's *Magnalia,* Margaret Fuller's *Woman in the Nineteenth Century,* Washington Irving's *Salmagundi,* and Isaac Watts's *Lyrics.* Chamberlain must have been an avid public library patron during her later years in Lowell.[128]

Besides libraries, Lowell's many cultural and educational programs constituted a fertile ground of ideas and aesthetic experiences enriching Chamberlain's writings. In the *Star of Bethlehem* (1841), Eliphalet Case describes the "spacious hall" accommodating twelve hundred people located in the town hall's second story. Here were held "political meetings, and a free discussion of moral, religious and other questions." Factory women also patronized the lectures "on literary, scientific and moral" topics hosted Tuesday and Wednesday evenings by the Lowell Lyceum and the Lowell Institute. Several kinds of musical programs were common, including sacred music from church-affiliated singing schools and performances by family groups, including the famous Hutchinson Family and Granite State Serenaders, both of New Hampshire. Songs ranged from the entertaining to those supporting causes such as woman suffrage and abolition. In the later 1840s, operatic instrumentalists and vocalists also began performing in Lowell.[129]

The city furnished plenty of other, less straitlaced entertainment as well. In an 1840s labor reform paper, *The Voice of Industry,* a writer observes that although Lowell was well supplied with libraries and lectures, the people were often too drained and exhausted by thirteen-hour workdays to avail themselves of instruction. Instead they sought lighter entertainment, such as "'Jim Crow' performances" and "the trashy, milk-and-water sentimentalities of the *Lady's Book* and *Olive Branch.*" Though considered improper by the middle class, dancing schools and ballrooms were frequented by some workers. Entertaining spectacles, as advertised in the *Lowell Courier,* included the New York Circus; "Grand Moving Dioramas of the cities of New Orleans, Louisville, [etc.]"; a dancing tattooed man; Monsieur Bihin, *"the giant of Belgium"*; "La Petit Taglioni, the Dancing Prodigy, only 6 years of age"; and "Mr. Love, the Unrivalled Polyphonist." Such entertainments could have contributed to the vitality and down-to-earth humor of Chamberlain's sketches.[130]

The Improvement Circle as Birthplace of the Lowell Offering

Since Chamberlain's writings were published not independently but through the medium of the *Lowell Offering* and *The New England Offering,* a consideration of the periodicals' history and objectives contributes to understanding her achievement. Chamberlain's marginalization as a Native woman writer has been compounded by the class-biased neglect of working-class women's writing. The production of laboring women with little education, the *Lowell Offering* has been often denigrated or ignored by scholars and other readers. Although the past thirty years have seen the remarkable growth of women's studies, the *Lowell Offering,* perhaps the first magazine written entirely by women, has received almost no attention from feminist scholars. While this and *The New England Offering* were reprinted in the 1970s after being more than one hundred years out of print, they are again currently out of print in paper, except for Benita Eisler's anthology of selected *Lowell Offering* writings.

Without Harriet Robinson's history of the *Lowell Offering* recorded in *Loom and Spindle* and her key to writers' pen names, it would be nearly impossible to identify Betsey Chamberlain or other writers. Robinson's writing experience parallels the troubled course of the *Lowell Offering* itself. By the late nineteenth century, the *Offering* had been virtually forgotten. Determined to chronicle this important women's achievement, Robinson was forced to finance the publication of *Loom and Spindle* herself, after four publishers rejected the manuscript.[131] Following publication in 1898, the book remained out of print and largely unknown until its reissue in 1976.

Twentieth-century treatment of the *Lowell Offering* has been riddled with half-truths and misconceptions. For one, scholars and other readers have often presumed that the *Lowell Offering* and *The New England Offering* were entirely the production of Euro-American Yankee women. Chamberlain's presence as a worker and writer shows that

Lowell was a somewhat more multicultural and tolerant community than has been thought. Nonetheless, some racial and ethnic intolerance plagued Lowell, since many Yankee workers resented the influx of Irish immigrants, and African Americans seem not to have been allowed to work in the mills at all. Surprisingly, Chamberlain, known for her "Indian blood," participated in the workers' Improvement Circle and contributed some pieces that were quite critical of Euro-American citizens' and the government's treatment of Native people. And Chamberlain's Native defenses were not the only ones to appear in the *Lowell Offering*. Like other nineteenth-century workers' periodicals, the *Offering* published writings that protested Native people's mistreatment.[132]

Lowell Offering writings were generated and shaped in the workers' Improvement Circles first organized in Lowell in the 1830s. For workers such as Chamberlain, who spent long days toiling at repetitive mill tasks, the Circles offered "delightful entertainments." Workers yearning for education relished these "intellectual banquets." That Chamberlain represents one factory-girl narrator "feasting upon the treasures of knowledge" found in books suggests how greatly she desired learning (p. 129). Although clergymen have often been given credit, the first Improvement Circles were in fact founded about 1836 and conducted by such factory women as Emeline Larcom and Harriot F. Curtis. According to Lucy Larcom (Emeline's sister), the early Circles gathered for "the writing and reading of their own literary compositions, with mutual criticism."[133]

In 1839 the Reverend Abel C. Thomas (1807–80) moved to Lowell, becoming pastor of the Second Universalist Church. There he established and presided over the Improvement Circle from which the *Lowell Offering* originated. Organized about January 1840, Thomas's Improvement Circle was one of seven meeting in Lowell by 1844. Thomas drew upon his prior experience as a Philadelphia printer to serve as the *Lowell Offering*'s first editor and publisher. The initial four issues were jointly edited by Thomas and the Reverend Thomas B. Thayer, who presided over an Improvement Circle meeting at the First Universalist Church. Mill women attending this Circle also contributed to the *Offering* until April 1841, when they began publishing their own periodical, *The Operatives' Magazine*.[134]

The Improvement Circles met fortnightly in church vestries, boardinghouses, and mills. As Harriet Hanson Robinson recalled, *Lowell*

Offering writings originated in the workers' reluctance to speak at the churches' Circles. The male and female attendees "were often asked to speak" but "persistently declined." Consequently, "they were invited to write what they desired to say, and send it, to be read anonymously at the next meeting." The women in particular contributed so many writings "that they very soon became the sole entertainment of what Mr. Thomas called 'these intellectual banquets,'" where "the writers furnish[ed] 'the feast of reason,' while all present participate[d] in 'the flow of soul.'" Similarly, Chamberlain's narrator in "A Vision of Truth" expresses feeling "truly delighted with the entertainment" of the Improvement Circle (p. 133). That she found Thomas's Circle a fruitful setting for learning and writing is underscored by his appreciation of her as "a constant Circle helper, [who] vitalized many pages of *The Offering* by humorous incidents and the wit of sound common sense." As Harriet Farley recalled, early Improvement Circle meetings were heavily attended, but attendance declined when the "novelty" wore off, although the number and quality of writings "gradually" increased over time.[135]

Thomas's memories of Improvement Circle activities differ somewhat from Robinson's. His *Autobiography* notes that from the outset, writing rather than speaking was the Circle's central activity: "Improvement in composition was the principal aim, and whosoever felt disposed, was invited to furnish original articles. These were corrected by the Pastors, (who were severally in charge of the Circles,) and publicly read at the meetings, with suggestive comments, to large assemblies. By this process, surprising advancement was visible among those who persevered, and several persons of extraordinary talent were discovered, mostly females."[136] Chamberlain must have been foremost among these. Clearly she found writing rewarding, since one reform proposed in her dream vision, "A New Society," is that women "each month, write at least enough to fill one page of imperial octavo" (p. 129). Submitting her compositions for public response probably helped her hone her skills, although it may also have restrained her from including more social criticism in her pieces.

All but five of Chamberlain's known writings—including her pro-Native pieces—were published during Thomas's editorship from October 1840 to August 1842. In this work, he seems to have been inspired by his Quaker background and his feminist leanings. As Robinson wrote, Thomas, "the grandson of a noted Quaker preacher (Abel

Thomas)," believed in women's ability and right to express themselves "both in speaking and in writing." (Significantly, several of Chamberlain's local-color sketches recall happy memories of socializing with Quakers in the Wolfeboro, New Hampshire, area.) Thomas expressed pride in having published "not only the first work written by factory girls, but also the first magazine . . . written exclusively by women in all the world." He considered the writers comparable to "the most gifted female authors in the land." When he moved away from Lowell in July 1842, he turned over the management of the *Lowell Offering* to three mill women: Harriet Farley, Harriet Lees, and Harriot F. Curtis. The following year Thomas married Maria Louise Palmer, who would become a woman suffrage activist.[137]

Twentieth-century scholars have sometimes implied that Lowell pastors colluded with mill management to suppress worker dissent. For instance, Philip S. Foner has written, "The circles were fostered and encouraged by the clergymen of Lowell and by the mill owners, who looked with favor upon their employees devoting themselves to culture rather than to complaining about their conditions in the mills and acting together to remedy them." Abel C. Thomas's writings, however, suggest that he did not ally himself with mill management. He published some writings censuring the "soul-less corporations" and advocating reforms. From 1841 to 1844, Thomas coedited and wrote for a religious paper, the *Star of Bethlehem,* published jointly in Lowell and another mill town, Manchester, New Hampshire. In an 1843 article, Thomas recalled his efforts to change mill working and living conditions: "During my residence in Lowell, I took occasion repeatedly to press certain improvements upon the attention of the several Corporations. Soul-less bodies are they, and it is hard to reach 'the quick,' where there appears to be little of the sort." His suggestions included better-ventilated boardinghouses, workers' bathing facilities, and a relief fund for ill employees. In his final *Lowell Offering* editorial, Thomas sought similar benefits, including libraries for workers. Although he found discussion of the "manufacturing system" inconsistent "with the design of the Offering," he included among his demands one considered radical at the time: "Diminution of the hours of mill-labor."[138]

No labor activist, Thomas nonetheless definitely empathized more with workers than with mill magnates. This empathy, along with his feminist leanings, constituted a progressive stance on human rights issues enabling his publication of Betsey Chamberlain's pro-Native writings. Thomas's ambivalent position on the *Lowell Offering*'s treatment of labor issues was perpetuated by subsequent editors, particularly Harriet Farley. In her editorials, Farley sometimes evaded or minimized pressing labor issues. For instance, in 1843 she wrote, "With wages, board, &c., we [the *Lowell Offering*] have nothing to do—these depend upon circumstances over which we can have no control." Nonetheless, the *Lowell Offering* under her editorship published a story, "The Mother and Daughter," in which women workers die in a mill fire as the direct result of management indifference or incompetence. An editorial militantly advocating a reduction in working hours bears her signature, "H. F." She wrote: "[R]eforms must come—some changes must be made—and sooner or later there will be an alteration and retrenchment of the hours of labor. Man was not made to be a mere beast of burden—far less woman. . . . [T]hough a manufactory may be the last stronghold of lengthened labor, yet it will finally be *stormed* and taken." Thus, the *Lowell Offering* under Farley's editorship, as under Thomas's, both acknowledges and evades labor problems.[139]

The periodical addresses many other social issues as well, including women's rights, class bias, the Irish famine, slavery, and persecution of Native people. Thus, as Cane and Alves argue in *"The Only Efficient Instrument": American Women Writers and the Periodical, 1837–1916,* such nineteenth-century women as the *Lowell Offering* writers found the periodical an avenue for "participation in the intellectual life and political discussions of their times."[140] For working-class and poor women, the small magazine certainly offered more accessible publication opportunities than did monograph or journal publication. As laboring women with little education, Chamberlain and the others must have found their publishing opportunity astonishing. In the rapidity of Chamberlain's composition and the liveliness of her pieces, one senses her heady enjoyment of the author role—and perhaps her awareness of its tenuous nature.

Writing for the Lowell Offering

A close look at *Lowell Offering* issues in which Betsey Chamberlain published yields further insights into her experience (Figure 13). In common with the other writers, she received some compensation. For

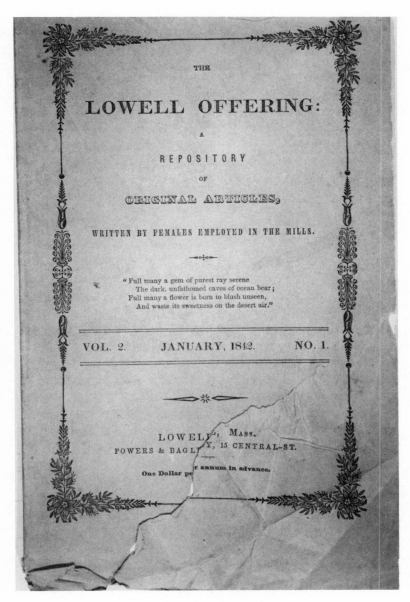

Fig. 13. Early cover, *Lowell Offering. Photograph by Judith Ranta*

the four earliest issues published October 1840 to March 1841, writers were given ten copies of issues for each published page of their writing. They might then realize a profit, of course, from selling the issues. By January 1843, as *Offering* editors indicate, writers received both "a stated compensation" (presumably monetary) and "a copy of the Offering." Chamberlain must have welcomed the extra money, though she may not have written initially with this in mind: many of her pieces were composed before writers received "compensation."[141]

Editorial notes in the first issues suggest that Chamberlain wrote many of her pieces quite early and rather quickly. Her Improvement Circle first met in January 1840, when Chamberlain probably began writing. By February 1841, she had composed seven sketches: "A Letter about Old Maids," "Recollections of an Old Maid. Number 1," "Recollections of an Old Maid. Number 2," "Old Maids and Old Bachelors," "Christmas," "Recollections of an Old Maid. Number 3," and "The Last Witch of Salmagundi." By March 1841, she had submitted three more pieces to the *Lowell Offering*: "Unfortunate La Brainard," "Recollections of My Childhood," and "The First Wedding in Salmagundi." The first of these was published in September 1841 under the title "La Brainard," an author's or editor's revision. Chamberlain continued to publish at the rate of one and often two pieces per month.[142]

Editors' comments support Robinson's remembrance of Chamberlain as "the most noted" early *Lowell Offering* writer. In the December 1840 issue's table of contents, Chamberlain's "Recollections of an Old Maid. Number 2" is presented as "Recollections of Betsey. Number 2." Apparently "Betsey" had gained some renown after publishing her first two pieces in the October issue. The humble moniker conveys her persona's appealingly earthy, humorous stance. The editors well understood her appeal. In notes preceding or following her pieces, they comment approvingly on "Betsey's" didacticism and local-color realism. At the head of "Recollections of an Old Maid. Number 2," the editors remark that "the two characters are introduced by way of contrast," urging that "the moral of each be attentively regarded." Following "The Last Witch of Salmagundi," they inform readers that here, as in "Christmas," the author "has not related fictions," since the "incidents as detailed actually occurred."[143]

Despite its early appeal, after 1840 Chamberlain would not often publish under the signature "Betsey." She signed subsequent pieces with three additional pen names: Tabitha, Jemima, and B. C. The use of pen names was not peculiar to the *Lowell Offering*. Writers for other early nineteenth-century workers' periodicals invariably published anonymously or pseudonymously. Nor was the use of multiple pen names unusual. Most *Offering* writers publishing as frequently as did Chamberlain employed four or more pseudonyms. Lucy Larcom, for instance, published under eight different signatures, and her sister Emeline seven. It is difficult to discern a pattern in Chamberlain's use of pseudonyms. While multiple signatures might suggest that more women wrote for the *Lowell Offering* than actually did, Chamberlain's writings belie this. She published two pieces in the same *Offering* issue using two different signatures as often as she published two in one issue under the same signature.

For the most part, pen names were chosen by the writers themselves. In an early editorial, Abel Thomas explains the procedures for assigning signatures. When submitting an article to the *Offering,* the writer was required to furnish her "real name and residence . . . as a guaranty that [the article was] *original."* The editors pledged to "sacredly regard the confidence reposed in them by the writers." Writers were asked to choose a "fictitious signature." If they did not supply a pen name, then the editors would publish their writings under their real names or initials. Thus the pieces signed "B. C." were probably those for which Chamberlain had not chosen a pen name. Her signatures Tabitha, Jemima, and Betsey were all old-fashioned, rural New England names appropriate for her local-color writings.[144]

During the time when Chamberlain published, *Lowell Offering* and *New England Offering* editors professed a broad-minded selection policy that permitted great freedom in subjects and styles. As Abel Thomas wrote: "The largest range of subject has been allowed, and the greatest variety of style indulged. . . . [I]n composition the style has been humorous or otherwise." Thomas's liberal editorial stance accommodated Chamberlain's Native protest writings, feminism, and humor. Harriet Farley as editor of *The New England Offering* also invited serious or humorous pieces upon a range of subjects. As she wrote in an editorial, "[A]rticles upon any subject shall be welcome to our pages; and nothing be rejected on account of the topic of which it treats. Prose or poetry, didactic or humorous, literal or fanciful, pathos or bathos, all shall have their respective place in our grateful estimation, and the pages of our magazine."[145] None of Chamberlain's controversial writings, however, appeared in *The New England Offering*.

In his autobiography Thomas recalled correcting the writings, but elsewhere he claims to have little edited *Lowell Offering* contributions. In an *Offering* editorial, he explains: "We have frequently been asked whether we do not re-write, or greatly alter, the articles furnished for publication? We answer, No. We *never* re-write an article; and we take fewer liberties with any communication than are claimed by the editorial craft every-where. Sometimes we expunge a word, and unfrequently an entire sentence; and very seldom we substitute a few words for an omitted passage—but the words so substituted have not averaged four to a page. Should we ever find it necessary to take greater or other liberties than these, we shall be careful to mention the fact." Thomas took pains not to alter the women's viewpoints and style. As he wrote in another editorial, he "resolved carefully to avoid any alteration which might affect the sentiment or style of the several writers." Likewise, Lucy Larcom observed, "We did not receive much criticism." In an 1882 article, Harriet H. Robinson cited Thomas's statement that heavily revised writings were not published in the *Offering*. As Thomas wrote, "Communications much amended in process of training the writers were rigidly excluded from print." Thus, it can be safely assumed that Chamberlain's *Lowell Offering* writings were not altered substantively beyond her original intentions.[146]

Despite a measure of tolerance and editorial noninterference, Betsey Chamberlain was negotiating a complex situation. As a mixed-race woman publishing in a periodical predominantly by and for Euro-Americans, the protection of her Euro-American descent enabled her to slip into her writings some angry responses to Natives' persecution. Anonymity afforded another kind of protection. While her identity was known to Abel Thomas and to the other writers and later female editors, Chamberlain was mostly unknown to her audience. She sometimes used her forum as a *Lowell Offering* writer to advocate for Native people, but in a muted way that would not jeopardize her opportunity to publish. In her *Offering* pieces, the ambivalent treatment of Native and Euro-American relations reflects the complexity of her position.

Since in its time the *Lowell Offering* enjoyed considerable renown and a fairly wide circulation, it can be assumed that Chamberlain's writings contributed their share to the vibrant mix of antebellum culture. In 1843 Harriet Farley wrote that the *Lowell Offering* had three hundred subscribers in New York State (not including New York City) and that their "subscription list [was] very good." There were subscribers in all of the states except some southern ones, and overseas in countries including England, Scotland, Ireland, and France.[147] Sales of early issues were vigorous, ranging from three thousand to more than five thousand copies per issue.[148] These figures are supported by two later nineteenth-century texts about Lucy Larcom. The unidentified preface writer of *The Poetical Works of Lucy Larcom* (1884) asserts that the *Lowell Offering* "had at one time four thousand subscribers." This figure is again cited in Daniel D. Addison's 1895 biography of Larcom. Interest in factory women's periodicals seemed to decline with time. In 1849, *The New England Offering* had only one thousand subscribers.[149] While it is unlikely that the magazines' Euro-American readers knew they were reading a Native author, they were nonetheless experiencing and being influenced by a Native mind and sensibility.

Chamberlain's Native Writings

While Chamberlain never explicitly identifies herself as Native, her words express much Native content as well as suggestions of her mixed heritage. References to Native people or significant pro-Native content are found in eight of her thirty-seven periodical pieces. Chamberlain's unusually frequent treatment of Native subjects offers further evidence of her "Indian blood," to quote Robinson's terms, and her identification with Native people.[150] Nonetheless, given the dominant society's genocidal persecution of Natives, it is not surprising that Chamberlain would refrain—at least in print—from openly identifying her bicultural heritage. In her autobiographical local-color sketches, Chamberlain suggests her ancestry in several narratorial self-portraits. As previously seen, the narrator of "Recollections of an Old Maid. Number 1" boldly describes herself in girlhood as having "a face as round as the full moon, and cheeks as red as peony." Hard work has rendered her "tough as a squaw" (p. 164). This pleased self-description of a tough, red-faced girl reflects Chamberlain's awareness that she differed from the Anglo-American ideal of the pale lady and suggests her heritage. (Chamberlain may have considered herself as resembling "a squaw" rather than being one, because she was not full-blood Native and did not live in a traditional Native community.)

In other reminiscences, Chamberlain's narrator describes her child-hood pleasure in "roam[ing] the fields for berries, and the meadows for flowers" (p. 211). The narrator of "Sabbath Morning" recalls child-hood happiness "gathering wild-flowers and berries, nuts and acorns." In the forest, she enjoys worshiping God amid the trees and birds, where "all nature pay[s] homage to the great Creator." As day breaks, the narrator exults in the "resplendent sun" (p. 132). Since two other texts, "Visit to a Grave-Yard" and "The Indian Pledge," reveal some knowledge of Algonkian religious beliefs, Chamberlain probably knew as well that these New England people were woodland hunter-gather-ers also practicing some agriculture. Thus, she often describes herself in childhood participating pleasurably in the gathering activities tradi-tionally performed by Northeast Native women. She also worships in some traditional Algonkian ways, regarding the forest and sun as sa-cred. As Pritchard explains: "To the Algonquin, the pine forests are God-built cathedrals where one can witness the presence of God. . . . Wabanaki people have the greatest reverence for the sun."[151] Cham-berlain represents her narrator worshiping the creator at sunrise in a forest rather than in a church.

In those of her writings with considerable Native content, Chamber-lain's narratorial stance veers from angry protest against their mistreat-ment to conventional representation of Native "savages." Chamberlain's earliest protest writing is found in her tale "The Indian Pledge" (1842), which resembles Northeastern Algonkian oral tales in its brev-ity, fictional nature, and effort "to teach a moral lesson."[152] The un-named Native hunter of Chamberlain's tale proves more honorable and a better Christian than a Euro-American man he encounters. Set in mid-eighteenth-century Connecticut ("the land of 'steady habits,'" p. 126), the story recounts the meeting of a Euro-American farmer, Ichabod, and a Pequot or Narragansett hunter suffering from hunger and thirst. In these particulars the story is faithful to history, since the elimination of their game animals and other food sources led to the migration or starvation of many New England Algonkian. When the Indian asks Ichabod for some food and drink, the white man lashes out: "Get you gone, you heathen dog!" (p. 126). Slowly withdrawing, the Indian collapses on the ground, but soon Ichabod's kindly wife, Mary, secretly brings him some food and drink. In gratitude, he gives her a feather as a token of future protection from Native attack against herself or her family.

In fact, the Indian long remembers his promise and later refrains from retaliating against Ichabod at an opportune moment. Native people's fidelity to their promises had been noted and appreciated by some Euro-Americans. In his *History of New-Hampshire* (1784), Jeremy Belknap relates the story of Elizabeth Hull Heard, a Euro-American Dover, New Hampshire, woman who in 1676 protected a Native boy from massacre. In return, the boy promised that she would never be harmed by his people. During an attack in 1689, the Natives recognized Heard and spared her life. This incident is found also in Cotton Mather's *Magnalia Christi Americana* (1702).[153] Not only would Chamberlain have known this story, but she may have been a direct descendant of Elizabeth Heard, as previously noted, making the story even more meaningful to her. The alliance of Euro-American women and Native people was a theme of some earlier women's fiction, including Lydia Maria Child's *Hobomok* (1824) and Catharine M. Sedgwick's *Hope Leslie* (1827), both titles readily available in Lowell libraries. Chamberlain makes the theme her own by placing her hunter on an equal footing with the Euro-American characters. While Child's and Sedgwick's Native characters are secondary to the main Euro-American ones, Chamberlain's is clearly superior to the Euro-American farmer, Ichabod.

This story, as well as "Visit to a Grave-Yard," reveals Chamberlain's knowledge of Algonkian, specifically Narragansett or Wampanoag, religious beliefs. If she did not acquire this knowledge from her own family or neighbors, Chamberlain may have gleaned it from her reading in Wolfeboro and Lowell. In "The Indian Pledge," the hunter tells the Euro-American woman, "Cantantowwit protect the white dove from the pounces of the eagle" (p. 127). Later when he feeds and shelters Ichabod, he tells him that his god, Cantantowwit, has urged him not to seek revenge against him (p. 128). Spelled sometimes as Kautantowwit (Chamberlain's spelling may have been altered by the *Lowell Offering*'s editors or publisher), this name for the "the great South-West God" was recorded by Roger Williams in his study of the Narragansett, *A Key into the Language of America* (1643). In *Magnalia Christi Americana*, Cotton Mather also noted that New England Indians' "chief God" was called *Kautantowit*. Since *Magnalia* was held by the Lowell City School Library, founded in 1844, it may well have been available two years earlier when Chamberlain published "The Indian Pledge." One can only speculate abut why she chose to incorporate explicit Narragansett rather than Abenaki lore in her writings. Her ancestry may have been Narragansett, or she may have wanted to include Native details more familiar to a southern New England audience, whom she considered her principal readership.[154]

Chamberlain's "Visit to a Grave-Yard" discusses Cantantowwit in even more detail. The piece is set during Indian Summer, which the narrator explains is "a name derived from the natives, who believe that it is caused by a wind, which they believe to be the breath of their great god Cantantowwit, to whom the souls of all good Indians go, after their decease" (p. 134). Chamberlain's effort to explain something about Cantantowwit and related Algonkian religious beliefs emphasizes her regard for Native people. In the cemetery the narrator perceives the divine in the "south-western breezes, as they breathed through the glowing trees, [which] seemed almost to articulate, and I fancied that I could hear the still small voice of the Eternal" (p. 134). Wampanoag and Narragansett belief holds that Cantantowwit's house, located in the southwest, is the place where their people go after death. Likewise in *Magnalia,* Mather recorded that Kautantowit dwells "in the south-west regions of Heaven." As he explained, the New England Indians believed that since all people possess "immortal *souls,*" after death those who "were godly, shall go to a splendid entertainment with *Kautantowit,* but otherwise must wander about in restless horror forever." Chamberlain may also have known a book held by the Lowell Middlesex Mechanic Association Library in 1840. In *Biography and History of the Indians of North America* (1837), Samuel G. Drake explains that Northeast Native people call their god "Kuttand" and believe "they came [originally] from the South-west, and return thence when they die." In "Visit to a Grave-Yard" and other writings, Chamberlain sometimes expresses Native knowledge directly and at other times only intimates it.[155]

Chamberlain's Native hunter receives Ichabod into his home, offering him food and shelter when he is lost in the forest. This kindness accords with many historical and literary accounts of Native people's assistance to early colonists. In his history of Native American people, Joseph Bruchac (Abenaki) devotes a chapter to the welcome offered the settlers by Natives, who shared their food, medicine, culture, and sometimes even their lands—though they did not expect to cede their lands or have them stolen outright, as often happened.[156] Thus, Chamberlain's hunter distinguishes between the settlers' lands and the "Indians' hunting-grounds," stressing the need for Euro-Americans to follow Native cultural practices (wearing a feather) when visiting Native lands (p. 127).

Two earlier literary representations of Native people's welcoming behavior anticipate such scenes in "The Indian Pledge." In *Traits of the Aborigines of America* (1822), Lydia Sigourney's speaker recounts the hospitality that many early Algonkians offered Europeans. This book was held by the Lowell Circulating Library in 1834. Like Chamberlain's Native hunter, Sigourney's Indian dwells in a "hut" and shares his food and bed with the settlers:

> . . . [T]he slight-constructed hut
> Furnish'd his shelter, and its doors spread wide
> To every wandering stranger. There his cup,
> His simple meal, his lowly couch of skins
> Were hospitably shared.

In John Greenleaf Whittier's "The Indian's Tale" (1831), the New England Native speaker, whose home is also a "hut," describes his people's aiding the needy English:

> There came unto my father's hut,
>   A wan, weak creature of distress;
> The red man's door is never shut
>   Against the lone and shelterless;
> And when he knelt before his feet,
>   My father led the stranger in—
> He gave him of his hunter-meat.

While Sigourney's poem often strongly denounces Euro-American mistreatment of Native people, both her text and Whittier's reiterate the notions of Native disappearance and the superiority of Christianity to Native religions.[157] In some respects these texts anticipate Chamberlain's story, but Chamberlain more strongly supports Native people, rejecting the notion of Native disappearance and illustrating the superiority of Algonkian religious practices.

At the conclusion of "The Indian Pledge," Chamberlain advocates for better treatment of Natives. As her characters part, the hunter tells Ichabod, "[W]hen you see a red man in need of kindness, do to him as you have been done by" (p. 128). Thus the hunter enacts the Algonkian custom of teaching by example, conveying "a Native lesson in compassion."[158] Besides encouraging more humane conduct, Chamberlain's story reverses the common Euro-American view of Natives as ignorant savages. Grateful, and ashamed of his misconduct, Ichabod "went home purified in heart, having learned a lesson of Christianity from an untutored savage" (p. 128).

The theme of Native people's superior religiosity or Christianity is found in other early texts, such as *Poor Sarah; or, The Indian Woman* (1820) and the writings of William Apess. *Poor Sarah* contrasts a poor, pious Christian Native, Sarah, and a less devout, privileged Euro-American woman. The theme of Euro-American Christians' hypocrisy and Native people's more sincere Christianity is found in many of Apess's writings, such as *The Experiences of Five Christian Indians of the Pequot Tribe* (1833). It also appears in the work of some early Native women writers discussed in Karen L. Kilcup's introduction to *Native American Women's Writing, 1800–1924*. Like these other early writers, Chamberlain introduces Christianity into "The Indian Pledge" primarily "to critique white society . . . underscor[ing] the inconsistencies between words and behavior." Not only does Chamberlain's Native character possess superior spirituality, but he far surpasses Ichabod in forest survival skills.[159]

Although Chamberlain generally avoids the heavy emphasis upon Native people's conversion found in such contemporary texts as *Poor Sarah* and William Apess's writings, she explores the theme of the spiritually superior Native in "The Indian Pledge"—but without transforming him into a Christian. Chamberlain makes it clear that her Native hunter's virtue springs from his belief in a Native god, Cantantowwit. In this regard, although "The Indian Pledge" is less developed than *Poor Sarah* and Apess's texts, it is more daring: it resists the pressure upon Native people to convert.

Like Chamberlain's local-color sketches, "The Indian Pledge" draws from oral traditions. As mentioned above, the tale resembles Northeastern Algonkian oral tales in its brevity and didacticism. It also shares some other characteristics of Native narratives, as specified in Kristin Herzog's discussion of oral traditions. Like those, "The Indian Pledge" is episodic and circular in structure. After their first encounter, Ichabod and the Native hunter meet a second time. The action circles from Ichabod's farm into the Native hunting grounds and then back to the farm. The tale's style and setting share the terseness and compression of Native oral narratives, with "motives and emotions remain[ing] unexplained." The characters are "intimately tied to [the] landscape" of eighteenth-century Connecticut. Lastly, Chamberlain's tale includes the irony often found in Native oral narratives, concluding with a satiric characterization of her compassionate and spiritual hunter as "an untutored savage" (p. 128). With such irony, she challenges racist notions of Native "heathens" and "savages."[160]

"The Indian Pledge" also reflects the influence of Lydia Maria Child's progressive writings, particularly "Adventure in the Woods," a children's story published in 1826 in Child's *Juvenile Miscellany*. Child's story, in turn, draws from earlier Native oral traditions and writings about Native women. Chamberlain's and Child's stories follow similar plot patterns, stressing the importance of cooperation between Native people and Euro-Americans. As in Chamberlain's "The Indian Pledge," set in eighteenth-century Connecticut, the setting of Child's story is historical. Set in colonial Boston, "Adventure in the Woods" represents the kindness of Mrs. Wilson, an English settler, in providing food to an ailing Algonkian woman, as Chamberlain's Mary feeds the starving Native hunter. In both stories the Native characters repay this charity in kind, aiding Euro-Americans lost in the forest and demonstrating Natives' superior knowledge and skill surviving in their homelands.[161]

While both stories follow a circular pattern and resonate in other ways, they also differ significantly, reflecting the authors' varying degrees of identification with Native people. Chamberlain's story represents more graphically the persecution that Euro-Americans inflicted upon Native people. The farmer denounces the hunter as a "heathen" and an "Indian dog," refusing to aid him. Child's story only suggests that there has been a lack of peace between the English settlers and the Natives. Her Native character is represented as more grateful for Euro-Americans' assistance and more obsequious in expressing that gratitude. But Chamberlain's hunter retains his dignity, even assuming the role of teacher to the misguided Ichabod. Thus Chamberlain's story reflects deeper knowledge of the bigotry facing Native people, and of their full humanity.

In her views on Natives, Chamberlain also participates in a dialogue with her sister *Lowell Offering* writers. "The Indian Pledge" responds quite directly to a story appearing earlier in 1842, Hannah Johnson's

"The Indian's Faith," whose title it echoes. Set in Connecticut, both stories feature major characters who are Narragansett, a band about whom—among white New Englanders, at least—more was known, published, and circulated than any other Native group at that time. Both stories interrogate the sincerity of whites' Christianity. Demonstrating that the Native hero is a better Christian than the white man, the stories challenge the Euro-American view of Natives as heathens.[162]

In some important ways, however, the stories differ. Johnson's tale is constructed so clumsily that the plot is hard to follow, while "The Indian Pledge" is coherent and fluid in construction. On the whole, "The Indian's Faith" typecasts Indians in derogatory or limiting ways. For instance, Johnson's Indians are "savages," and the Narragansett hero, Conancet, is a "noble sachem" and a "noble Indian."[163] Moreover, in Johnson's story the Narragansetts and whites are represented as equally destructive toward one another. In Chamberlain's "The Indian Pledge," Ichabod is clearly more destructive than the Native hunter, as is the case also in her "A Fire-Side Scene." Chamberlain's unnamed hunter is represented more as an ordinary human being who, admitting his temptation to avenge himself against Ichabod, chooses instead to follow the prompting of his deity, Cantantowwit. While Johnson's hero dies at the story's end, Chamberlain's hunter survives, returning to his forest life. Thus "The Indian Pledge" corrects biased notions of noble savages and vanishing Indians found in "The Indian's Faith."

Chamberlain's story also seems to respond to another earlier *Offering* piece, "The Lessons of Nature," by Ella [Harriet Farley]. In an Emersonian discussion of nature's sacred influence, Farley quotes two lines from Alexander Pope's "An Essay on Man" (1733–34), contending that even an uneducated Indian, "the humblest individual," can detect God in nature:

Lo! the poor Indian, whose untutored mind,
Sees God in clouds, and hears Him in the wind, &c.

At the conclusion of "The Indian Pledge," Chamberlain's narrator responds to Farley's piece by commenting sardonically on the "untutored savage," whom she represents as actually more sensitive and knowledgeable than the "educated" Euro-American farmer. In "The Lessons of Nature," Farley's narrator quotes approvingly from "An

Essay on Man" that one ought to "look thro' Nature up to Nature's God."[164] Native people, on the other hand, would tend to find God looking *at* or *with,* rather than through, Nature. Thus, in Chamberlain's "Visit to a Grave-Yard," the narrator hears the "voice of the Eternal" in the "south-western breezes."

"The Indian Pledge" might also be read as an allegory of Chamberlain's situation in Lowell at the time. In writing this story she tried to negotiate, or reconcile her Native heritage with living and working conditions there. The Native hunter could be a mask for Chamberlain herself, who, after enduring the Euro-American man's contemptuous rebuff, is offered food and drink by a white woman. Likewise, Chamberlain undoubtedly faced racism in her quest to earn a living and found a measure of acceptance from the Euro-American workers at Lowell. The story's Native hunter reassures the white woman that no harm will come to her from his people. Accordingly, Chamberlain attempted to preserve her livelihood by assuring her coworkers of her goodwill. Still, in this story she could not refrain from venting some anger at the Euro-American man's cruelty.

Seven Indian-themed writings in later *Lowell Offering* issues reveal Chamberlain's coworkers' assumptions of Euro-American superiority and Native people's inferiority, suggesting the bigotry that Chamberlain faced in Lowell. Understanding nineteenth-century anti-Native racism helps to elucidate the rage of her pieces "A Fire-Side Scene" and "The Delusion of the Heart" (not included in this volume). Though several of the other *Offering* writings show sympathy for the wrongs done to Native people, such expressions are usually clouded by bias. In Mariam R. Green's ballad "The Indians," Native "treach'ry" is caused by white betrayal:

> That red man was driven from all that was dear,
>> Whose hearts hospitality swayed;
> Who greeted the haughty white man with a cheer,
>> Till taught treach'ry by being betrayed.

Still, Green's speaker assumes that Native people—rather simple children of Nature—are doomed to disappear. The least biased of the *Lowell Offering* writings, besides Chamberlain's, is Pumen's "The Dark Side." The narrator contends that "the red man's wrongs shall be redressed. . . . and [he will] be known and acknowledged as a brother in humanity." If Pumen or any other *Offering* writers were not also Native, then their position as lowly factory girls may have contributed to their identification with the oppressed Indians.[165]

Despite some expressions of sympathy for and identification with Native people, bigotry tends to overshadow open-mindedness and tolerance in most of the Indian-themed pieces by *Lowell Offering* writers. These convey a strong assumption of Euro-American superiority. Jane S. Welch's "Plea for the Indian" concludes with a wish that the Natives' "uncultivated minds be taught to appreciate the high value of civilization and learning," as well as Christianity. In her sketch of Pocahontas, Harriet Farley distinguishes her from other Natives by her ability to recognize the English as a "nobler race of beings . . . a race superior in mind, and far more beautiful in person." As in the other pieces, Farley's narrator assumes that the Natives are rapidly disappearing. The narrator explains, "The departure of that dark race is like that of clouds, which pass away before the morning sun." Given the bias conveyed in Farley's writings, it is no wonder that few of Chamberlain's pieces, and none of her pro-Native ones, were published in the *Lowell Offering* and *The New England Offering* during Farley's tenure as coeditor from November 1843 to March 1850. Chamberlain's angry pieces are elucidated by awareness of the anti-Native bigotry existing in the community where she lived, worked, and wrote.[166]

Her most direct expression of resistance to Native persecution is found in "A Fire-Side Scene" (1842). In this brief sketch of a Euro-American family gathered at their hearth, the author powerfully juxtaposes the homey fireside scene with a relation of Euro-American cruelty in the burning of Native villages. She also brilliantly compares one use of fire with another. Fireside gatherings and storytelling commonly occurred in country towns such as the one where Chamberlain grew up. In his history of Tuftonboro, New Hampshire, a small town just north of Wolfeboro, John W. Hayley recalls that in his nineteenth-century childhood, "the incidents of the Indian wars were a frequent topic of conversation around the fireside."[167] The children of Chamberlain's sketch urge Uncle David to recount his experience "burning the Miami Indians" (p. 125). Uncomfortable and reluctant at first, Uncle David finally complies.

He recalls his participation as a United States Army soldier in the burning of the Miami on 20 August 1794. Relieved that the Indians were only "heathens," Uncle David describes the army's surrounding the Native villages and burning alive all the inhabitants, including women and children. Again and again, he rationalizes the army's actions with the observation that the Miami were only "heathens." This scornful epithet resounds also in Chamberlain's "The Indian Pledge," when Ichabod contemptuously calls the Algonkian hunter a "heathen." This may well have been a painful issue for Chamberlain, since she or her family members could have suffered the insult from their Euro-American neighbors. Her writings associate white racism with early American religious notions rather than with skin color, as we might more readily assume today. In "A New Society," her factory-girl narrator redefines "heathen," removing the misnomer from Natives and simultaneously making a feminist statement. For her narrator, a heathen is "every father of a family who neglects to give his daughters the same advantages for an education which he gives his sons" (p. 129).

To return to "A Fire-Side Scene," Chamberlain deepens the text's social criticism when one of the children asks Uncle David, "[D]o you think 'Uncle Sam' is a Christian, to give you a pension for being in *that* scrape?" (p. 126). Again Chamberlain raises the problem of Euro-American Christians' sincerity and sanctity, casting doubt as well upon the government's morality. She does not identify the battle, but a crucial one in Native history did take place on 20 August 1794: the Battle of Fallen Timbers, in which many New Hampshire soldiers fought. At Fort Miami on the Maumee River (in present-day Ohio), Michikinikwa, or Little Turtle (Miami/Mahican), and Weyapiersenwah, or Blue Jacket (Shawnee), led a confederation of Miami, Ojibwa, Delaware, Potawatomi, Shawnee, and Ottawa bands against federal troops headed by General "Mad" Anthony Wayne. The Natives' defeat led to their loss of huge portions of the Northwest Territory. That Chamberlain knew the battle's date, as well as some vivid details, and long after wrote "A Fire-Side Scene," again demonstrates her identification and empathy with Native people.

Some of the most important precedents for Chamberlain's Native protests can be found in the writings of William Apess (Pequot). The prolific Apess penned a number of angry, eloquent diatribes against Natives' persecution, such as his *Eulogy on King Philip* (1836). As in Chamberlain's "A Fire-Side Scene," Apess's narrator derides the Euro-American view of Native people as heathens and savages.[168] He also questions Euro-Americans' vaunted benevolence and the sincerity of their Christianity: "Another act of humanity for Christians, as they call themselves, that one Captain Standish, gathering some fruit and provisions, goes forward with a black and hypocritical heart and pretends to prepare a feast for the Indians; and when they sit down to eat, they seize the Indians' knives hanging about their necks, and stab them to the heart. The white people call this stabbing, feasting the savages. We suppose it might well mean themselves, their conduct being more like savages than Christians."[169] Apess's challenges to Euro-American hypocrisy and cruelty offered models of courage for Betsey Chamberlain in composing and publishing her own protest writings.

Among Euro-Americans, Lydia Maria Child's juvenile text *The First Settlers of New-England* (1829) strongly anticipates Chamberlain's Native protest writings. Given her intellectual, Native, and feminist interests, Chamberlain probably knew Child's writings. In the introduction to *The First Settlers,* Child explains that her aim is to correct misconceptions about Native people and influence her juvenile readers to take future action to relieve their unwarranted suffering. Like Apess and Chamberlain, Child questions Euro-Americans' integrity, showing "that the treatment they [Native people] have met with from the usurpers of their soil has been, and continues to be, in direct violation of the religious and civil institutions which we have heretofore so nobly defended, and by which we profess to be governed." She impugns the Christianity—and plain good sense—of the Pilgrim settlers, who "whilst they were systematically planning the destruction of the Indians, . . . were sharply engaged in discussing with each other points of faith altogether unimportant or incomprehensible." Child's courage in challenging both Native people's historical and continuing persecution and the "wisdom" of the founding fathers must have helped inspire Chamberlain to publish her Native and feminist protest writings.[170]

Child cites many occurrences of massacre and other injustices perpetrated by English settlers against Natives. Her chapter on the Narragansett cites an unidentified writer's description of a seventeenth-century English attack, anticipating Chamberlain's treatment of the Miami massacre in "A Fire-Side Scene." This passage also appeared earlier in Washington Irving's very popular *Sketch Book* (1819–20), attributed to the "Ms. of the Rev. W. Ruggles." Irving cites Ruggles's description of "the shrieks and cries" of the fiery attack's Narragansett victims and the guilty reactions of some Euro-American soldiers: "The burning of the wigwams, the shrieks and cries of the women and children, and the yelling of the warriors, exhibited a most horrible and affecting scene, so that it greatly moved some of the soldiers. They were in *much doubt* then, and afterwards seriously inquired, whether burning their enemies alive could be consistent with humanity, and the benevolent principles of the Gospel."[171]

Chamberlain's character Uncle David describes the attack against the Miami in terms quite similar to Ruggles's: "Yes, we burned them all up—women, children, and all. Oh, their horrid yells and groans! how many times I have heard them in my dreams" (pp. 125–26). In Uncle David's anxiety about his own participation, Chamberlain echoes the remorse that Ruggles attributes to some of the New England soldiers. Like Ruggles's and Child's writings, Chamberlain's "A Fire-Side Scene" challenges the sincerity of Euro-Americans' avowed piety.

While many other Euro-American literary treatments of Native people represent them as inferior, ignorant, and brutish or dehumanize them as noble savages, a vein of sympathy and protest against their mistreatment can be traced in Euro-American literature to the eighteenth century. Sympathetic writings on Indians include: Benjamin Franklin's *Remarks Concerning the Savages of North America* (1784); Philip Freneau's "The Indian Student" and "Lines Occasioned by a Visit to an Old Indian Burying Ground" (1788); Washington Irving's "Philip of Pokanoket," in *The Sketch Book* (1819–20); James W. Eastburn's *Yamoyden* (1820); James Kirke Paulding's *Koningsmarke, The Long Finne* (1823); Lydia Maria Child's *Hobomok* (1824) and *The First Settlers of New-England* (1829); William Cullen Bryant's "An Indian at the Burial-Place of His Fathers" (1824–25, reprinted, interestingly, in the *Cherokee Phoenix* 2, no. 17 [29 July 1829]); Catharine M. Sedgwick's *Hope Leslie* (1827); and John Augustus Stone's play *Metamora; or, The Last of the Wampanoags* (1829). The last was a great hit, according to Richard Moody, with over two hundred performances in sixty years. *Metamora* was the most successful of more than seventy-five nineteenth-century "Indian dramas."[172]

Chamberlain seems to have known the play, borrowing from it. The hero, Metamora (representing the Wampanoag leader known as King Philip), gives Oceana, a Euro-American woman, an eagle feather to wear as a token of protection, just as in Chamberlain's "Indian Pledge" the hunter gives the farm wife a feather as an emblem of protection from Native aggression. Although Chamberlain borrowed from *Meta-mora*, she did so selectively, rejecting the assumption of the vanishing Indian. As Colin G. Calloway observes in his work on New England Native people after King Philip's War, nineteenth-century Euro-American literary treatments of Natives tended to assume they "were a doomed race." In such texts, final scenes often feature the "last" Indian's departure, thereby perpetuating the imperialistic concept of Native extinction. Although Metamora's dying speech is filled with condemnations of the cruel Euro-American conquerors ("My curses on you, white men! . . . Murderers! The last of the Wampanoags' curse be on you!"), the passage marks the disappearance of "the last of the Wampanoags." In contrast, Chamberlain's Native characters do not disappear with her texts' conclusions. Thus, though she borrowed from Euro-American writings on Indians, she borrowed judiciously, reject-ing Christian conversion and the notion of Indians as a vanishing people.[173]

Not long after publishing her two Indian defenses in the *Lowell Offering,* Chamberlain contributed a story so different that it is hard to believe it was written by the same person. A sensational seduction tale partly set on the American frontier, "The Delusion of the Heart" in-cludes the kind of treatment of Indian "savages" that one associates with Euro-American authors. The Natives are a threatening back-ground presence, troubling the lives of the Euro-American main char-acters: "Scarce had the settlers recovered from the murderous depradations of the Corees and Tuscaroras, when another calamity befel them. A party of Yamosees came upon them, and their settle-ment was again laid waste. Charles had been absent on a journey, and late at night, on his return, he came within sight of his home; the work of destruction was nearly complete; the flames of the burning hamlet were ascending. He drew nigh, and saw the savages about to leave the place."[174] Thus, in burning the settlement, the Natives are responsible for the same kind of fiery devastation perpetrated against them by Euro-Americans in "A Fire-Side Scene." In this regard "The Delusion of the Heart" to some degree neutralizes the critique of Euro-American oppression in Chamberlain's earlier writings.

In her *Lowell Offering* writings, Chamberlain's ambivalent treatment of Native subjects reflects the divided consciousness of her bicultural position, as well as her efforts to negotiate her situation publishing in a periodical written predominantly by and for Euro-Americans. For a nineteenth-century mixed-race person writing in an era of intense persecution of Natives, the urge to identify with the oppressor must have been enormous. The conflict can be seen in the work of other nineteenth-century mixed-race writers as well. In her angry pro-Indian poem "The Natives of America" (1841), Ann Plato's speaker addresses Native people's suffering since "Columbus came afar" and "we fell in cruel hands . . . Of cruel oppression." But in an essay, "Decision of Character," published in the same volume, Plato's narrator praises Columbus for "the greatness of his mind." The same kind of internal conflict may have led another nineteenth-century mixed-race author, William Apess, to append to his otherwise intensely pro-Native *A Son of the Forest* the condescending dialect poem "Indian Hymn," including such lines as "God lub poo Indian in da wood, / So me lub God, and dat be good." The editor, Barry O'Connell, admits finding it mystifying "why Apess would have chosen to reproduce it." Plato's antithetical views of Columbus are as puzzling as Chamberlain's publication of "The Delusion of the Heart" following "The Indian Pledge" and "A Fire-Side Scene."[175]

Chamberlain may have been responding to pressure from Euro-American *Lowell Offering* writers, editors, and readers. Undoubtedly, some—perhaps many—found the critique of racism in "The Indian Pledge" and "A Fire-Side Scene" objectionable. "The Delusion of the Heart" may have been calculated to appease the dominant community by presenting the "other side" of the Indian problem. Chamberlain thereby preserved her opportunity to publish in the workers' magazines. Yet the Native depredations against Euro-Americans in "The Delusion of the Heart" serve as well to express, albeit indirectly, murderous anger at Euro-American oppression. Apess's writings vividly convey the racism endured by antebellum New England Algonkian. In *The Experiences of Five Christian Indians,* he explains, "It was thought no crime for old and young to hiss at the poor Indians." He describes enduring the "calumny heaped upon us by the whites to an intense degree."[176] Trying to survive in such a climate, Chamberlain would have experienced more than enough provocation to an anger that found an outlet in her story's Native ravages.

The Dream Vision Writings

While not explicitly Native in content, Chamberlain's dream visions reveal Algonkian cultural influences. For the *Lowell Offering,* she composed four brief, prose dream visions: "A Vision of Truth," "A New Society," "Sabbath Morning," and "A Reverie." These are her only writings, except "Christmas," that touch upon factory working and living conditions. While Chamberlain wrote much less about factory work and life than did other *Lowell Offering* contributors, her dream visions express wishes either to flee from Lowell or to reform living and working conditions.

The dream vision is a fairly common genre in the *Lowell Offering* and other nineteenth-century periodicals, yet virtually no scholarship exists on this genre in nineteenth-century U.S. writing, perhaps because periodicals have been little studied or because the form has been deemed subliterary. Twenty-one prose dream visions were published in the *Lowell Offering,* and another nine prose pieces recount waking visions. Most *Lowell Offering* dream visions are strongly influenced by John Bunyan's famous dream allegory, *The Pilgrim's Progress* (1678). After the Bible, this was probably the book most familiar to and revered by antebellum mill workers. While the majority (fifteen, to be exact) of the *Lowell Offering* dream visions are, like *The Pilgrim's Progress,* allegorical and heavily didactic, only one of Betsey Chamberlain's four pieces is allegorical: "A Vision of Truth." The beautiful tree of this piece represents the *Lowell Offering,* but the text lacks the moral and religious didacticism of other allegorical *Offering* dream visions. Chamberlain's "A New Society" is the only *Lowell Offering* dream vision to advance any reform of living and working conditions. Those advocated by other *Offering* dream visions involve their narrators' private, usually moral, betterment. Chamberlain's Native lineage, as well as her maturity and strong individuality, contributes to her texts' distinctiveness.[177]

All the *Offering* dream visions, including Chamberlain's, operate on the ancient premise that dreams express truth, found in both classic Western literature and Native American dream songs. Nonetheless, Chamberlain's visions employ many fewer of the Bunyanesque conventions found in other *Offering* writings. The typical *Lowell Offering* dream vision's narrator falls asleep in a bucolic setting, often beside a river or stream, and dreams the events of the tale. In N. S. L.'s "An Allegory," the narrator dozes off "on the bank of a murmuring stream" and dreams of being led first by Ignorance and then Learning, who teaches her to value study. The figure of the guide, found throughout *The Pilgrim's Progress* and other classic Western dream visions, also appears in many *Lowell Offering* visions. In Eliza Jane Cate's "Garden of Life," a kindly, intelligent female guide cautions the dreamer not to admire the most beautiful garden plants, but to appreciate instead the modest and humble violet.[178]

Both N. S. L.'s and Cate's visions possess the allegorical, strongly didactic quality of most *Lowell Offering* dream visions. In contrast, Chamberlain's allegorical "Vision of Truth" does not correct the dreamer's behavior, but rather deepens her appreciation for the *Lowell Offering*. Her didactic dream vision, "A Reverie," is much more whimsical than similar *Offering* texts. The narrator is instructed by a mermaid rather than by grave, Bunyanesque, personified abstractions, such as Learning or Faith. Less apt to ascribe Puritan guilt to their protagonists, Chamberlain's visions lack the personified abstractions as characters found in other *Lowell Offering* dream visions, although such characters do appear in several of her other writings (Necessity in "Old Maids and Old Bachelors," Memory in "Origin of Small Talk").

Again as in Bunyan, many *Lowell Offering* dream visions involve a survey of some realm emblematic of moral or spiritual struggle. In S. T.'s "An Afternoon Ramble," the narrator, guided by a being "of divine beauty and loveliness," soars and observes crowds of people, cities, thrones, and kings. Viewing "a steep hill" on which many people are climbing, the narrator finally learns to be content with her lot. While Chamberlain's "A Reverie" also involves a visit to a marvelous realm, her site—a jeweled island with lounging mermaids—differs markedly from the steep hills and striving, worldly cities of other *Offering* visions.[179]

Chamberlain's dream visions are also more apt to express discontent and refrain from condemning or revising that feeling, as do other *Lowell Offering* authors. Some dissatisfaction is voiced by the factory-girl narrator of Lucy Larcom's "A Flower Dream," who chafes at her "life of ignoble drudgery." But then her dream teaches her to be happy even in a lowly sphere.[180] In Chamberlain's "A Reverie," the unhappy factory-girl narrator also learns to accept—though perhaps not unreservedly—her difficulties. But in two other visions, "A New Society" and "Sabbath Morning," discontent with mill life remains unreproved and unchanged by the dreams. The former proposes some radical reforms, including an eight-hour workday—at a time when people were struggling unsuccessfully for the ten-hour day—and equal pay and educational opportunities for men and women. This piece raises the question of whether Chamberlain participated in the 1834 and 1836 Lowell women's strikes protesting against wage reductions. In 1834 some eight hundred women turned out from the mills, and two years later the strikers numbered as high as two thousand, or nearly one-third of the female workforce. Given her individualism and the views expressed in "A New Society," most likely Chamberlain did participate. One can only surmise, since the strikers' names have apparently not been preserved. Chamberlain's reformist writings wholly surmount the contented "life of ignoble drudgery" promoted in many other *Offering* dream visions. Although most of the other writers avoid challenging mill conditions, many of their dreamers are jolted awake by clanging factory bells. This suggests a desire to escape the mills, at least via the writing of dream visions.

In "A New Society" and "A Reverie," Chamberlain's challenges to Lowell living and working conditions resemble reformist dream visions, presumably Euro-American-authored, that appeared in other 1840s labor papers. One such piece, "The Factory Inquisition, or American Bastille," was published in *The Working Man's Advocate* (New York) in 1844. Falling asleep, the narrator dreams of visiting "Mr. Employer's counting room." Observing factory management perpetrating injustices against workers, the narrator perceives the room's evil. Although the narrator acquires some insight, his gaining knowledge is less important than the text's exposure of social evils. Likewise, "A Dream" by "That *Other* Factory Girl," published in the *Voice of Industry,* exposes social ills. The dreaming narrator envisions a situation in which she is an observer rather than a participant. Contrasting the corrupt mill management and the poor, virtuous factory girl, the dream rebalances the social scales by meting out justice on the Judgment Day. Rather than acquiring new personal insight, this narrator gains instead the satisfaction of seeing injustice exposed and rectified.[181]

While these visions share Chamberlain's aim of social criticism, they differ somewhat from hers in tone and content. In the other labor papers, dream visions are impersonal and sardonic, serving principally as vehicles for protest against working and living conditions. In contrast, Chamberlain's personal visions impart new insights or wisdom to the dreaming narrator-self. Their tone is idealistic, envisioning idyllic conditions. While the aim of social criticism is not lacking in Chamberlain's dream visions, it is subordinated to the acquisition of personal wisdom.

Chamberlain's dreaming narrators participate in the action, gaining profound and often personal knowledge. In this respect, these writings partake of Native dream song tradition. Dream visions and songs are found in nearly all Native cultures of the United States. In *Native American Literature,* Andrew Wiget explains, "Dream songs occur in every area of the native North America." To Native people, dreams, both personal and sacred, are "considered the source of wisdom and creativity." As Wiget states: "Nothing is more personal than one's dreams, which constitute a secret well of power from which one can draw strength and general spiritual renewal."[182] Chamberlain's visions recount the dreaming narrator-self's transforming or renewing experience. Moreover, her dreamers transcend ordinary experience, often surmounting boundaries of space and time. In Algonkian culture, it is believed that dreamers can overcome such constraints. According to Pritchard's *No Word for Time: The Way of the Algonquin People,* dreamers can enter "the spirit world," where "[c]lock time can seem to skip backwards or forwards, and some say even physical time travel is possible." With experience, one learns that waking and dreaming life merge, that "this [waking] life is little different from a dream."[183]

Time travel forms the basis of Chamberlain's progressive "A New Society." In both this and "A Reverie," she blurs the boundary between waking and sleeping. As the narrator of "A New Society" sits reading and thinking, suddenly a boy enters to hand her a document dated 1860. Thus, before the reader realizes, the narrator has fallen asleep and begun dreaming. By failing to mark the division between waking and sleeping, the author suggests the closeness of these states. The 1860 document cites resolutions adopted at the Annual Meeting of the Society for the Promotion of Industry, Virtue and Knowledge. This progressive organization advocates equal pay and educational opportunities for men and women, as well as an eight-hour workday. Chamberlain's visions often end with a return to the disappointing present, and this one is no exception. Leaving her room to seek her housemates, the narrator stumbles on the stairs and awakens to a present in which women do not possess equal educational opportunities or pay, and the typical workday spans fourteen hours. Still, the dreamer has acquired insight into possible reforms.

The visions of "A Reverie" and "Sabbath Morning" also project ideal realms, transcending the dissatisfying present. "A Reverie's" opening places the reader immediately into the dream without indicating that it is one, again conflating waking and sleeping states. The reader shifts from a prosaic opening sentence—"I was crossing the bridge near the Merrimack counting-room" (p. 130)—to a resplendent vision of mermaids lounging on a bejeweled river island. When the dreamer admires the mermaids' beauty and "unrestrained freedom," one of them counsels her not to envy "their comparatively useless lives." Although the mill woman's "earthly pilgrimage" has been one of "losses, crosses and disappointments," she enjoys the human advantages of knowing, reasoning, and acting. The narrator is abruptly awakened by her overseer's rebuke for idleness. After her dream flight from mill work's hardships, she resumes her "task at picking cloth" (p. 131), having gained insight into the value of human reason and responsibility. "A Reverie" blends elements of Native dream song tradition with the Protestant work ethic of Chamberlain's Euro-American forebears.

"Sabbath Morning" opens on a Sunday in "the busy city of Lowell," where the homesick narrator longs for happier childhood days in rural New Hampshire. Falling asleep, she is carried back "in fancy's car" to her beloved Lake Winnipesaukee. This vision's Native features include dream travel and reverence for nature. The narrator longs to "pay to Nature's God the sacrifice of praise" (pp. 131–32). On her dream visit to "Winipisiogee," she admires the waters, forest, birds, rising sun, "glittering summits of the rocks, and the shining sides of the opposite mountains." Exulting in the glorious beauty, the narrator suddenly awakens to realize sadly that she "had only been dreaming" (p. 133). Her disappointment in returning to Lowell thus registers an implicit protest against mill conditions and an even deeper one against her Native estrangement from Euro-American industrial society.

Chamberlain's fourth dream vision, the allegorical "Vision of Truth," again conveys a Native reverence for nature's beauty and healing potential, as well as a profound appreciation for the Improvement Circle and the *Lowell Offering*. After attending a delightful session of the Circle, the happy narrator falls asleep and dreams of "traveling in a strange country." A guide takes her to an Edenic "grove, cultivated by the hand of man" (p. 133). On a hill grows an enormous, beautiful tree, carefully described in three paragraphs. The tree produces abundant leaves "for the healing of the nations." Named *Mental Knowledge*, the tree sprouts leaves of the *Lowell Offering,* gathered by people coming from all directions (p. 134). Besides suggestions of Native dream visions and herbal medicine, this conveys Chamberlain's characteristic idealism. She promotes culture, education, and peace among diverse peoples. As in her other dream visions' conclusions, the narrator is abruptly awakened, this time by "the first morning bell" (p. 134). This one, however, does not leave the narrator disappointed, since she awakens to a world where her vision of culture and the *Lowell Offering* fully lives. In this case, the dream deepens her appreciation of their far-reaching value.[184]

Village Sketches

While Chamberlain's dream visions explore ideal realms, her local-color essays recount events in the quotidian realm of rural New Hampshire. Like the visions, the sketches were composed with a didactic intent, although they often treat odd, whimsical occurrences. In her first published piece, "A Letter about Old Maids," the author addresses the reader directly, explaining her plan to produce "chiefly recollections of simple country girls." Unconcerned about readers' opinion of her style, she cares only that "the *moral* be remembered and regarded" (p. 158). Indeed, many of her didactic village sketches represent women, and Chamberlain wrote more of these than anything else. Of her thirty-seven periodical pieces, twenty-eight are autobiographically based village sketches.

They are brief reminiscences of life in and around Chamberlain's hometown of Wolfeboro, New Hampshire. Although some of the texts' events predate her life, she usually finds a way to relate them to the narrator-self. These pieces are most strongly influenced by the village-sketches tradition as developed by Washington Irving, Mary Russell Mitford, Sarah J. Hale, and Catharine Sedgwick. The texts also reveal evidence of oral literature, including Native and New England storytelling. Often focusing upon women, the sketches examine the quality of women's lives, advocating changes in societal views and treatment of them. Like other local-color writers, Chamberlain draws many of her characters from society's margins. Both women and men, these include poor, elderly women; old maids and old bachelors; Quakers; Native people; African-American servants; day laborers; and the mentally ill. In such people's ostracism and mistreatment, Chamberlain exposes society's unacknowledged injustices, often pleading for greater tolerance. Some circumstances and events in and around her fictional hometown, dubbed "Salmagundi," are corroborated in local histories of Wolfeboro and surrounding towns. Chamberlain alters and shapes occurrences, especially those connected with family troubles, to suit her rhetorical purposes, revealing the truth while protecting her family's privacy. Thus, she again demonstrates her concern with shielding her family and preserving her opportunity to publish.

Although Chamberlain's village sketches convey information about her life and family, they cannot be considered autobiography, because their main subject is not Chamberlain herself. Still, the writings have autobiographical qualities important to consider, since the written autobiography and memoir are among the foremost genres worked by Native women in the postcontact era. In their study *American Indian Women: Telling Their Lives,* Gretchen M. Bataille and Kathleen Mullins Sands explain that autobiography is not an indigenous oral genre. In telling their own stories, Native women fuse elements from both Native oral tradition and Euro-American written conventions. Andrew Wiget traces the origins principally to oral tradition. Native written autobiography developed from storytelling, a central element of Algonkian culture.[185] In creating her village sketches, Chamberlain participated in the storytelling tradition that was a vital feature of her culture.

Chamberlain's sketches reflect oral literary traditions in several ways. Most of her plots are not invented but are drawn from a shared fund of family stories or local lore. "The First Dish of Tea" relates an incident in Chamberlain's great-great-grandmother's life that must have been told and retold by several generations. Likewise, other sketches recount local events preceding Chamberlain's life that must have been told to her. "The First Wedding in Salmagundi" describes the 1766 nuptials of Reuben and Sarah Libby, related as well in Parker's 1901 *History of the Town of Wolfeborough.*[186] Chamberlain's narrator explains that a neighbor told her this story, which must have been repeated over the years by many local residents. "The Black Glove" and "The Old Farm-House" recount Wolfeboro stories found in published histories such as Parker's. Chamberlain regarded herself less as a solitary creator of plots and characters than as a recorder and reshaper of collectively created stories transmitted within her rural New Hampshire community.

Her stories and sketches follow New England folktale traditions, as seen in John Greenleaf Whittier's writings, especially *Legends of New England* (1831), and in the collections of "stories and legends" compiled in the early twentieth century by Eva A. Speare and published as *New Hampshire Folk Tales* and *More New Hampshire Folk Tales*. Since Whittier came from a poor farming background and worked in such occupations as shoemaking and school teaching, he was a writer of special interest to Lowell workers. In fact, in the 1840s he spent an interval in the town, attended Improvement Circles, befriended *Lowell Offering* writers such as Lucy Larcom, and published a book about his experiences, *The Stranger in Lowell* (1845). Found in at least several Lowell libraries, his writings were well known by workers there.

Legends of New England includes many Native stories and descriptions of Euro-American encounters with Native people. Whittier acknowledges the great contribution of Algonkian oral traditions to New England folk literature. In *Supernaturalism of New England* (1847), he suggests that New England folk traditions "have been modified, and . . . *acclimated,* by commingling with those of the original inhabitants." Whittier's interest in Native traditions is tinged, however, by his often-expressed views of them as savages who have "departed forever." Although *Legends* was not widely available in New England, some of Chamberlain's tales so much resemble his that she must have been influenced by the book, or at least by the same traditions.

Both authors' writings are based upon local events, some of which the narrator has witnessed and others only heard secondhand. Like Chamberlain's "La Brainard," Whittier's "Rattlesnake Hunter" concerns a man who accidentally murders someone dear to him and spends the rest of his life a poor, wandering outcast. In several witchcraft legends, Whittier's representations of poor elderly women accused of sundry acts of magic anticipate such sketches by Chamberlain. With a similar wry humor, Whittier writes: "Many of her neighbors were ready to make oath that they had been haunted by old Alice, in the shape of a black cat . . . that she had bewitched their swine, and rendered their cattle unruly—nay, more than one good wife averred, that she had bewitched their churns and prevented the butter from forming. . . . In short, it would be idle to attempt a description of the almost innumerable feats of witchcraft ascribed to the withered and decrepid Alice."[187] Chamberlain's witchcraft writings are more sympathetic to the accused women, reflecting her feminism.

Wishing to preserve old New Hampshire tales passed down in their families and communities, women from many areas contributed in the early 1930s to Eva Speare's collections. Like Chamberlain, Speare chronicles Native and pioneer life, witchcraft and superstitions, town eccentrics and famous persons, and other noteworthy local events. Speare's texts attest to a vital tradition of women's oral literary culture in early New Hampshire, as seen also in Chamberlain's writings. The preservation of local stories was the province of women, and, according to Speare, Native women contributed to New Hampshire oral literature. As she explains, "The legends were related by Indian women, remnants of tribes who were sheltered at the fireplaces in the log cabins by kindly settlers in time of need." She distinguishes Native "legends" from Euro-American "stories," suggesting that the latter were more factual and reliable.[188]

Speare's stories, like Chamberlain's, are presented as "true events, not fiction."[189] Still, the line of demarcation in both Chamberlain and Speare is uncertain, with some embellishments added by storytellers or previous writers. Both Speare's folktales and Chamberlain's sketches are largely impersonal, revealing little or nothing about the authors or narrators. Emphasizing incident, the writers leave emotions and motivations mostly unexplored. Chamberlain's sketches can be distinguished from Speare's, however, by their common use of a colloquial, first-person voice and by the insertion into many of her texts of passages from ballads and other poetry.

Although the village sketches' narrator—a surrogate for Chamberlain herself—often participates in recounted events, her presence is one of a muted observer's. Chamberlain connects events to herself and furnishes some introspective glimpses, but she never makes her own subjectivity and experience the focus. Telling Ruth A.'s story in "Recollections of an Old Maid. Number 1," the narrator recalls being "at her wedding" (p. 166). Likewise, in recounting the experience of another girlhood neighbor, Caroline B., the narrator mentions, "I was sent for in haste to assist at the bridal preparations," after which she attended her through a "long nervous fever" (p. 167). In "The First Wedding in Salmagundi," Chamberlain's narrator reveals that in childhood she was "the greatest rogue in the family" (p. 187). The narrator of "Cousin Mary" reflects that she possesses a "more turbulent spirit" than that of the meek and gentle Mary, whom she counsels and attends in illness (p. 147). Despite these personal asides, the sketches' focus remains on her neighbors and community rather than on Chamberlain herself.

This "self-effacement" is characteristic as well of other early Native women's life stories, as noted in Bataille and Sands's *American Indian Women: Telling Their Lives.* Some oral aspects that Bataille and Sands identify in Native women's autobiography appear as well in Chamberlain's local sketches. These include "emphasis on event, . . . concern with landscape, [and] affirmation of cultural values and tribal solidarity." Like other Native women's life stories, Chamberlain's are "retrospective rather than introspective."[190] As much a historian as a writer, Chamberlain records significant events from her community's past.

Several other characteristics of early Native women's life stories can be found in Chamberlain's sketches. Bataille and Sands note the writers' modesty and willingness to sacrifice for family members. Similarly, Chamberlain submerges her identity to promote family and community welfare. Another indispensable quality of Native women is humor.[191] With a surface lightness, Chamberlain's pieces are sometimes quite funny, as in the opening of "The Last Witch of Salmagundi." The narrator observes, "Among the first settlers of New England, it was considered as necessary to have a Witch in every parish, as it was to have a Parson, or Physician—and perhaps even more necessary, for whole townships have been destitute of both Parson and Physician, when there was no lack of witches" (p. 153). Like other instances of Chamberlain's wit, this passage entertains while subtly challenging unjust local customs, such as the scapegoating of old women. The author attributes great social value and efficacy to laughter. The narrator of "The Last Witch of Salmagundi" later observes "that the wild vagaries in which the light-hearted often indulge . . . will often do what reason, philosophy and religion fail to accomplish" (p. 156). Through humor people may alter adverse social conditions, such as the suffering resulting from witchcraft charges, previously resistant to the efforts of clergy and other male authorities. Chamberlain's socially potent humor is thoroughly democratic, since it can be exercised by women, children, working-class men, and other marginalized community members.

Although Chamberlain's narrators sometimes commend—perhaps not without irony—the Euro-American townspeople's "worthy ancestors" (p. 153), her sketches usually focus upon society's edges. Her sympathy extends to marginal figures such as poor elderly women, old maids, laborers, drunks, Native people, African-American servants, the mentally deranged, and Quakers. Like the writers discussed in Fetterley and Pryse's *American Women Regionalists, 1850–1910,* Chamberlain refrains from belittling her subjects in the way that some prominent (male) local colorists did. Instead, she writes with empathy, "present[ing] regional experience from within, so as to engage the reader's sympathy and identification."[192] Although Chamberlain credits the English writer Mary Russell Mitford with influencing her own writing, her sketches can be distinguished from Mitford's by their darker social vision, derived in part from her Puritan inheritance, as well as from identification with oppressed Native people.

In "Our Town: How It Looked," Chamberlain's narrator explains her intention of imitating Mitford's admired collection of sketches, *Our Village* (1824–32): "How beautifully has Miss Mitford delineated to us the scenes and events of our village. The English collection of cottage and castle, of hut and hall. . . . With these has she intermingled the more interesting scenery of the heart, and made all other pictures but scene-curtains to its simple dramas,—its every-day tragedy and comedy. . . . And why, then, may we not portray our town" (p. 200). Chamberlain's sketches thus support Josephine Donovan's contention in *New England Local Color Literature* that "American women writers derived undoubtedly from Mitford rather than Irving."[193] Still, Chamberlain's choosing to call Wolfeboro "Salmagundi" reflects some of Irving's influence. As in Irving's satirical essays and poems published in *Salmagundi; or, the Whim-Whams and Opinions of Launcelot Langstaff, Esq. & Others* (1807–08), Chamberlain's choice of the name Salmagundi signifies her intent to produce satirical, humorous writings, lightly travestying Wolfeboro society. Irving's humor especially influenced the raucous and burlesque tone of Chamberlain's early pieces.

Mitford was the major influence upon Chamberlain's writings, sharing with her an attention to common people. In *Our Village,* Mitford's narrator remarks that rather than writing about "fine mansions finely peopled," she will represent "cottages and cottage-like houses . . . with inhabitants whose faces are as familiar to us as the flowers in our garden." Likewise, Chamberlain sketches the experience "of simple country girls" and other ordinary New England people. Chamberlain's debt to Mitford was recognized by her contemporaries. In 1841 a writer reviewing the *Lowell Offering* for the *North American Review* observed: " 'Recollections of an Old Maid,' are charming sketches of still human life, which Miss Mitford's self would not need to blush to own."[194] From Mitford and other early local colorists, Chamberlain learned that literature could represent—and even foreground—the experience of the poor farm and laboring people familiar to her.

Chamberlain was likely also influenced by such American writers as Sarah Josepha Hale and Catharine Maria Sedgwick. Hale's writings were particularly influential, since she was also from New Hampshire and set many of her sketches there or elsewhere in New England. Hale's early writings include her novel *Northwood* (1827) and two collections of sketches, *Sketches of American Character* (1831) and *Traits of American Life* (1835). Both *Northwood* and *Sketches of American Character* are included among the holdings of the Lowell Circulating Library in 1834. Although Donovan contends that *Northwood* "was perhaps the first work to include real details of the New England locale," Hale's women characters tend to be "quiet, obedient, never offer opinions, and spend their time on domestic chores."[195] In contrast, Chamberlain's portraits embody a forthright feminism, and her settings are rendered more realistically than *Northwood*'s romanticized version of rural New England.

Chamberlain's contemporaries admired her local-color writings. In 1844 Charles Knight, an English editor and publisher, assisted by Harriet Martineau, assembled an anthology of *Lowell Offering* writings entitled *Mind amongst the Spindles: A Selection from the Lowell Offering,* reprinted the following year in Boston. Of thirty-seven pieces included, six were penned by Betsey Chamberlain—an especially impressive figure considering that at least seventy women contributed to the *Offering.* For *Mind amongst the Spindles,* Knight and Martineau chose Chamberlain's "The First Wedding in Salmagundi," "The Whortleberry Excursion," "The Sugar-Making Excursion," "The Indian Pledge," "The First Dish of Tea," and "Witchcraft," attributed to the pseudonyms Tabitha and Jemima. In his introduction, Knight appreciates Tabitha as a "simple, unpretending narrator of old American scenes and customs," and Jemima for "prettily describ[ing] two little home-scenes." While Knight magnifies the simplicity and prettiness of Chamberlain's writings, sidestepping their dark tones and complexities, he astutely values their contribution to American local-color writing.[196]

Chamberlain's sketches were also admired by other *Offering* writers, judging from imitations of them published in later issues. This exemplifies the camaraderie and mutual support the women shared, making the *Lowell Offering* and other achievements possible. As Harriet Robinson reminisced years later, "It was not so much individual as collective thought and aspiration, that made the Lowell *Offering* possible." Chamberlain also recalls such collective effort in "A New Society," when her narrator likens the *Offering* to a tree composed of many different tendrils and branches. From 1843 to 1845, when Chamberlain had left Lowell and ceased writing for the *Lowell Offering,* her humor was especially missed by the other contributors. At the opening of "The Party," by Patty [Harriet Farley], two women discuss the Improvement Circle. One remarks, "I wish that old maid Betsey would write again, or some other funny old soul." The other character complies by producing an earthy, humorous sketch of country life, reminiscent of Chamberlain's sketches. Patty's country women, with their "great round faces, and bright eyes, and red cheeks," even resemble Chamberlain's childhood self-portrait in "Recollections of an Old Maid. Number 1." Harriot F. Curtis, writing as "Kate," contributed a sketch of hearty back-country women that even more closely echoes Chamberlain's self-portrait. Kate's narrator describes her aunt as having "a face as large and as round as a pumpkin, brown as a berry, and cheeks that rivalled a peony," and being almost as wide as she was tall. Chamberlain's rural sketches were imitated in a host of subsequent *Offering* writings. The praise and imitation of her sister writers shows that Chamberlain was admired and regarded by them as a pacesetter.[197]

Women's Rights

Chamberlain emerges as a leader in terms of her woman-centered and feminist qualities. Taken as a whole, her body of work makes a stronger feminist statement than can be found in that of not only other *Lowell Offering* writers but also many other antebellum female literary writers. Her experience as a single mother working to support herself and her children may partly account for her distinctive feminism. Her Native heritage also furnished a source of feminist vision. She had probably heard or read about the famous female leaders, known as "Suncksqua" or "Squaw Sachems," of seventeenth-century New England Native bands. These powerful women included Awashonks (Sakonnet), Weetamoo (Pocasset), and a woman identified in written histories as the "Massachusetts Queen." Also renowned and closer to Chamberlain's lifetime were the Mohawk leader Molly Brant (1736?–96) and the Abenaki doctor Molly Ockett (1740?–1816). Chamberlain likely drew some of her assurance of women's value and rights from the examples of these Native leaders and healers.[198]

She must have also known the ideas and published writings and speeches of Anglo-American feminists, such as Judith Sargent Murray, Fanny Wright, and Sarah and Angelina Grimké. In the 1790s, Murray published essays in the *Massachusetts Magazine* affirming women's equality with men and advocating an expansion of women's educational opportunities. In the 1820s and 1830s, the Scottish Fanny Wright toured the United States, speaking and publishing essays supporting such causes as women's education and labor rights. The abolitionist sisters Sarah and Angelina Grimké published pieces in the 1830s challenging women's oppression, upholding their equality with men, and advocating improvements in female education.

Chamberlain joined her voice to those of earlier feminists. In two village sketches, her narrator contends that women deserve rights and privileges of which men unjustly deprive them. Women are barred from political participation, the narrator of "Our Town. Number 2" protests. In Salmagundi the narrator was not allowed to attend town meetings because she was a woman, "one of the unprivileged sex" (p. 202). Apparently, women's participation in politics, including the right to vote, had been matters of public concern in Chamberlain's childhood hometown. The narrator of "Recollections of My Childhood" recalls a subject considered in school debates: "Ought females to be allowed the right of suffrage?" (p. 214).

In the part-allegorical "Origin of Small Talk," Chamberlain's narrator objects to men's restriction of women's speech and their right to education and culture. "*{U}ncivilized* man," she protests, creates laws that "deprive woman of the means of mental culture to which she is justly entitled" (p. 162). This sketch also revises the Adam and Eve story, representing Eve as the more industrious and generous of the pair. Envious Adam, like too many nineteenth-century men, "often ridiculed Eve for her small-talk" (p. 163). In her characteristically clever, light-hearted style, Chamberlain challenges her culture's misogyny.

Chamberlain imbues many of her pieces with humor, ranging in tone from the farcical to the bitingly ironic. Since this role was one seldom assumed by women writers of her era, Chamberlain, along with Tabitha Tenney and Caroline Kirkland, stands as one of the pioneering American female humor writers. Her humor may have been part of her Native inheritance and perhaps in some measure a price she paid for acceptance in Lowell. As Laurel Ulrich observes in *The Age of Homespun*, early New England Native people were famous among their Euro-American neighbors for their "droll wit," whereby "[t]hey entertained as well as outraged their neighbors."[199]

Chamberlain's humor often serves as a powerful dimension of her feminism. The narrator of her local-color sketches assumes the authoritative stance of her townspeople's observer, albeit a generous one. Nancy A. Walker, in her important study of American women's humor, *A Very Serious Thing,* explores the relationship between social subordination and the power conferred by humor. As she observes, "To be a woman and a humorist is to confront and subvert the very power that keeps women powerless."[200] The force of Chamberlain's wit is especially evident in her satirical treatment of influential men's foibles. Unlike other early female writers such as Tabitha Tenney and Frances Whitcher, who mock women's weaknesses or the social roles available to them, Chamberlain usually aims her jibes at men, especially the pillars of her New Hampshire community.

In satirizing her townspeople, Chamberlain was likely influenced by Caroline Kirkland's amusing sketches of a Michigan frontier settlement, published as *A New Home—Who'll Follow?* (1839). Kirkland's renditions of "commonplace occurrences" and "everyday people," in a manner "decidedly low," resemble Chamberlain's later representations of "simple country girls." Both authors acknowledged their debt to the English sketch writer Mary Russell Mitford. *A New Home—Who'll Follow?* was held by several Lowell libraries, including those of the Lowell City School and the First Unitarian Church. Writing of her youthful experience in the mills, Lucy Larcom remembered being "delighted" by Kirkland's novel, her "first real Western book." She and her friends found its "genuine pioneer-flavor delicious." As it presaged Larcom's subsequent move to frontier Illinois, so the book may have helped prepare Chamberlain for her settlement in the same state.[201]

An earlier novel known to Chamberlain was *Female Quixotism: Exhibited in the Romantic Opinions and Extravagant Adventures of Dorcasina Sheldon* (1801), by Tabitha G. Tenney of New Hampshire. In "Recollections of an Old Maid. Number 3," Chamberlain's narrator describes "Dorcasina Sheldon" as one of "the three popular novels of the day" (p. 174). Tenney's text satirizes the unrealistically romantic notions about life and love that novels purveyed to women, ideas that, combined with their lack of education, left them particularly vulnerable to exploitation and disillusionment. In "Recollections of an Old Maid. Number 1," Chamberlain pursues a similar purpose in her representation of the pampered and affected Ruth.

More often, however, Chamberlain makes men—particularly influential ones—the targets of her humor. Her satire of the Squire's stinginess in "The Last Witch of Salmagundi" is a particularly good example. Rather than grant to Margaret, a poor elderly woman, her husband's estate to which she is rightfully entitled, the Squire gives her a "nine pence." As Chamberlain's narrator remarks, "Margaret was supported by the Town for some little time previous to her death; and once, when the Squire visited her, he gave her a nine pence to stop her clamor for Uncle Joe's money, and as she was never known to spend it, he thought it would not be necessary to give her any more" (p. 155). Thus Chamberlain unmasks the sham underlying the Squire's power and benificence, opposing as well the unjust treatment of old women. Chamberlain's satires most immediately anticipate Fanny Fern's and Frances Whitcher's wildly successful humorous writings of the 1850s and 1860s.

Some of Chamberlain's most forthright and hopeful feminism is found in her dream vision, "A New Society," set in 1860. Like the idealism of her other dream visions, "A New Society" conveys great optimism about women's and labor's future. As the nineteenth century progressed, the achievements of the women's rights and labor movements partly met Chamberlain's hopes, although early twenty-first century U.S. society has still not fully attained the human rights she envisioned for 1860.

Besides the polemical and satirical pieces discussed above, Chamberlain expressed her feminism less directly but just as powerfully in several village sketches representing individual rural New Hampshire women. These pieces examine the quality of women's lives, often advocating changes in societal views and treatment of them. Chamberlain's inherent belief in women's value shapes her writing's woman-centered quality. The characters include a range of women, from young unmarried ones to old maids to poor, aged widows. In some texts Chamberlain examines problems in courtship and marriage, often challenging conventional views.

In several pieces about common New Hampshire women, Chamberlain promotes the causes of women's education and improved treatment of old women. "Recollections of an Old Maid. Number 3" includes a remarkably early, sympathetic portrait of a female intellectual, a "literary lady, poetess, blue-stocking, or whatever else you may please to call her" (p. 169). Sarah D., known by the narrator in her youth, is the only child of a poor farmer. Unlike many fathers, Sarah's encourages her intellectual interests, teaching her mathematics and grammar. In her teen years Sarah works during the day, contributing to her family's income, and spends her evenings studying: "Sarah . . . plied the spinning wheel in the day-time, and studied Euclid with her father in the evening" (p. 171). She becomes so skilled at mathematics that the village boys come to her for assistance with their schoolwork. Although Sarah soon marries a butcher and becomes a mother, the narrator shows that her education still benefits her. As Sarah tells the narrator, her schooling makes her a better wife and mother, able to advise her husband and children. The sketch ends with Sarah's contention that "a cultivated mind" can help any woman, no matter how "obscure and toilsome" her "station of life" (p. 176).

In many of Chamberlain's pieces, however, heterosexual courtship and marriage cause problems for women. Marriage is particularly problematic when it becomes a woman's sole vocation, as it is for the eponymous heroine of "Cousin Mary." Here Chamberlain shows the dangers of rearing women for wifehood and motherhood without at least the kinds of intellectual opportunities enjoyed by Sarah D. When Cousin Mary believes herself abandoned by her fiancé, she suffers a breakdown that soon leads to her death. In thus critiquing women's relegation to the separate domestic sphere, Chamberlain speaks from the position of a woman working in the public sphere, supporting herself and publishing her writings. This experience, as well as her marital disappointments, must have shown her that women possessed desires unfulfilled in the domestic sphere alone. Imparting her special insight as an early nineteenth-century woman laboring in the public sphere, Chamberlain transforms her lowly social position as a factory girl into one of authoritative commentary on women's plight.

Even though her position grants her a certain authority, Chamberlain refrains from lecturing on the dangers of training women only for marriage and motherhood. Instead, she arranges the elements of "Cousin Mary" so that the facts speak for themselves. As her narrator describes Mary's upbringing: "Mary was taught to think that the only proper sphere of woman was the domestic circle, and that as a wife alone could she be truly happy, and respectable. For this end was she educated, and every thought and faculty were early directed to a preparation for that station which she would undoubtedly occupy" (p. 140). A shy and gentle girl excelling at the household arts of spinning, weaving, cooking, washing, and the rest, Mary sets her heart upon one suitor, Daniel Parsons, by whom she is courted for seven years.

Failing to understand Mary's heart, Daniel withdraws from the relationship to test her love. His seeming abandonment devastates Mary. As she tells the narrator, "[W]hen I laid my head upon my pillow it was with the wish that I might never raise it again, and then my brain began to whirl, and the blood kept boiling into it, and sounds like the crash of buildings, and the yells of wild beasts went through my ears, and then I lay like one almost benumbed" (p. 146). Chamberlain thus shows the terrible dangers to which cultivation for the domestic sphere alone and consequent overdependence on men expose women. Mary soon develops consumption, and even Daniel's renewed devotion cannot stay her disease's course. She dies on the very day she and Daniel were to be married, a victim of both the domestic sphere's narrowness and man's callousness or obtuseness.

Chamberlain's critique of marriage probably derives as much from Euro-American feminism as from Native sources. According to Susan Hazen-Hammond's book of Native American tales about women, love gone wrong or the "rejected suitor is a common theme in Native American stories." Romantic failures often lead to "murder, revenge, and death."[202] While Cousin Mary's plight is perhaps the worst, it is only one of Chamberlain's sketches interrogating women's experience of courtship and marriage. In "Our Physician," the character Polly T. is unable to marry because of her homeliness. In "Recollections of an Old Maid. Number 2," a beautiful woman, Caroline B., contracts a "nervous fever" following her husband's abandonment of her (p. 167).

The Quaker husband in "The Whortleberry Excursion" describes bringing his new bride home to the "cage" he has prepared for her (p. 218). After another man abducts his betrothed in "The Husking," a young man retrieves and marries her quickly. In the narrator's words, the ceremony enacts a kind of imprisonment, "confining the rogues for life, without the aid of constable, jury, or judge" (p. 192). These pieces reflect Chamberlain's skeptical view of marriage, particularly for women, and her belief that their opportunities should be expanded beyond the home.

Marginal Women: Witches and Old Maids

Margaret, "The Last Witch of Salmagundi," suffers both as a wife and as an elderly woman accused of witchcraft. This sketch is one of two addressing witchcraft and one of several defending aged women's rights and dignity, a concern dear to Chamberlain. For many years Margaret lives unhappily with a husband whose miserliness and poor judgment deprive her of any income after his death. Through the remainder of her life Margaret, a town pauper, subsists on public charity. Considered a witch by some, she is blamed for local misfortunes. The text includes a plea for better treatment of old women and abandonment of "the foolish idea of witchcraft" (p. 156).

The local-color sketch "Witchcraft" also challenges the rural phenomenon of scapegoating old women by accusing them of practicing magic. The narrator recounts such beliefs "in the township of B." (probably Brookfield, New Hampshire), where two elderly women were long considered witches: "[F]or a long series of years, all the mishaps within many miles were laid to [their] spiritual agency." Hoping to dispel "the mists of error," Chamberlain's narrator exposes this folly and men's cruelty toward women and even toward animals considered witches (pp. 176–78). The sketch recounts two incidents in which fearful men brutally kill animals believed to be bewitched. For Chamberlain's narrator, recollection of these events evokes "so many disagreeable sensations" that she is unable to write much about them (p. 178). Her narrator's response reveals Chamberlain's identification with the mistreated and her Native regard for animals.

While she rejects belief in witchcraft because it leads to persecution of women, Chamberlain's sketches on the subject convey with spirit

and humor information about some early nineteenth-century folk beliefs. These pieces reveal their author's close familiarity with, and
hearty enjoyment of, Anglo-American, Algonkian, and other kinds of
American folklore. Her folklore motifs appear as well in other American legends and folk beliefs. According to William S. Simmons's *Spirit
of the New England Tribes: Indian History and Folklore, 1620–1984,* the
theme of witches causing illness in cattle is prevalent in British and
Anglo-American folklore; in both "The Last Witch of Salamagundi"
and "Witchcraft," the old women considered witches are thought to
have caused illness in farm animals. The widow Goodwin of "Witchcraft" is believed to "ride" a male neighbor at night as one would a
horse. This motif of the "witch rider" is common, according to Simmons, in Anglo-American, Afro-American, and British legends. Further, witches' ability to transform themselves into animals is found in
Native, Afro-American, and Anglo-American folklore. Margaret in
"The Last Witch in Salmagundi" is believed to have once turned herself into a mouse, and some townspeople believe that the widow Goodwin could project her spirit into a calf's body (pp. 154, 177).[203]

Besides transmitting some of her community's folklore, Chamberlain could have created her witchcraft sketches to express covertly her
own sense of difference and marginality as a part-Native woman. As
Benjamin B. Thatcher wrote, early New Englanders viewed witchcraft
and "powowing" as among the Natives' chief "sins." Native women,
especially older ones, were often characterized as hags and witches.
Charles Brockden Brown's *Edgar Huntly* (1799) includes a portrait of
a strange, solitary, aged Lenni Lenape woman called "Old Deb" and
"Queen Mab," whose "voice was sharp and shrill, and her gesticula-
tions . . . vehement and grotesque." In the popular play *Metamora*
(1829), a Euro-American crowd taunts Metamora's wife, Nahmeokee,
just released from wrongful imprisonment, with being a "witch, hag"
and a "[f]oul Indian witch." Jennet, a Euro-American character in
Catharine Sedgwick's *Hope Leslie* (1827), suspects two Native female
characters, Magawisca and Nelema, of witchcraft. As Jennet remarks,
"The girl [Magawisca] is ever going to Nelema's hut, and of moonlight
nights too, when they say witches work their will—birds of a feather
flock together." At different times, both Magawisca and Nelema are
wrongfully jailed by the Puritan settlers.[204]

Given the racist misogyny facing nineteenth-century Native
women, a mixed-race woman writer such as Chamberlain would prob-

ably have been reluctant to address Native women's problems directly, especially when writing for a predominantly Euro-American periodical. Significantly, her identifiably Native characters are male. Still, her treatment of witchcraft enabled her to explore indirectly the issues faced by Native and mixed-race New England women. She could express her own sense of marginality and alienation as well, while still protecting herself, her family, and her opportunity to publish.

Besides challenging marginal women's persecution, Chamberlain strove to improve their lives by representing the unappreciated worth of such women. She championed the cause of old maids, another denigrated group. A contested figure in earlier writing, the never-married woman had been defended by such writers as Sarah Hale and Catharine Sedgwick; in 1835, both published apologia for old maids. Mrs. Carvill, the narrator of Hale's "An Old Maid," tries to convince the misogynist Mr. Burton of her friend Miss Atherton's worth. Showing the value of single women's lives, Mrs. Carvill challenges the social pressures pushing women into marriage: "I think it highly injurious to my own sex, and to society, that our young girls should be educated only with a view to marriage." Likewise Mrs. Seton, the narrator of Sedgwick's "Old Maids," draws portraits of several exemplary spinsters, advocating that all women "reverence themselves."[205]

In her writings about old maids, Chamberlain takes their defense one step further by casting her narrator as one. Not only is she an old maid, she is appealingly comical and spunky. The narrator enumerates the merits of "that unlucky, derided, and almost despised set of females." While caring for many townspeople, single women "form a large proportion of our authoresses; they are the founders and pillars of Anti-Slavery, Moral Reform, and all sorts of religious and charitable societies." Their industry and compassion benefit many neighbors: "[W]ere it not for old maids, the sick would suffer for want of care, the children would have to do without stockings, and the flax would never be spun; the lambs and goslins would all die, and the old bachelors would go ragged." Chamberlain half-humorously reveals society's mistake in denigrating whole classes of women. Furthermore, her sympathetic treatment of these women anticipates Margaret Fuller's defense in the American feminist classics "The Great Lawsuit" (1843) and *Woman in the Nineteenth Century* (1845).[206]

Chamberlain's most compelling treatment of a marginal woman is found in the local-color sketch "Aunt 'Dear Soul.'" An indigent elderly woman living alone in a "poor abode" on the outskirts of the narrator's hometown, Aunt Dear Soul embodies some of the qualities Chamberlain most values, such as independence, fruitful industry, closeness to nature, and generosity. Refusing to seek shelter in the local poorhouse, Aunt Dear Soul takes action to support herself. In this piece, as in "A Reverie," Chamberlain shows how greatly she values women's opportunity and capacity "to reason, and to act" (p. 131).

Like a Native woman, Aunt Dear Soul subsists upon outdoor work, gathering from nature's plenty to distribute among her neighbors: "Aunt Dear Soul picked cranberries, blueberries, strawberries, and all sorts of berries, for a living; she brought the housewives roots and fern-buds for their beer; she gathered nuts and apples for a share of the proceeds; stripped bark for dye-stuff, and picked the stray brush in the woodland, for her own hearth-stone. . . . When there was no vagrant work to do, then Aunt Dear Soul lived an unusually vagrant life. She visited all the neighbors for miles away, carrying a large satchel for the expected gifts." (pp. 137–38)

As she strolls the countryside, her neighbors provide her with gifts of food and clothing in return for her sincere, unfailing kindness. Conveyed through words of encouragement and praise, her kindness extends to all, young and old. Anticipating Mary Wilkins Freeman's and Sarah Orne Jewett's local-color sketches of poor, elderly, rural women, Chamberlain shows that society wrongly ostracizes such women as Aunt Dear Soul. The qualities that Chamberlain values most, in fact, are found in such marginal, apparently useless members of society. As a middle-aged, mixed-race woman, Chamberlain thus explores her own difference and resists the social forces that would marginalize her. In creating this loving portrait of "Aunt Dear Soul," she honors her Native grandmothers.

Reading Betsey Chamberlain's writings and researching her life reveal the rewards of studying "ordinary" Americans. Unpretentious and formally uneducated beyond grade school, Chamberlain produced writings as fresh as her rural New Hampshire home—despite working twelve to fourteen hours a day in the mills. Her folk pieces also offer rare insights into the experience and subjectivity of a mixed-race New England woman. Graced with a profusion of colorful and vivid elements, her texts effect a compelling fusion of Native and Euro-American oral and literary cultures, demonstrating that New England Native people not only survived but contributed their share to the evolving American society.

Part Two

BETSEY CHAMBERLAIN'S
WRITINGS

ONE

Native Tales and Dream Visions

A Fire-Side Scene

A HUGE ROCK-MAPLE FIRE was burning brightly on the old kitchen hearth, which was nicely swept with a new hemlock broom, and surrounded by a group of smiling boys and girls, with uncle David in their midst.

"Come, uncle David," said Frank, "tell us about burning the Miami Indians."

Uncle David gave a shrug with his shoulders, scratched his head, rolled the tobacco over and over in his mouth, gave a deep sigh, and said, "Oh, that was a horrid affair! The Miamis had the most beautiful fields of corn my eyes ever beheld; it was then in the milk,—just fit to roast,—and our army destroyed the whole."

"But," said Frank, "that is not what I asked you to tell—tell us about burning the Indians."

"Well, Frank, I suppose I must tell you something about it," said uncle David, "but I would rather not, for the thoughts which the remembrance of that horrid massacre sets afloat, curdle the blood in my veins. I am glad the Indians were heathen—had they been Christians, I should dread meeting their souls in another world.—It was the 20th of August 1794, that our army met the Indians on the banks of the Miami, and gained a complete victory over them.[1] We lost something like an hundred of our men, and to revenge our loss, we managed matters so adroitly that we surrounded their villages, set them on fire, and every Indian that tried to escape was driven with the point of the bayonet back into the flames, and burned up alive. Yes, we burned them all up—women, children, and all. Oh, their horrid yells and groans! how many times I have heard them in my dreams. I am glad the Indians were heathen."

"And what else did you do, uncle David," said Frank, "besides massacreing the poor Indians, burning their villages, and all such cruel things?"

"Oh," said uncle David, "we roasted the Indians' hogs and corn, and our army had fine picking, I assure you."

"Uncle David," said Frank, after a long pause, "do you think 'Uncle Sam' is a Christian, to give you a pension for being in *that* scrape?"

"Why—yes—sartin," said uncle David, with evident perturbation, "they were heathen, boy—they were heathen—wheugh—wheugh— Frank, draw Uncle David a mug of cider to clear the cobwebs from his throat, and he will sing, 'Hail Independence.'"[2]

Tabitha.

The Indian Pledge

On the door-steps of a cottage in the land of "steady habits,"[3] some ninety or an hundred years since, might, on a soft evening in June, have been seen a sturdy young farmer, preparing his scythes for the coming hay-making season. So intent was he upon his work, that he heeded not the approach of a tall Indian, accoutred[4] for a hunting expedition, until "Will you give an unfortunate hunter some supper and lodging for the night?" in a tone of supplication, caught his ear.

The farmer raised his eyes from his work, and darting fury from beneath a pair of shaggy eye-brows, he exclaimed, "Heathen, Indian dog, begone! you shall have nothing here."

"But I am very hungry," said the Indian; "give only a crust of bread and a bone, to strengthen me on my journey."

"Get you gone, you heathen dog!" said the farmer; "I have nothing for you."

"Give me but a cup of cold water," said the Indian, "for I am very faint."

This appeal was not more successful than the others. Reiterated abuse, and to be told to drink when he came to a river, was all he could obtain from one who bore the name of Christian! But the supplicating appeal fell not unheeded on the ear of one of finer mould and more sensibility. The farmer's youthful bride heard the whole, as she sat hushing her infant to rest; and from the open casement she watched the poor Indian, until she saw his dusky form sink, apparently exhausted, on the ground, at no great distance from her dwelling. Ascertaining that her husband was too busied with his work to notice her, she was soon at the Indian's side, with a pitcher of milk, and a napkin filled with bread and cheese. "Will my red brother slake his thirst with some milk?" said this angel of mercy; and as he essayed to comply with her invitation, she untied the napkin, and bade him eat and be refreshed.

"Cantantowwit[5] protect the white dove from the pounces of the eagle," said the Indian; "for *her* sake the unfledged young shall be safe in their nest, and her red brother will not seek to be revenged."

He then drew a bunch of feathers from his bosom, and plucking one of the longest, gave it to her, and said, "When the white dove's mate flies over the Indians' hunting-grounds, bid him wear this on his head."

*　　　*　　　*

The summer had passed away. Harvest-time had come and gone, and preparations had been made for a hunting excursion by the neighbors. Our young farmer was to be one of the party; but on the eve of their departure he had strange misgivings relative to his safety. No doubt his imagination was haunted by the form of the Indian, whom, in the preceding summer, he had treated so harshly.

The morning that witnessed the departure of the hunters, was one of surpassing beauty. Not a cloud was to be seen, save one that gathered on the brow of Ichabod, (our young farmer,) as he attempted to tear a feather from his hunting-cap, which was sewed fast to it. His wife arrested his hand, while she whispered in his ear, and a slight quiver agitated his lips as he said, "Well, Mary, if you think this feather will protect me from the arrows of the red-skins, I'll e'en let it remain." Ichabod donned his cap, shouldered his rifle, and the hunters were soon on their way in quest of game.

The day wore away as was usual with people on a like excursion; and at night-fall they took shelter in the den of a bear, whose flesh served for supper, and whose skin spread on bruin's bed of leaves, pillowed their heads through a long November night.

With the first dawn of morning, the hunters left their rude shelter and resumed their chase. Ichabod, by some mishap, soon separated from his companions, and in trying to join them, got bewildered. He wandered all day in the forest, and just as the sun was receding from sight, and he was about sinking down in despair, he espied an Indian hut. With mingled emotions of hope and fear, he bent his steps towards it; and meeting an Indian at the door, he asked him to direct him to the nearest white settlement.

"If the weary hunter will rest till morning, the eagle will show him the way to the nest of his white dove," said the Indian, as he took Ichabod by the hand and led him within his hut. The Indian gave him a supper of parched corn and venison, and spread the skins of animals which he had taken in hunting, for his bed.

The light had hardly begun to streak the east, when the Indian awoke Ichabod, and after a slight repast, the twain started for the settlement of the whites. Late in the afternoon, as they emerged from a thick wood, Ichabod with joy espied his home. A heartfelt ejaculation had scarce escaped his lips, when the Indian stepped before him, and turning around, stared him full in the face, and inquired if he had any recollection of a previous acquaintance with his red brother. Upon being answered in the negative, the Indian said, "Five moons ago when I was faint and weary, you called me an Indian dog, and drove me from your door. I might now be revenged; but Cantantowwit bids me tell you to go home; and hereafter, when you see a red man in need of kindness, do to him as you have been done by. Farewell."

The Indian having said this, turned upon his heel, and was soon out of sight. Ichabod was abashed. He went home purified in heart, having learned a lesson of Christianity from an untutored savage.

Tabitha.

A New Society

"Dreams are but interludes which fancy makes;
When monarch reason sleeps, this mimic wakes:
Compounds a medley of disjointed things,
A court of cobblers, a mob of kings.
Light fumes are merry, grosser fumes are sad;
Both are the reasonable soul run mad:—
And many forms and things in sleep we see,
That neither were, nor are—but haply yet may be."[6]

It was Saturday night. The toils of the week were at an end; and, seated at the table with my book, I was feasting upon the treasures of knowledge which it contained. One by one my companions had left me, until I was alone. How long I continued to read I know not; but I had closed my book, and sat ruminating upon the many changes and events which are continually taking place in this transitory world of ours. My reverie was disturbed by the opening of the door, and a little boy entered the room, who, handing me a paper, retired without speaking. I unfolded the paper, and the first article which caught my eye was headed, "Annual Meeting of the Society for the promotion of Industry, Virtue and Knowledge." It read as follows: "At the annual meeting of this society, the following resolutions were unanimously adopted:

"1. *Resolved,* That every father of a family who neglects to give his daughters the same advantages for an education which he gives his sons, shall be expelled from this society, and be considered a heathen."

"2. *Resolved,* That no member of this society shall exact more than eight hours of labour, out of every twenty-four, of any person in his or her employment."[7]

"3. *Resolved,* That, as the laborer is worthy of his hire,[8] the price for labor shall be sufficient to enable the working-people to pay a proper attention to scientific and literary pursuits."

"4. *Resolved,* That the wages of females shall be equal to the wages of males, that they may be enabled to maintain proper independence of character, and virtuous deportment."

"5. *Resolved,* That no young gentleman of this society shall be allowed to be of age, or to transact business for himself, until he shall have a good knowledge of the English language, understand book-keeping, both by single and double entry, and be capable of transacting all town business."

"6. *Resolved,* That no young lady belonging to this society shall be considered marriageable, who does not understand how to manage the affairs of the kitchen, and who does not, each month, write at least enough to fill one page of imperial octavo."[9]

"7. *Resolved,* That we will not patronize the writings of any person who does not spend at least three hours in each day, when

health will permit, either in manual labor, or in some employment which will be a public benefit, and which shall not apper-
tain to literary pursuits."

"8. *Resolved,* That each member of this society shall spend three
hours in each day in the cultivation of the mental faculties, or
forfeit membership, extraordinaries excepted."

"9. *Resolved,* That industry, virtue and knowledge, (not wealth and
titles,) shall be the standard of respectability for this society."

I stopped at the ninth resolution, to ponder upon what I had read;
and I thought it was remarkably strange that I had not before heard
of this society. There was a gentle tap at the door, and a gentleman
entered the room, with a modest request for subscribers to a new
periodical which was about to be issued from the press. I showed him
what I had been reading. He glanced his eyes upon it, and exclaimed,
"Oh happy America! Thrice happy land of Freedom! Thy example
shall yet free all nations from the galling chains of mental bondage;
and teach to earth's remotest ends, in what true happiness consists!"

By reading the remainder of the article, I learned that this society,
and its auxiliaries, already numbered more than two-thirds of the population of the United States, and was rapidly increasing; but the date
puzzled me extremely; it was April 1, 1860.

The agent for the new periodical reminded me of his business. I ran
up stairs to ascertain if any of our girls would become subscribers; but
before reaching the chambers, I stumbled, and awoke.

Tabitha.

A Reverie

I was crossing the bridge near the Merrimack counting-room.[10] The
evening was dark, and as I stopped to view the reflection of the well-
lighted factory on the waters of the canal, soft music swelled upon the
breeze in wild, harmonious strains. It drew near, and swept beneath
the bridge; and on the water a beautiful little island arose. Its glossy
surface of emerald green was beautifully interspersed with pearl and
coral. A jasper wall was round about it, against which reclined a company of mermaids, with their sea-green hair flowing loosely over their
shoulders. Their highly polished foreheads and arched eyebrows—their

laughing eyes, glancing from beneath long silken lashes—noses of that peculiar contour that at once bespeaks elevation and tenderness— mouths and chins classically formed, and complexions of the delicate red and white of the apple-blossom—busts that a modern belle might envy—arms exquisitely formed, and a delicate hand with taper fin- gers,—contrasted strikingly with the scaly, fish-like appearance of their lower extremities.

Their wild song was accompanied with the music of reeds, which blended melodiously with their voices, and as I stood entranced, I could not help expressing a wish that I was a mermaid, that I might be free from care, and enjoy unrestrained freedom; then might I ride on the bosom of the waters, or explore the bottom of the mighty deep, and search out all its treasures.

The music ceased, and one of the mermaids thus addressed me: "Child of earth, envy not the Naiads[11] of the deep their comparatively useless lives. Though losses, crosses[12] and disappointments have been the lot of your earthly pilgrimage, give not way to useless repining; but consider that you were born to know, to reason, and to act. Throw off this dreaming, melancholy garb, and put on the mantle of sober and cheerful wisdom, and walk in the light which God has given.[13] You will thus experience more enjoyment on earth, than is vouchsafed to the nymphs of the ocean."

As she spoke, the Merrimack yard vanished, and a turbulent sea extended far as the eye could reach. Wave rolled on wave, mountain high, and the beautiful little island, with its inhabitants, was washed from sight. A shudder ran through my frame, and a well-known voice sounded in my ear, "The cloth has come in—'nine mills'* are soon lost by being idle." I raised my head from my cloth-frame, where I had been sleeping, and prepared to resume my task at picking cloth.[14]

B. C.

Sabbath Morning

It was a beautiful sabbath morning, and I had arisen earlier than usual. The tranquil hours had just given Aurora[15] the tint of the rose, and dispelled the vapours of the night that hovered over the shadowy

---

*The price of a certain amount of work.

earth, while the sun's first rays tinged with radiant purple the half-enlightened clouds. It was a time for thought and reflection; and imagination carried me back to the years of childhood, when with a light step and merry heart I used to trip through the dewy grass, and hie to the wild-wood, that I might hear the birds, when they first awoke, begin to chant their morning songs. And I longed for the days of other years, that, far from the busy city of Lowell, I might again see Nature celebrate the returning light, and pay to Nature's God the sacrifice of praise.[16]

Thus far had I proceeded with my communication, intending to delineate the various beauties which, in other days and far away, would, on a lovely sabbath morn, enchant my eyes and ears, and inspire my heart with a holy transport, awakening a desire to join in the rapturous employment of praising the great Author of all things. But my feelings overcame me, and my trembling hand refused to do its office. I threw down my pen, and burying my face in my handkerchief, a friendly shower of tears came to my relief. A visit from Morpheus[17] hushed each rising sigh; and seated in fancy's[18] car, imagination soon placed me on a huge rock which jutted over the limpid waters of my own loved Winipisiogee.[19] Through the grey mist of the morning I could discern the islands of Varney and Barndoor, with their green pastures and shady groves; also Rattlesnake island, with its tall cedars. Behind me was the wood, where in by-gone days I had spent many hours in the delightful employment of gathering wild-flowers and berries, nuts and acorns; and where I had watched the squirrel, as he hopped from tree to tree, and listened to the songs of the robin and bob-a-lincon,[20] and sometimes chased the fox to his hiding-place. The returning day soon awoke the winged inhabitants of the grove, and they began to pour forth the melody of their little throats, to the praise of Him who gave them voice and melody. The resplendent sun, darting his rays from behind the woods, giving light and color to re-animated nature, now decked with smiles and new-born graces the whole enchanting prospect. The glittering summits of the rocks, and the shining sides of the opposite mountains, sent up exhalations which, mixing with the pure air of the morning as they arose, reminded me of the smoke of burnt-offerings, which anciently ascended from the altar of God's chosen people.[21] In this smiling morn I could see all nature paying homage to the great Creator, and the language of my heart was, Let my voice reach Thy throne, O Lord, before that of Thy other creatures! In the grey twilight, at the dawn of the morning, while the birds and beasts yet sleep, may my solitary prayer find acceptance, and invite the reviving creation to praise Thee! Praise the Lord, oh my soul![22]

I awoke, and felt a sadness at heart to think that I had only been dreaming.

Tabitha.

A Vision of Truth

Yesterday, I was visited by a very dear friend, of whose society I had been deprived for nearly three years. So happy a day I had not enjoyed during his absence. Many were the topics of conversation; and among others, we noticed the various improvements, which, during our separation, had been made in the industrious city of Lowell. This naturally introduced the Improvement Circle;[23] and I proposed that we should spend the evening by attending a meeting thereof—to which he joyfully agreed. We went, and were truly delighted with the entertainment. After retiring to rest, the day spent so pleasantly was lived over in imagination, and the train of thought which accompanied it, kept me awake a long time; and when I slept, it was only to dream.

I fancied that I was travelling in a strange country, attended by a guide; and presently we entered a beautiful grove, cultivated by the hand of man. The trees were covered with beautiful foliage, and blooming flowers shed their fragrance all around. The birds were tuning their throats to melody. All nature was decked in smiles. "How enchanting the scene here presented! What a feast for those who delight to see nature in all her loveliness!" said I to my guide.—"It is truly delightful," said he. "But come with me to yonder hill, and I will show you what has been a matter of astonishment to many."

I assented, and he led me to a green eminence, on which grew a tree, different from any thing of which I had ever formed a conception. Its trunk was unlike other trees; for it appeared to be composed of small tendrils, interwoven with each other; and yet the tall straight trunk, at a slight glance, appeared to be much like the trunk of an oak. It had numberless branches, some straight, others waving; but all combined, formed a most beautiful tree—a tree which I can better imagine than describe.

"Of what clime is this tree a native," said I to my guide.—"Of our own America," he replied; "but the seeds grew in different sections of the country. These seeds were germinated in flower-pots, in the cotton mills, and by a botanist transplanted to this spot. You perceive that the trunk is composed of different plants, and yet entwined so as to appear like one tree. The branches, you also perceive, bear different kinds of fruit; and yet all are nutritious. This tree is somewhat similar to one of which we read in the Apocalypse—for it yields its fruit every month, and its leaves are for the healing of the nations."[24]

While he yet spake, people were coming in all directions, to gather the leaves, which were hung together in clusters, and so much alike, that it would be difficult to distinguish one from another. As the clusters were broken off, new ones were budding for the next harvest. I asked my guide what maladies they would heal. "Oh," said he, "maladies of the mind." "And what," I enquired, "is the name of this wonderful tree?" He led me to the other side of it, and showed me the words, *Mental Knowledge,* carved on the trunk; and plucking several clusters of leaves, he showed me, Lowell Offering, on the outside of each. I was about to make some remarks, when the first morning bell awoke me.

Tabitha.

Visit to a Grave-Yard

It was in that charming season of the year called the Indian Summer, (a name derived from the natives, who believe that it is caused by a wind, which they believe to be the breath of their great god Cantantowwit, to whom the souls of all good Indians go, after their decease,) that I visited the burial-place of my friends, and took a last view of a spot where many times and oft I have loved to linger.

It was late in the afternoon of a beautiful day. The air was perfectly transparent, and the clouds which were floating in the sky, were of the purest azure, tinged with gold. The south-western breezes, as they breathed through the glowing trees, seemed almost to articulate, and I fancied that I could hear the still small voice[25] of the Eternal, whispering of life and immortality beyond the grave; and oh! how did I long to lie down and sleep in that hallowed spot!

As the sun slowly descended, leaving behind him a line of crimson to mark his path-way to rest, each cloud in the spacious firmament floated majestically to the western sky, and stood there in "grandeur magnificent," arrayed in all the gorgeous and brilliant hues of the rainbow. There as they stood, catching the parting rays of the king of day, and transforming them to different hues, I fancied those clouds to be the aerial couches of the spirits of those loved ones whose bodies lay slumbering beneath my feet; and how gladly would I have *then* laid down my earthly vestments, and soared away to that western sky! But it could not be—for my pilgrimage was not ended.

I turned from this scene of surpassing beauty, and another met my eye. In an easterly direction, the sun's rays yet lingered on the top of a lofty mountain, whose trees were of every hue, from the deep green of the spruce and fir, to the palest yellow of the autumn leaf; and there, above that mountain's top, was the most beautiful rainbow my eyes ever beheld. Beautiful even in death was the foliage of the trees on that mountain—but more beautiful was the bow of Omnipotence, arched over its top.[26]

The beautiful tints soon faded away in the gray twilight—but they still remain bright on the tablet of Memory. Long, long did I linger on that hallowed spot; and not until the shades of night had gathered thick around me, did I retrace the path that led me thither.

B. C.

TWO

"The Unprivileged Sex": Women's Concerns

Aunt "Dear Soul"

IN A LITTLE COT,[27] far away in the outskirts of "our town," lived Aunt Dear Soul; a poor and humble widow, whose gray hairs told of years and sorrows, whose coarse garb spoke of poverty and thriftlessness, and whose poor abode told of privation and discomfort. The poor-house, not very far away, would have been opened to her as an asylum; but with a Yankee feeling of independence, which seemed not amiss in the daughter of a Revolutionary soldier, she would have resented an invitation to share its privileges; and she still clung to the home of her fathers.

An old cow, with a mottled back, was all that now remained of the barn-yard herd; and, whether it was because the spots upon her hide reminded her owner of the freckled lily of the field, or whether she would fain bestow upon the valued creature the most significant epithet of beauty and endearment, I know not; but Aunt Dear Soul's "Cow Lily" was as well known as herself. The gentle beast picked up a comfortable living by the way-side in summer; and if, when in early spring or desolate autumn, she ventured through an open gate, and helped herself to a few stalks, or some fragrant hay, she was never beaten nor driven away. After quietly satisfying her hunger, she would depart, and the refreshment received would be transferred to Aunt Dear Soul in a rich liquid blessing. The boys never stoned her, the girls, stroked her sleek sides, and murmured "Cow Lily," in tones of affection; and the meek creature passed on, through the cow-paths of life, with no greater sorrow than an irregular sustenance, and the trouble of getting it. As with the beast, so with the owner. Aunt Dear Soul picked cranberries, blueberries, strawberries, and all sorts of berries, for a living; she brought the housewives roots and fern-buds for their beer; she gathered nuts and apples for a share of the proceeds; stripped bark for dye-stuff, and picked the stray brush in the woodland, for her own hearth-stone. For Aunt Dear Soul had a hearth, with a pair of "black dogs"[28] to keep her fire in proper order; and the innovation of a stove would to her have been intolerable. When there was no vagrant work to do, then Aunt Dear Soul lived an unusually vagrant life. She visited all the neighbors for miles away, carrying a large satchel for the expected gifts, and returning every night with treasures of fruits, cakes, broken meats, old clothes, or worn household stuffs, and with the remembrance of kind looks and words. But why were all so kind to Aunt Dear Soul? It was because the spirit of kindness dwelt in her—exhibited in her homely way, but appreciated and returned. "Why, you dear soul!" she would say to the boy "with shining morning face," shining with evaporated tears, as he limped unwillingly to school.[29] "Why, you dear soul! how beautiful you look with your clean apron on, and your books in your hand, and your new cap and trowsers; you dear soul, you!" and the boy was mollified in an instant. Pleased with himself, with Aunt Dear Soul, and even with the prospect before him, he tripped gaily along, forgetting past tears and future spelling-lessons. "Why, you dear soul!" she would say to the little girl, who sat in her mother's door-way, looking pale from her efforts to finish her task at the needle, breaking her thread and pricking her fingers, in her perturbation. "Why, you dear soul! how beautiful you can sew! you will make all the shirts in the family, soon;" and the child, pleased and encouraged, would stitch on with a light heart and nimble fingers.

"Why, you dear soul!" she would exclaim to the distressed mother of half-a-dozen little ones, who, with one child in her lap and another in the cradle, would look as if almost sorry to see Aunt Dear Soul enter the door. "You dear soul! how beautiful you look, with your babies all around you! and such beautiful babies, too!" and the young mother, flattered in a vulnerable point, would direct Aunt Dear Soul to a soft arm chair, and invite her to a welcome dinner. True, it was all flattery; but all liked it. It was from Aunt Dear Soul, and could not offend; for, like all *true* flattery, it was based upon something real.

Much as Aunt Dear Soul went around, and various as were the listeners to her gossip, she never made mischief. There was an instinct which preserved her from the repetition of aught that could cause serious trouble; and Mrs. A., of one sewing society, knew only that Mrs. B. was chosen president of another; but not that she had said, "she hoped affairs would go on under her management better than some that she knew of."

The different religious factions abused each other in the presence of Aunt Dear Soul, and received in reply only her quiet assertion—"I likes 'em all."

Would it not be well if there were more Aunt Dear Souls in all society? The world could not be much the worse, and may there not be lack of those who feel only kindness, and see only beauty; and from the fountains in their own hearts, send forth an unfailing gush to all around them?

I had just returned from a residence of some years in Lowell, and for one or two more, had not seen Aunt Dear Soul. It was a pleasant morning, and I heard footsteps that I knew, approaching the open door. It was Aunt Dear Soul, who gave a start that would have done honor to Mrs. Siddons,[30] if it was acting, and then, after a long, earnest look, stretched forth her hands, with a glad cry, "Why, you dear soul! is it you? I thought it was *some great lady*. Why, you don't grow a bit older, and are twice as handsome! you dear soul! How glad your ma'am must be to have you come home, you dear soul, looking so beautiful, and bringing her all these nice things. It is'nt every body that has got such a gal, you dear soul!"

Who, after this flattery, but would feel strengthened in all purposes of filial piety, rewarded for all self-sacrifice, and gratified with the acknowledgment of duties well done, even by one as humble as Aunt Dear Soul?

And not the daughter only was pleased, but the mother felt a renewal of pride and joy, and bestirred herself to get an extra dinner for Aunt Dear Soul.

Betsey.

Cousin Mary

Do you not think my Cousin Mary was beautiful? yet I know not why you should, unless it is because her name was Mary. I have seen all sorts of Marys; the tall, and the short; the thick, and the thin; the ashy white, and the florid red; yet never do I see the name of Mary in a book, but it comes associated with some picture of gentle retiring beauty, such as was hers who sleeps beneath a marble stone, in our village burying-ground. And that name is also connected with higher thoughts than those of mere personal loveliness. The Marys of Scripture—what visions of spiritual beauty cluster around their names, from the purity, and trust, of the virgin mother of our Lord, the holy love, and unwavering resignation of the listener of Bethany, to the remorse, devotion, and confiding faith of the Magdalen—it is all high, ennobling, moral beauty.[31] There are Marys also in history—Marys of a queenly line, and almost unearthly beauty, and other Marys of story, and of song. There is the Mary of Cowper, the Mary of Burns, of Byron, and of him (I have forgotten his name) who wrote the sweet "Lament for Mary."[32] It is also linked with other and dearer thoughts, for who, among us, has not a mother, sister, daughter, or at least an Aunt Mary; at all events I feel quite confident that you have each a Cousin Mary. Yes, I have now *a* Cousin Mary, but not *the* cousin of whom I intend to write. I have not her, except in memory, and from that she will never be lost.

My Cousin Mary was young when I was grown a woman; and I love to think of her now, as when I watched her then, maturing in the seclusion of her lowly, peaceful home, like some sweet violet in its shady bed; and when I marked the still and modest girl, mingling with the noisier and more mirthful beauties of our village, I saw that it was not in those gay circles that Cousin Mary was to find her happiness. My Aunt Polly (Mary was named for her mother)[33] was hardly the right one to be entrusted with the charge of one so gentle and affectionate as her pretty daughter. She was married young to my Uncle Obadiah, and all of her sisters (there were eight of them) had found partners for life ere they had reached their twentieth year; and she seemed to think that every female, at least all related to her, were born to be married. Mary was taught to think that the only proper sphere of woman was the domestic circle, and that as a wife alone could she be truly happy, and respectable. For this end was she educated, and every thought and faculty were early directed to a preparation for that station which she would undoubtedly occupy.

It may not here be amiss to give an account of the course which was considered necessary, in those old times, to prepare a female for the important duties which would then devolve upon her. To make good bread, butter, and cheese, were of course *sine qua nons*;[34] and there were many other things nearly, if not quite, as indispensable. They must know how to card, spin, and weave; knit footings, skirts and drawers; make soap, sausages, candles, beer, and their own wedding-cake; color the boys' summer frocks, and trowsers with yellow-oak bark, and so many other things, of which a modern fine lady has probably never heard. Early in life the daughters of a farmer "well to do in the world" commenced that course of thrift, economy, and forethought, which rendered our mothers fit partners for the sturdy yeomanry of New England. Where there were several daughters, the work was divided between them, according to their different capacities, or inclinations; one doing the carding, another the spinning, and another the weaving, while a fourth assisted her mother to wash, bake, and brew. If the farm was large, and the family too small to do all of the work, some poor neighbor's daughter, Hitty, Sally, or Dolly, was hired to assist them. She was never called a servant, or domestic, but spun, eat, and slept with the daughters of her employers, and very often became the bride of their eldest son. Jonathan, Hezekiah, Eliphalet, or whatever else his name might be; at all events usually made her the subject of his initiating exercises in the mysteries of gallantry, such as sitting on the bars, while she was milking, waiting to carry her pail for her, and beguiling the time by talking about "father's crops, steers, and heifers," or the state of his meadow and woodland, and similar interesting subjects. Perhaps if he was naturally romantic, or really smitten by the charms of the fair damsel, his conversation would take a more elevated turn, and he would talk about the moon, or may be of the stars and clouds. These attentions were often followed by those of a more pointed character, such as waiting upon her to and from singing schools, meetings, weddings, and merry-makings; and it was often the case that, when the mother was called upon to part with one daughter, her son was ready to bring her another.

But I must not too long digress from Cousin Mary. She was an only child, and, as her father's farm was a small one, no other help was considered necessary in the performance of their household duties. Before her twelfth year was completed, she could spin, cook, and wash as well as her mother, and make full as good butter. Patch-work quilts were already completed, done in what, in our modern way of speaking, would be called mason-work, or perhaps mosaic. Indeed, girls in those days often exercised themselves in all the figures of Euclid, while making their quilts, though they were wholly unconscious of these practical illustrations of geometry.[35] Cousin Mary was the only girl I ever knew, who had *two* quilts, made in the fashion of what is called "Job's troubles;"[36] and there used to be an old saying that no one who ever commenced such work would live to complete it. I am happy to be able to inform all who may wish to exhibit such an evidence of industry, that they need not fear, from this cause, an untimely death, for I have known some who have lived to mature years, and slept under a weight of "troubles" of their own making.

As Mary had no brother or sister, she enjoyed the same privileges as the daughters of their more wealthy neighbors, and was allowed as much wool and flax as she would make up; and her future marriage portion was to be, like theirs, not so much a criterion of her father's wealth, as of her own industry. She worked like a beaver, and had not only the requisite pillow-case full of stockings before she was engaged, but also divers rag-mats, and strip carpets; blue and white woollen coverlids,[37] and a huge pile of blankets, sheets, and pillow-cases. She had also towels, and table-linen of her own weaving, done in patterns manifold. There was hukkabuk, diamond, bird's-eye, lock and compass, lemon and orange peel, chariot wheels, seven stars, nine snowballs, true lover's knots, and many others. She had from childhood possessed a little flock of geese and hens, of her own rearing, the products of which were some feather beds, and sundry articles, which she had purchased, with the eggs sold at the village store; among which were a silk gown, a chip hat, a fur tippet, and a pair of gold ear-knobs.[38] These articles were of course kept very choice, and only worn upon particular occasions.

Mary was, I think, about eighteen years of age, when she first received the attentions of Daniel Parsons. He was the younger son of a wealthy farmer, and my Aunt Polly was much pleased with the prospect of a match, which she thought would conduce to the happiness and advantage of her daughter. She was continually talking about it to Mary, and expatiating upon the felicities, and increase of dignity, appertaining to the marriage state. Though I think that my aunt did well to prepare Mary's thoughts for an event which would probably occur to her, yet such constant disquisitions, as though it was something inevitable, were not judicious. It would have been better to have taught her that marriage, though an event that might possibly, or would probably, yet was not one that must, assuredly, constitute her future happiness; and that misery and degradation were not necessary concomitants of a single state.

But so it was, and Mary was taught to consider herself a wife in prospective; and, from the time that Daniel Parsons began to make his stated weekly visits, she looked upon him as her future husband. But she did not feel in any hurry to marry. O no; a courtship of a dozen years was, in those days, considered nothing out of the way; and for seven years was Cousin Mary the affianced one of Daniel Parsons, without people's troubling themselves about the time when they should be man and wife. At length the customary observations were made, that they should think it was high time that Daniel and Mary were married, and they saw nothing in the world to hinder, and wonder was expressed that the courtship had not come to a crisis before. And then there were suspicions, and surmises, and doubts, and fears, and some thought that they never would be united, and others that they never had intended to be, or that Daniel could do far better, or that Mary should remain single, to take care of her parents, in their declining years.

Such observations, of course, were more frequently made when Daniel expressed his determination to leave home, for a time, and seek his fortune, or obtain a better acquaintance with the world, in the city. Aunt Polly was not at all discomposed at this. She was glad that Mary was to be left with her a short time longer, though still pleased at the thought of resigning her, at some future time, to an enterprising husband. Whatever Cousin Mary felt, she said nothing—at least, nothing expressive of much feeling upon the subject—and I supposed, as did many others, that if Daniel should not return, or should find a more pleasing partner in his new place of residence, she could easily withdraw her affections from him, if not transfer them to some one else. But we did not give her credit for the warmth and constancy of feeling, which she really possessed. I had supposed that to be a wife, a housekeeper, to go about a home of her own, as she now did about her father's house, was her highest aim. But how much was I mistaken. Because she was reserved, and concealed the strength of her feelings, I presumed she did not possess it; and when some months had passed away, and no Daniel returned to Cousin Mary, and she still went on with her accustomed household duties, as busy, and *apparently* as cheerful as ever, I supposed that she had forgotten him, as he had probably forgotten her.

Sometimes I would ask her when she was to be married, and her reply would usually be, "Never: why should I wish to leave this happy home? I can never have a better one." But Aunt Polly would always call out, "I am glad that Mary does not wish to leave us yet, and that Daniel does not think of marrying at present. It is pleasant to think that we shall live together awhile longer."

I knew that Mary did not correspond with Daniel, but the few letters, which he wrote to his parents, were always forwarded, by them, to her, and he received accounts of her health and welfare through the same medium. They were both unaccustomed to the use of the pen, and it was, in those days, a stranger thing for country lovers to correspond than to neglect it; so that circumstance, of itself, occasioned but little uneasiness.

But at length Daniel returned, for a short time, to his father's house. Every body was upon the watch to see how matters would go on between him and Cousin Mary. I must confess that I sat down to my chamber window, with a feeling of more than usual solicitude the next Sunday evening after his arrival. I thought of the many times when I had seen him, on his "winding way," just about sundown, with his hair nicely brushed, his handkerchief tied about his neck in a neat square knot, his shoes well greased, and his very walk bespeaking an errand of unusual importance. And there Cousin Mary would sit and wait for him, in the best fore-room, with her pink calico gown on, and a white vandyke, and her best morocco shoes,[39] and all things around her arranged with even more than ordinary care.

I thought of all this, but I felt that a change had now come over the spirit of Daniel's dream. He had learned to wear a watch, cravat, and long coat; could smoke cigars, and sing songs; wore pomatum on his hair, and "Day & Martin" on his boots; and was altogether quite a spruce young gentleman.[40]

But he did not go near Cousin Mary that day, nor the next, nor even the next; and when they did meet, it was as strangers, rather than those who had once been lovers. At length, Daniel went back again, and country gossips loudly proclaimed the fact that Mary was a deserted girl. Aunt Polly said she did not care; Mary was far too good for him, and she knew of many others who would be glad to marry her, and she doubted not that she would soon find a better husband. I said nothing to my cousin about it. I felt that she would be better pleased if this subject were entirely dropped, and I do not approve of the meddling which is so common in all love affairs. Where there is happiness, let them enjoy it in that peaceful quiet so dear to every mind of delicacy, and where there is misery and disappointment, let the wrung heart recover itself in secrecy and silence.

But though, upon one subject, I said nothing to Cousin Mary, I watched her as closely as I could, without offending her. I saw enough. She talked, and laughed, and worked as much as ever, but her form began to waste, her hands grew thin, there was a hollow circle around her eyes, and when she thought herself unobserved, the smile was changed to a sigh. At last Aunt Polly sent for me to come there, for Mary was sick. She did not know what was the matter, but thought she had taken a violent cold. I went, and found her seated in her little chamber in an attitude of the deepest dejection.

"Mary," said I, as I raised the head which had rested on her hands— "dear Cousin Mary, tell me what is the matter?"

"Nothing," said she—"nothing in particular. I cannot work, and my mother is alarmed about me. Nothing is the matter but a head-ache, and *that will soon be over.*"

She uttered the last words in a low impressive tone, and I calmly replied, "Mary, you must tell me all. I can at least sympathize with you, and perhaps advise and console you. I know some things now, for I at least have not been wholly deceived."

"Oh," said she, bitterly, "I have tried to deceive you all. I have been a hypocrite this long time, but I can be one no longer. My strength and spirits have utterly failed me. I do not sleep; I have had no quiet rest for months; I can do nothing now but die. I shall sleep soundly then, and not till then."

"Mary," said I, earnestly, "you must not talk so; you must not feel so; you must overcome this; you can do it, and for your parents' sake, who have no other child but you, and for your own sake, you must not give way to this weakness. Rouse yourself, and be as though this had never happened. Be yourself; you have the kindest of parents, an excellent home, and many friends. You are young, and life should still be dear to you. It is dear when you have once thrown off this worse than weakness, and become what you once have been."

"That time will never be," was Mary's bitter reply. "It cannot be. I know all that you *would* say, and more than you *could* say. I *have* tried to rouse myself, but my efforts have been like those of a miserable dreamer. I try to awake, and to be once more in the happy world about me, but the dreadful bands still keep me down. I am like one in chains, and when it seems for a moment as though I might burst them asunder, the effort only convinces me more surely of my own weakness. Do not tell me that *I can* overcome this, for I assure you that *I cannot.* I despise and hate myself for it, but I can do nothing but pray for rest and peace in the slumber of the grave."

"Tell me, Mary, all that has happened, and let me know what has thus depressed you."

"I cannot tell you all, nor but very little. When I first began to suspect that Daniel might prove untrue, I felt as though such suspicions were the suggestions of the adversary,[41] and would not harbor them. I kept hoping on, and hoping against hope, and satisfying myself, by every reasoning, that I had been unjust to him; and putting the construction[42] which I most wished upon his absence and silence; and at length, when he returned, I avoided a meeting as long as possible that I might not *know* that my fears were true, that I might not be deprived of all hope; and when I did see him, I tried so hard to appear indifferent, though I feared that the truth must sometime be known. But he did not know then that I felt it, nor did any one. I returned that evening to my parents, and sat and tried to talk with them, and to appear as though nothing had disturbed me; but when I laid my head upon my pillow it was with the wish that I might never raise it again, and then my brain began to whirl, and the blood kept boiling into it, and sounds like the crash of buildings, and the yells of wild beasts went through my ears, and then I lay like one almost benumbed, and conscious of naught but life and misery."

Mary was not naturally romantic, she had never read novels, and I felt, as she poured forth her feelings in the quick earnest language of passion, how deeply she had loved, and how much she had been wronged. I trembled as she opened her heart to me, for there is no frankness like that of a reserved mind when it has once thrown aside all concealment.

"Mary," said I, at length, "I see that you cannot yet become indifferent, but you must change your feelings. Learn to despise him for his fickleness, and hate him for his cruelty."

"I cannot," said she; "I feel myself too unworthy and despicable to despise any one; and I cannot hate—it is not in my nature; neither do I wish that a love which *has* made me happy, and which *might* have gladdened a long life, to change to that dark passion as I am about to enter another world."

She buried her face in her hands, and I could say nothing more, for I felt my own more turbulent spirit rebuked by the meekness of the gentle girl. I had seen love come upon others, brightening with its sunshine their young existence; and I had seen disappointment follow, like a tempest, bringing darkness and desolation in its train; but it passed away, and all again was green and beautiful; but upon Cousin Mary it had come like the withering blight, which penetrates the very earth, and carries destruction to every root and stem. I saw that for her "the life of life" was o'er, and life had naught but death in store. Yet no one else knew it, no one suspected it, "for every string had snapped so silently—Quivered and bled unseen."[43]

A physician was called to her, who said that the symptoms were those of consumption,[44] but she might be saved by judicious care and watchfulness. From that time I did not leave her, but we spoke no more upon that one subject. I endeavored to arouse and cheer her, but in vain. She had exerted herself as long as possible, and now she wished to be left in peace. Once I brought to her the child of a neighbor, with the hope that its innocent playfulness would effect what I had not been able to perform, but she turned away from it, and I saw that there were tears in her eyes. Yet I could not see her die without making one more effort to save her.

She was reserved; she had concealed, even from me, the strength of her attachment to her lover. How probable then that he was totally unconscious of it; her pride had enabled her to appear indifferent, he perhaps thought her cold and heartless; at all events, he could not know how every idea of future happiness had been linked with thoughts of him; how that affection was inwoven with every fibre of her heart; if he knew it all, he certainly must return to her. I wrote, without her knowledge, a letter to Daniel Parsons, and it had the desired effect. He was soon with us, and when he beheld the wan cheek, and sunken eye, of Cousin Mary, his heart smote him for the ruin he had wrought. His former affection returned, and he wished, if possible, to restore her to happiness.

"But you deceived me," said he to her; "I thought that you cared but little for me, and therefore I put your feelings to the test; and when I left home the last time, it was with the assurance that you never had really loved me."

"I saw that a change had taken place in you," was Mary's reply, "and I thought it greater than it really was. I could not bear that you should think I cherished a feeling which was to meet no return. I believed that your love was gone, and only wished to hide my own till I rested with the dead."

"You must not talk of dying," said Parsons to her. "You shall live, and we will yet be happy."

He was indeed resolved that if affection, and the most constant attention, could restore her, she should yet be his; and again a roseate glow came upon Mary's cheek, and a sparkle to her eye, but they were flickering and evanescent. Preparations were made for their marriage, and the journey which was to follow it, and from which was hoped the most beneficial results. The day was fixed, and all was ready, but it was as I had feared—the excitement, the reaction of feeling had been too great, and on the very evening appointed for the wedding they bade each other a last farewell.

We clad her that night in white robes, but they were not those she had prepared for the bridal; and when we had arrayed her in garments for the grave, he who had thought then to have been her husband, came to look upon her as she lay in the sleep of death. He lifted the shroud from the lifeless form, and gazed long and earnestly upon that countenance, which never more might beam with love, and hope, and trust in him. He shed no tear, but his face was pale as that of the dead, and his lips quivered as he pressed them, for the last time, to the marble brow; then, gently replacing the shroud, he turned away, and never looked at her again. He has been true to her memory, and the most beautiful monument, in our burying-ground, is that which marks her last resting place. Faithfully are all the duties of his life performed, but when I see him now, with a countenance, which, spite of[45] its calmness, bears the impress of an enduring sorrow, I cannot but regret that he must have received so severe a lesson, before he could understand the heart of Cousin Mary.

Betsey.

Fortune-Telling. A Narrative of Salmagundi

I will inform the reader, first of all, that I do not altogether approve of fortune-telling; nevertheless, it may sometimes be practised with perfect propriety. The practice of turning cups after tea,[46] in which many young ladies often indulge, might be a means of giving timely caution, for the purpose of persuading thoughtless young people to desist from practices, or to forsake company, that would be likely to lead them to ruin, without seeming to meddle with the conduct or affairs of others; a thing which was practiced, "many a time and oft," by an old bachelor of my acquaintance.

This bachelor had become quite notorious for fortune-telling—not that he knew any thing respecting futurity;—no, he only judged effect from cause; and being almost always at leisure, and of good manners— also possessing excellent conversational powers—he was a welcome guest at all convivial parties, quiltings, huskings, or any other merry-making which the good people of Salmagundi chose to make.[47]

In this little village there lived an old lady, who, having no daughters of her own, looked upon every girl in the village with an interest amounting almost to maternal solicitude. The girls all truly loved the old lady, and were never more happy than when, seated in her neat little parlour, they listened to some legend of olden time, which Aunt Nancy (as we girls familiarly called her) would cull from the well-supplied storehouse of her cranium, for our amusement.

One autumn, Aunt Nancy made a quilting, to which all the girls were invited. We had promised ourselves much merriment at this quilting; for we thought that Aunt Nancy, agreeably to her usual practice, would tell us some of the choicest and rarest of her stories. But she, good lady, was that afternoon afflicted with a nervous headache, and we had rather a sorry time. To make amends for this unforeseen disappointment, Aunt Nancy sent for "black Bartholomew," as we sportively called him, to take tea with us, and tell our fortunes. This movement was highly gratifying to the most of us, and a joyous and merry time had we.

The most of us had nothing told, but what was intended for the amusement of the time present; and as it would be uninteresting to the reader, I omit particulars. But there were two of our number whose fortunes were of a different stamp; and the "black man" augured much of misery.[48] The young ladies' fortunes, however, depended much upon the course of conduct which they themselves pursued; and Bartholomew pointed out a way for them to escape the evils which hung impending over them, and threatened (as he said) to destroy their peace for time and eternity.

One of these young ladies was the natural daughter of Capt. Richard Salter, the commander of a merchant-man, that sailed from Portsmouth to Liverpool. Her mother, who had retired into the country to hide her disgrace,[49] had by her engaging manners gained the affections of a very worthy farmer, and became his wife. And this truly benevolent man, ever bestowed upon Harriet S. the same kind care, which he did upon his own children.

Harriet grew up a lovely and promising girl. So modest and retiring was she, that she might well be compared to the violet. It was seldom that she could be persuaded to join in any of our youthful sports, and when she did, it was with a manner which told that she yielded to the entreaties of her companions, more from a desire to please others, than because she took any pleasure in them herself. Every mother in the village who had a wild, giddy daughter, would frequently, when reprimanding her for her follies, express a wish, that her child was but half so well behaved as Harriet S.; and the girls themselves would sometimes wish the same; but oftener would they bid their mothers remember that "still water runs deep."

Harriet's mother, before her marriage, had spent more than a year in my father's family, assisting my mother in her domestic affairs; and after my mother's death was very kind to me. This brought Harriet (who was but six months my junior) and myself, as a thing in course, to become acquainted. I possessed her confidence in a good degree; and was fully persuaded that her retiring manners were, in a great measure, owing to a too keen sensibility; for she was feelingly alive to the shade which her mother's early misfortunes had cast upon her birth.

Harriet and Eleanor J. were the last whose fortunes were told. When Bartholomew fixed his large black eyes upon the hazel orbs of Harriet, and with an ominous shake of the head, read off her future destiny, I felt angry with him, while every better feeling of my nature was absorbed in pity for the unfortunate Harriet. "Harriet," said the oracle, "beware! beware! Here in this cup I see sins, crimes, and a living witness of dishonour![50] Yes, I see—what do I see? I see a long dreary road, that leads to another kingdom! And here! yes, here in this road is a female, a lone wanderer! She is fleeing from the home of her childhood, to hide her disgrace. The road is watered with her tears! She wishes she had listened to the warning of 'black Bartholomew'; but now it is too late! more I dare not tell. Stop! I here see a way of escape. Harriet, there is a serpent that will lead you to ruin, unless you banish him from your presence.[51] Rouse yourself! Seek your happiness in a virtuous course of conduct; your amusements, in the company of your young companions. In their youthful and innocent sports, you will find more true enjoyment, than you possibly can in the company which you have kept of late. Notwithstanding what is past, you may yet be respected and happy. This, however, depends upon yourself. If you escape threatened evils until you are eighteen years of age, there will be but little danger in future."

Here Bartholomew stopped, and turning to Eleanor J., took her cup. He turned it round, and round; then fetching a deep sigh, he looked full in the face of Eleanor. A moment's pause, another sigh, and he re-commenced his augury.

"Eleanor," said he, "I see in this cup a female who is bowed down with premature old age. She is sitting alone; and by the light of a few embers, patching her children's clothes. The little ones are in a corner of the room, sleeping on a bed of straw. The winds are whistling through the cracks and crevices of her lowly habitation. The broken windows are stuffed with rags. It is past twelve. The stillness of the dark night is disturbed by vociferations. The door is thrown open, and a bloated wretch staggers into the room! With an uplifted cane, he approaches the trembling woman! All beyond is darkness. Eleanor," said he, after a moment's pause, "give Joseph the mitten,[52] and escape threatened evil."

Eleanor and myself were to spend the night with Aunt Nancy, who, having recovered from her headache, sat with us until a very late hour; and many were the merry stories of by-gone days which she rehearsed. The old clock had struck eleven, and we were about to seek repose, when a gentle tap at the door called our attention. Uncle Jonathan went to the door, where he met "black Bartholomew," who requested his assistance in leading home a young man from a neighboring grog-shop,[53] who was a little worse for liquor. Uncle Jonathan, who was ever ready to do a neighbor a kindness, took his lantern, (the night being very dark,) and sallied out to give his aid in leading home the inebriate. Eleanor and myself, with the curiosity common to youthful females, followed him, to ascertain who the unfortunate fool might be. But what was our surprise, when we found him to be none other than Joseph R., the beau of Eleanor; a young man who had hitherto borne an unimpeachable character!

"Well," said Eleanor, "I will take up with 'blackey's' advice, although, in consequence, I may have to live a poor, despised old maid, and dry up, until I am blown away in some north-westerly gale." "That's right, my own good gal," said Aunt Nancy, who had overheard her.

What effect Bartholomew's prognostications had upon Harriet S., was not known; for she became more retiring than ever, and at length shunned all society. Her step-father had a brother living in Lower Canada, who had often written to his brother, requesting him to dispose of his property in Salmagundi, and come to reside with him in Canada. This request he complied with, sometime in the winter following the incidents which I have related; but from motives of convenience, left his family behind him, making arrangements to return for them in early sleighing[54] in the following winter.

The next summer, many were the dark hints which were handed from one to another, respecting Harriet S. Her appearance too plainly told her situation; and at length it was rumored that she would be the means of breaking up the family of Andrew L., their nearest neighbor. About mid-summer, Harriet's step-father returned to Salmagundi, and had Andrew arrested. He was discharged upon giving notes (with good bonds as security) for the sum of several hundred dollars. After this, Harriet accompanied her step-father to Canada—thus literally fulfilling Bartholomew's prognostications; a thing which she might have avoided, had she but given heed to his warnings.

It was not till after these circumstances took place, that Bartholomew told what induced him to tell Harriet's fortune in the manner which he did. He then related, that he had frequently seen Andrew and Harriet walking by the side of Lake Winnipisiogee, with no other company; and also, had often seen them sitting together in Harriet's chamber, at late hours; and judging what the result of such a course might be, he thought it to be his duty to give timely warning.

A number of years afterwards, a gentleman from Salmagundi, while on a visit in Canada, called upon Harriet. He found her in a miserable log hut, spinning tow,[55] and surrounded by several ragged children— the largest of which bore no resemblance to the others, but was the living image of Andrew L.

Eleanor J. adhered to her resolution. She gave Joseph R. the mitten in good earnest, and although he asked a thousand pardons, and promised, on his bended knees, never to be overtaken in a like fault in future, she remained inexorable. Many of the "wise ones" of Salmagundi blamed Eleanor at first; but in after years, when Joseph became a confirmed sot,[56] they applauded her conduct.

Eleanor was some years on the wrong side of thirty, when a rich and very worthy man, who had lately had the misfortune to bury a very amiable wife, paid her his addresses. After a short acquaintance they were married; and thus far has Eleanor, by a judicious course of conduct, justified her husband's choice of a partner. The prospect now is, that she will glide happily through life, a blessing to others, and truly blessed herself. Eleanor's husband stands high in the estimation of his fellow citizens. He is now Chief Justice of one of the Courts in the County where he resides. Eleanor says that she shall always approve of fortune-telling, and also think highly of old bachelors—since it was an old bachelor, who, by telling her fortune, saved her from destruction.

The above is no fiction, but merely a statement of facts that actually occurred.

Tabitha.

The Last Witch of Salmagundi

Among the first settlers of New England, it was considered as necessary to have a Witch in every parish,[57] as it was to have a Parson, or Physician—and perhaps even more necessary, for whole townships have been destitute of both Parson and Physician, when there was no lack of witches. What real utility there was in having a witch, I was never able to ascertain. I only know that the most of the mishaps which befel[58] our worthy ancestors were ascribed to witchcraft.

In order to do things according to established rules, when the little village of Salmagundi was first settled, the good people selected the homeliest old woman in the whole Parish, for their witch. Gimmer, Tickle-pitcher, old Trot, old Peg, &c., were the several names by which she was known; but her real name was Margaret.

Margaret and her husband did not live in much matrimonial felicity, for they neither ate, drank nor lodged together. The husband of Margaret, Uncle Joe, as he was usually called, was of rather a miserly turn. He was never known to spend a cent of money for any thing,— not because he had it not to spend, for it was generally known that he often received money in payment for oxen, young cattle, sheep, and sometimes for jobs of work.—This money he kept in an old sap-trough,[59] which was buried in some sly nook in the woods; the place being concealed by leaves, underbrush, &c. A Frenchman, by the name of Tossy, who lived hard-by[60] Uncle Joe's, had a son who often searched the woods for the purpose of finding Uncle Joe's sap-trough. One spring, Uncle Joe sold a yoke of oxen[61] for fifty dollars, and received cash in hand for payment. Young Tossy was determined, that whenever this money was deposited, he would know the place of concealment; and he accordingly watched the movements of Uncle Joe, until he saw him deposit it with his former stock. The lad made a number of petty depredations on the contents of the *sap-trough,* which coming to Uncle Joe's knowledge, he thought that the woods was no longer a safe place for his treasure, and he removed it to the house of one, whom, (for distinction's sake,) I shall call Uncle Daniel; taking as security, a writing, specifying the sum, and acknowledging the receipt of the same. This memorandum he lodged with Squire P.[62] for safe keeping. Soon after this transaction, Uncle Joe "went the way of all living," having first given his heirs to understand where they might find his money.

Soon after Uncle Joe's death, his heirs applied to Uncle Daniel and Squire P., for the contents of the sap-trough; when, lo! both of them were entirely ignorant of the affair, and for want of proof, the matter rested with all save Margaret.

Margaret was loud and long in her threats; and the gossips of Salmagundi soon saw that old Peg was busy with the affairs of these two men. If any of Uncle Daniel's cattle or sheep sickened or died, old Peg had bewitched them. If the dairy and poultry yards were less profitable than formerly, old Peg had been to work. If the butter was longer than usual in coming, old Peg was in the churn. And it has been said, that one fourth of July, Uncle Daniel took a little too much of "O be joyful,"[63] and as he came staggering home, his children asked, What is the matter with father? and his good wife replied, Oh, dear! your father is bewitched,—Squire P., in looking over his papers, discovered that many of them had been nibbled by the mice; and several that were very valuable were nearly destroyed; but the gossips said that old Gimmer nibbled them when she turned into a mouse to search for her husband's receipt. Squire P's potash-kettle[64] burst, and it seemed to be almost a miracle that he did not lose his life by the accident; and the gossips said that old Gimmer would have killed him *then,* if his brother had not been a preacher. There was a cabinet-maker in the village who owned a lot of Norway pine timber, and he used to supply the Squire with fuel for his potash. He had refused to pay the customary price, and afterward when he would have paid it, the cabinet-maker would not trade with him; and having to use hard wood, the heat being more intense, caused his kettle to burst. But this fact was overlooked by even the Squire; and, confident that he should never again prosper in the potash business, he gave it up entirely. He was afterward invested with a number of Town Offices, and at the time of Margaret's death, (for witches will die, although many good people say that they are carried off bodily) he was first Selectman[65] for the Town of Salmagundi.

Margaret was supported by the Town for some little time previous to her death; and once, when the Squire visited her, he gave her a nine pence to stop her clamor for Uncle Joe's money, and as she was never known to spend it, he thought it would not be necessary to give her any more.—Soon after Margaret's death, the cabinet-maker mentioned in his family some of the circumstances, and spake of the unrighteousness of letting Margaret die a Town pauper; and said, that the first time he should cut his finger, he would write to the selectmen and that his epistle should be signed *Peg.* A few days after this, while busily engaged in sharpening a plane-iron, one of his children hit her head against his elbow and caused him to cut his finger rather severely; whereupon he would have flown into a passion had not his eldest daughter, (who was something of the humor of her father,) said "Well, father, that is a lucky hit; for you can now write old Peg's letter to the selectmen;" and holding a broken teacup to catch the blood, while with her lively sallies, she restored him to good humor, he shortly sat down, and with the blood wrote the following letter:

To the Honorable, the Selectmen of Salmagundi, Greeting: Believing that it would be satisfactory to my acquaintances to know of my safe arrival at this place, and having an opportunity of sending by one of our out-posts, who is going to Earth for the purpose of buying a lot of Norway-pine wood of the cabinet-maker who lives in your village, which wood is wanted here to light quick fire for the new comers,—I embrace the opportunity to write.

I met with nothing worth relating, in my journey to the river Styx. At the ferry, Charon refused to take me into his boat, until I told him who I was; he then, in consideration of the hard usage I had received in your town, agreed to carry me over for a fourpence, being half the usual fare,—thanks to Squire P. for the ninepence which he gave me; were it not for that, I don't know how long I should have remained on the other side of the river.[66] With the remaining four-pence, I shall pay for the conveyance of this letter to you.

When I was summoned to appear before Radamanthus, Uncle Joe, (who is employed to saw wood,) begged to accompany me. After hearing what I had to say for myself, (my story being corroborated by the testimony of Uncle Joe,) Radamanthus told me that I should have a place in the Royal Palace as maid of honor to Queen Proserpine. And King Pluto has given orders to Radamanthus, that all who have had any hand in making me appear as a witch, or who have ascribed any misfortune which has happened to them through their own misdeeds, improvidence, or negligence, to the agency of witchcraft, or have in any manner treated me ill, shall be very severely condemned. I send you this news for a warning, that you may treat old women better, and give up the foolish idea of witchcraft, and learn to be honest in all your doings.

Peg.

To be left at the door of the old meeting-house in Salmagundi.

This letter was found at the door of the meeting-house, and carried to the first selectman, who was sorely frightened upon reading it. And he soon ascertained that a large quantity of Norway-pine wood had disappeared from the cabinet-maker's lot. After this, he sent for Uncle Daniel, and they held a long conversation. Uncle Daniel was more shrewd than the Squire; and after cogitating the matter thoroughly, they came to the conclusion that either the cabinet-maker, or friend Samuel the shoemaker, had written the letter, as they had both of them been known to possess a knack at scribbling. They concluded to keep the letter a secret; but it took air, as every thing of the kind will; and the many sly jokes and witticisms which it occasioned, prevented the good people of the village from ever after having a witch; thus proving beyond a doubt, that the wild vagaries in which the light-hearted often indulge, (however much they are condemned by many good people) will often do what reason, philosophy and religion fail to accomplish. That this letter put a stop to witchcraft in Salmagundi cannot be doubted, since it is a well known fact, that while the adjacent villages still have their witches, the good people of this village have none. They ascribe their mishaps to bad management, oversight, misdeeds, and the thousand and one other misfortunes which are attendants upon mortality.

I cannot close without stating, that Squire P. died in despair, and Uncle Daniel has sunk from a state of affluence, to the most abject poverty.

Tabitha.

A Letter about Old Maids

Mr. Editor:—I am one of that unlucky, derided, and almost despised set of females, called spinsters, single sisters, lay-nuns, &c.; but who are more usually known by the appellation of Old Maids. That I have never been married, is not my own fault, for I never refused an offer in my life, neither have I by disdain, coldness, or indifference, kept my male acquaintance at a distance. I have always had, and still retain, a great respect for the marriage state, and for those of my friends who, from right motives, have entered into it. I believe, what I presume will not here be doubted, that it is an institution ordained by the All-wise Disposer of human affairs, for the promotion of the happiness of mankind in general; but I think it was a part of that wise design, that there should be *Old Maids*.

The first reason I shall give in support of this opinion, is, that they are not only very useful, but even extremely necessary; for how many homes are rendered happy, after the departure from them of sons and daughters into the wide world, by the continuance of the old maid?—she who is now to be the light, life and joy of those who would otherwise be sad and solitary. How many parents are cheered and consoled, in the decline and departure of life, by her who remains to repay their care of her early years, by the constant and much needed attentions which can only be rendered by the old maid! How many married sisters, when trial and sorrow come to their homes and hearts, look for help and consolation from the one of their number who remains free from such cares, the ever ready and sympathizing old maid! How many widowed brothers have, with perfect confidence, consigned their motherless children to the love and care of the trusty old maid! Oh, many a little orphan has never felt its mother's loss, while sheltered by the kindly affection of some soft-hearted old maid! And who is usually the nurse in sickness, the friend in affliction, the help in every time of need, but the old maid?

These have ever been her duties and her pleasures; but in later times, old maids have taken a more conspicuous part. They form a large proportion of our authoresses; they are the founders and pillars of Anti-Slavery, Moral Reform, and all sorts of religious and charitable societies; and last, (though not least,) in country towns where no weekly sheet[67] is published, they are extremely useful in carrying the news.

For these reasons, I think we must all acknowledge that there is a great need of old maids; and this want has been provided for by the greater number of females who outlive the years of infancy, than of males. Some assert that more are *born;* but at all events they do not *die* so easily. Of the males who arrive at years of manhood, some die on the high seas, or in battle, or in foreign climes, or in distant parts of their own land, where they have been attacked by disease, and died for want of the judicious care of an old maid. So that all will allow, there must be quite a surplus of the female sex, who can be nothing more or less than *old maids.*

But all this reasoning in favor of *them* goes directly against old bachelors; for I do not see that they are either useful or necessary, at least not more useful for remaining single, (present company always excepted—) and had they been *needed,* more males would have been allowed to arrive at years of bachelorship.

Having thus introduced myself, and shown the utility of the tribe to which I belong, I reveal it as my design to furnish certain recollections of my youthful days. They are chiefly recollections of simple country girls, the companions of my earlier years, of whom the greater number are now wives and mothers. I shall care but little what opinions are entertained or expressed in relation to the style of composition, if the *moral* be remembered and regarded.

Betsey.

Old Maids and Old Bachelors. Their Relative Value in Society

CHAPTER I

I had seated myself at my table, with the intention of writing a chapter on the good influence which that valuable portion of the community, vulgarly called old maids, exert upon society. Being often called an old maid myself, (because of my eccentricities, to which I have an undoubted right, inasmuch as I honestly inherited them, and also because I have lost my front teeth, by a kick from the wild colt of uncle Obadiah Time,)[68]—it may well be supposed that I shall be on the side of the old maids; and I leave it for those who do not know any better, to write in favor of old bachelors.

I had consulted quite a number of spinsters who are about my own age, (being, as the old song says, "twice six, twice seven, twice twenty and eleven," abating one of the twenty's and the eleven,) and we all agreed, that old maids exerted a better influence on society, than did the old bachelors. I had headed my communication with a quotation from an old Scotch poem. It was the following:

"Auld nature swears, the lovely dears,
 Her noblest work, she classes O:
 Her prentic' han', she try'd on man,
 An' then she made the lassies O."[69]

Before I had time to add another word, my chamber door flew open, and in stalked an old woman. She fixed her large saucer eyes upon my face, and then pointing to my paper, said, "You are wrong." Wrong! said I; why am I wrong? "You are wrong," said she, "in supposing that nature had any hand in making either old maids or old bachelors." If nature did not make them, said I, pray tell me who did make them? "*I* made them myself," said she. And pray lady, I replied, tell me who you are, that I may correct my error. "My name," said she, "is Necessity; and I dwell in the Valley of Want." Well, thought I, that is rather queer. But it argues that it is necessary that there should be old bachelors, and also old maids, and I will look around me, and see what good is done by each party; and then I will give my thoughts upon the subject.

On investigating the matter, I found that each class was a benefit to society. I looked back to the days of childhood, and called to mind the whole bevy of old maids who lived in the vicinity of the home of my early years. I called to mind the many good qualities of Miss N., the good old maid who kept house for my father after my mother's death; and I remembered the opinion of old Mr. C., the oracle of the village, who said, that were it not for the old maids, the sick would suffer for want of care, the children would have to do without stockings, and the flax would never be spun; the lambs and goslins would all die, and the old bachelors would go ragged. My father said that the old maids were neat and industrious; and that it would be impossible to do without them; but he really thought that hopes of trapping the schoolmaster, (who by the way was an old bachelor,) made them a little more circumspect than they would otherwise have been.

One autumn, Miss N. made a quilting, and according to the custom in all *country* villages, the old bachelors were invited. They were five in number; and it really diverts me now, to think how spruce they looked. They wore high heeled, picked-toed shoes, with enormous copper buckles, grey ribbed stockings, gartered above the knee, courderoy inexpressibles, reaching just below the knee, and fastened with steel buckles about the size of a half dollar, their color a pale drab; their vests were what was called swan-down, striped with all the colors of the rainbow; coats of green cloth, with brass buttons, large as the top of a tea cup, hung loosely on their shoulders; their cravats were white, tied in a huge double bow under the chin, and dangling upon a ruffle bosomed shirtee, which was crimped with all imaginable nicety; their heads were powdered, hair combed back behind, and done up in a cue. My father rallied them for being dressed so much in uniform, and told them he really thought they had a design upon his house-keeper. They assured him that they had not; that they were only careful about their dress to avoid the criticism of the old maids; and the schoolmaster observed, "Were it not for the clapper tongues of the old maids, few bachelors would care how they looked, or what they did." Aye, said my father, I always thought it was *your* influence that made the old maids the amiable, useful beings which they are; but I now find that were it not for *their* influence, you would be but dead letters, mere blanks in society.

CHAPTER 2

The good precepts, and the better *examples,* of the old maids and old bachelors of the little village of Salmagundi, were not lost; for the children grew up in all the habits of industry which could be desirable. The girls (myself excepted) were all married; and to this day are considered patterns of neatness and humility; and they ascribe all their virtues to the instruction which they received from the old maids in whose society they spent much of their time, when they were children. The boys ripened into manhood under the instruction of the village *school master;* and many of them are now competent, (in the estimation of their fellow citizens,) to fill the highest offices in a republican government, with credit to themselves and honor to their country.

I cannot drop this subject without giving some particulars relative to the most unpromising boy in the village. This boy's mother was in what is called a bed-ridden state; and the care of her domestic affairs devolved upon an old maid, who was familiarly called aunt Sarah. She belonged to the Society of Friends, and was a universal favorite in the village. One cold morning, little Harry refused to go to school, whereupon aunt Sarah gave him a hearty box upon the ear, at the same time saying, "Harry, thee don't know what is good for thyself; if thee did, thee would never refuse to go to school; mind what I tell thee, Harry—if thee don't pay better attention to thy book, thee will never be a School-Master, *that* thee never will." Aunt Sarah's words sunk deep into the heart of Harry, (owing I suppose to the fact, that they were boxed into his head;) and from that time he resolved to emulate the old bachelor who taught the village school. Harry is now in the full vigor of manhood; he has been a member of the Legislature for several years,—also Chief Justice of the Court of Common Pleas for the county in which he resides; and I have been told that he will be a *candidate* for Governor, at the ensuing election; and his acquaintances say, that he will yet live in the White House at Washington. Harry has accumulated a large property, and lives in good style. The poor never go empty handed from his threshold, for he is known and acknowledged as their benefactor; their blessings rest upon his head, and their prayers ascend as incense to Heaven in his behalf.

Harry says he owes his prosperity entirely to the influence of the old bachelor who taught the village school. And the old bachelor would have been (according to his own statement) but a mere blank in society, had it not been for the influence of the old maids.

If I may be allowed to judge from these and many other facts, which have come within the compass of my observation, I shall give it as my candid opinion, that old maids exert a much better influence on society than do the old bachelors.

Tabitha.

Origin of Small Talk

Much has been said, and much written, upon the loquacity of woman; and much has she been ridiculed for her aptness in conversation. Her natural sociability has been termed, in derision, "the gift of the gab"; and man, vain, lordly man, would fain deprive her of the right of unrestrained "freedom of speech." By many she has been called "silly woman"; and by some, her intellect is allowed to be barely sufficient to understand what man may require of her. And although in America, it is allowed that "all mankind are entitled to equal rights," language is so tortured, that *mankind* means only the male part of the species. And *uncivilized* man cannot be content with ordaining laws which deprive woman of the means of mental culture to which she is justly entitled, but he would fain have her be silent, and live and die like a vegetable.

Such were my meditations, after listening to a dissertation upon the "nothingness of female chit-chat." What a pity, thought I, that some philosopher could not assign a plain, common-sense, philosophical cause, for this talkative propensity in woman, and thus silence every objection, in the mind of man, against her sociability!

While my thoughts were busy with this subject, a gentle tap at my chamber door disturbed my reverie. I opened the door, when, instead of the friend I expected, I met Memory, a little urchin who often intrudes upon my hours of retirement, and sometimes kindly lends his assistance in searching the chronicles in the upper story, for traditions of by-gone days. Having nothing of consequence with which to divert my visitor, I proposed that he should search for a tradition which would give a clue to the origin of small talk. He soon found, in a sly corner, an old, soiled manuscript, from which, with some difficulty, I transcribed the following:

When our first parents were placed in the garden of Eden, they had not the faculty of communicating their thoughts to each other.[70] Their guardian angel, perceiving that their happiness would be augmented could they but have the gift of speech, brought them a present of twelve baskets, filled with chit-chat; and having strewed the contents upon the ground, he thus addressed them: "Although this present is designed for you both, what each one gathers shall be his or her own exclusive property; and *who* would be profited, must be diligent and active in gathering it up."

Adam, from some cause or other, was in one of those surly moods, which many, very many of his sons, often indulge; and he gathered only three baskets full; while his nimble, and more industrious partner, collected and laid by for her own use the other nine.

The benevolence of Eve would not suffer her to hoard up this treasure; but from time to time, as there was necessity, she culled the
choicest, and bestowed it with an unbounded charity upon Adam. Eve
found that she was not a loser by being liberal with her gifts; for
however much she bestowed, her baskets were always full; and not
only full, but they were continually enlarging. Adam found that he
had not made a very judicious choice, in his selection of chit-chat; for
his baskets ever retained their original size. His niggardly disposition
suffered him to part with very little of their contents, and he almost
always added to his store the bounty of his benevolent help-meet; yet
his baskets were never heaped. Out of sheer envy, he often ridiculed
Eve for her small-talk—a sin which has been visited upon his sons
from generation to generation.

Tabitha.

Recollections of an Old Maid. Number *1*

There was but one young lady in our village:—I mean by this, that
there was but one young female who did not work. The word *lady* has
now a very indefinite signification. It means, sometimes, merely a female; sometimes, a female distinguished from most of her sex by ele-
gance of mind, or appearance; and sometimes again, one whose claims
to distinction are those of birth or wealth. But those of every class and
character who can contrive to worry away their lives without being of
any benefit to "that vulgar herd," the world in general, have a great
desire to appropriate this cognomen[71] to themselves; and as people are
apt to designate others by the names which they assume, so those are
often called ladies (*par excellence*) who do no work.

Widow A. had but one pretty little daughter, and as she had also a
pretty little house and farm, she thought these were very sufficient
reasons for making herself a slave to her child. She early discovered
that her little girl had a very delicate constitution; and instead of invig-
orating it by work and exercise, she pampered and nursed her, till she
looked as though she was indeed *born* (to use her mother's expression)
to be a lady.

Ruth A. had been sheltered from the morning breeze, the midday
sun, and the evening dew; till she was as pale and slender as the lily of

the vale, and her little soft white hands would of themselves have been a sufficient guarantee for her claims to ladyship.

Now though I in my young days was about as broad as I was long, with a face as round as the full moon, and cheeks as red as peony, and owned a pair of hands which had been lengthened and widened, thickened and roughened, reddened and toughened, by long and intimate acquaintance with the wash-tub, scouring-cloth, and broomstick; though I was as tough as a squaw, and could not have been persuaded that I had a nerve about me, yet I never looked at Ruthy without blessing my stars that I was not "a natural born lady." I picked the prettiest flowers, and the earliest berries, and carried them to my genteel friend, because I thought her an object of pity; yet the Widow A. was proud of an honor shared by no other mother in the village, and often regretted that she had not called her child Henrietta, or Georgiana, or Seraphina, or Celestina, or some such beautiful name. But she had been overpowered by the solicitations of her husband's mother, who wished to give her own name to her only grand-child, and had promised to bequeath to it her only silk gown, her best feather-bed, a string of gold beads, a great gold ring, and half-a-dozen little stubbed silver spoons. So Ruth or Ruthy, (for we girls had reversed the usual method of familiarizing a name by shortening it,) grew up a perfect lady in every thing but her old fashioned name. She played on the piano, read a great deal of poetry, had delicate nerves, the dyspepsia,[72] and long finger-nails, and was in all such respects well fitted to be the mistress of a *parlor*.

Although the sole object of her mother's devotion, though cared for, and watched over, as few girls can be, she never appeared lively, and seldom in any degree cheerful. She had always the headache, or the tooth-ache, or some other ache, which sent a frown across her fair brow, and that hilarity, which is the result of health and vigor, was never experienced by her. Her books were scribbled over with such quotations as, "O Mother Earth, take back thy child;" and

> I am weary, I am weary,
>   And now within my breast
> There dwells but one, one only wish,
>   It is, to be at rest.

And again:—

> I know that soon my time must come,
> And I shall be glad to go;
> For the world at best is a weary place,
> And my pulse is getting low.[73]

Now all this sentimentality was not affected. It was an expression of her real feelings; for life could have but little of enjoyment for one who spent it as she had done. I feel confident that Ruthy's presentiments of an early grave would have been fulfilled, had her mother's life been spared.

When Widow A. was taken suddenly and dangerously ill, and informed by her physicians that there was no hope of recovery, her mind instantly reverted to the helpless child she must leave behind. That last sickness was embittered by self-reproach for the past, and dark forebodings of the future. "She has no other friend," said she bitterly, "and O what will she do when I am gone?"

It was in vain that Ruthy, whose every faculty was now for the first time roused to exertion, endeavoured to calm and comfort her; it was in vain that she constantly reiterated her assurance, that she should find many earthly friends, and that even if she did not, still He who is the Father of the fatherless, and the orphan's protector, would surely be her God. Still the mother could not feel at ease, and when the Widow A. was laid in her last low home, there were many who repeated her last expression, What will become of Ruthy?

Her mother's foolish indulgence had almost beggared her, for the house and farm were already mortgaged, and Ruthy must maintain herself or get some one to maintain her. "She could not dig, to beg she was ashamed;" so what did she do but get married; and to one of the last men I should have thought she could have fancied.[74] He was a great, brawny, shaggy-headed widower, with not indeed seven heads and ten horns—but with what I should have thought would have been quite as frightful to her, namely, seven children and ten cows.[75] He had also men-servants and maid-servants, oxen and horses, dogs, sheep, and poultry, and all the other appurtenances of a large farm.

That Ruthy could be spared from manual labor, I felt assured, but I thought that the care, noise, and turmoil, must soon kill her. I was at her wedding, and when I saw her stand beside that stout, rough-looking man, with a flush upon her cheek, which would have been unnoticed upon a complexion less delicate, I thought of a lamb covered with garlands, and laid upon the altar of sacrifice. For one moment there seemed to be a coffin before my eyes, and a sweet pale face was within it; and then I saw the grave of Widow A. and an open one beside it. But I banished these fancies, and was gay with the rest.

Now that Ruthy has been a wife for many years, I can conceive of her reasons for marrying as she did. She had been a petted child, and now that she could be one no longer, she wished to find in a partner for life, one who, with the affection of a husband, should unite the doating fondness of a parent. She was deficient in energy of mind, and vigor of intellect; but she had strong affections, and it was through these that her character was to be renovated. She had discovered at her mother's sick-bed that *she could act;* and with increased action came the ability and desire to do more; and she felt confident that in her companion she had found one who would excuse all deficiencies, when he saw them accompanied by endeavors to do well. A word of reproach, or laugh of derision, might wholly have discouraged her; but she has never received it; and her husband's indulgence has been repaid by the warmest affection, and utmost eagerness to perform every duty of her station, in which she succeeds wonderfully.

I am now a sallow, withered old maid, but Ruthy's step is quicker and firmer, her eye brighter, and her cheek far more rosy than at the age of sixteen. She fears neither the sun nor the rain; she can make both butter and cheese; she has almost wholly given up the piano, but plays admirably upon the cook-stove; and is in all respects an excellent wife, and a tender mother, both to her own children, and to those of her predecessor.

Betsey.

Recollections of an Old Maid. Number 2

Caroline B. was the beauty of our village. In almost every town the beauty is considered the female of most consequence; and seldom can town or city boast of a girl so lovely as Caroline. There is much of beauty in our earth, but there is no other like that which sometimes shines forth in a female countenance; and so thought all our young beaux, for they all loved to look at Caroline. In talents, education, or sprightliness, she was not superior to her companions, yet before she was eighteen years of age she had received an offer from every young man in the village who dared aspire to such loveliness. They were all refused, for the idea had been early instilled into her mind that her beauty was given to make her fortune; that though a poor country girl, she was designed by nature to be the wife of some very rich man; and she waited very impatiently for his appearance. At length a young merchant from Boston, who had been reconnoitering[76] among the White Mountains, came to our village to visit some relatives. He saw Caroline, and of course fell in love with her—an offer quickly followed, which was as quickly accepted, and I was sent for in haste to assist at the bridal preparations.

I loved Caroline too well to be satisfied with all this, but I could say nothing—the bridegroom was evidently in love, and the bride I knew to be so amiable, modest and gentle, that I thought his kindness must always continue. With a proud heart he carried her to a city home, and there she fluttered in plumes and satins for one short year. During that time she was the admired slave of fashion and etiquette—she was in bondage to a set of laws, the basis of which seemed to be, that nature was always vulgar, and that to be polite and refined was to act, look and speak as unnaturally as possible. Had this continued long she must have become a heartless, despicable woman; but she was delivered from it by the failure of her husband, which was attended by so many suspicious and mortifying circumstances, that it determined him to leave the city, and seek his fortune elsewhere. Meanwhile Caroline was to return to her country home—yet she would rather have gone with *him,* she cared not whither. She had shared his prosperity, and why, she asked, should she not be with him in adversity—she had been nurtured in poverty—she could bear it any where—she could enjoy it with him, and to return in such a manner to the home she had so proudly left, O she would rather go and live with him in a miserable cabin, or in no cabin at all. But her entreaties were of no avail. Her husband was determined to go unencumbered, and Caroline returned to her parents. In the long nervous fever which followed her arrival I was her constant attendant, and when she was slowly recovering, I encouraged her in the bright hopes she had formed of future peaceful days with the husband she still so fondly loved. But she has been sadly disappointed. Years have passed, and not even a letter has come to tell of the welfare of him she cannot forget. She who was once the village beauty is now the village tailoress; she looks forward to a life of privation and toil, cheered only by the sympathy of early friends, especially of the one who is now an old maid. As for her villain of a husband, no one knows any thing about him, excepting the members of our Female Samaritan Society,[77] who all say that he is in Texas.

_____

The next who comes to my memory is Jane C.; and I think of her now because she was the ugliest looking girl amongst us. She was as rough and brown as a ploughed field—her face was short and her nose was long; her eyes were light and staring; and as for her mouth, I do not know but it would now be all the fashion, for it was *a la* Victoria.[78] Before she was a dozen years old, she was taught to consider herself as cut out for an old maid, and that there had been no mistake in the making. She entered society young, and immediately put her old-maidship upon her as a garment, which was to cover all defects of person and manners. She was of a gay, joyous disposition, and none could see her without observing that if she had got to be an old maid, she was determined to enjoy herself while she was a young one. She laughed and chattered and frolicked with the beaux, in a manner which was half-way between the freedom of a sister, and that of a betrothed bride; yet she was innocent withal, as the truly light-hearted must ever be. No young man avoided her, for her very looks seemed to say, "I am very conscious that I am the plainest mortal that ever lived, and I do not expect you to fall in love with me; and I shall take especial care that I do not fall in love with *you.*" She was very much liked by our bashful young bachelors, especially those who had just entered the frolicking circle, and hardly knew how to take care of *themselves,* much less of a *partner.* But Jane could take care of herself and of them too; and she never wanted attendants, tho' she had neither beauty, talents or accomplishments to recommend her—no, not even the magic of a little foot and hand.

Well, a young man took up his abode in our village as a merchant—so he styled himself—that is, he kept an assortment of calico and molasses, thread-lace and board-nails, Jews-harps[79] and spelling-books, Russia-linen and stick-liquorice, black satin and brown sugar, white muslins and blue crockery, hard soap and fish-hooks, pins, needles, tobacco, brooms, handkerchiefs, ribbons, candles, and as his advertisement stated, many other articles too numerous to mention. He was one of those who are resolved never to marry, unless they can find someone who is perfect, and not even then if they have not made their fortune. But though not a marrying man, yet he valued to enjoy the society of the ladies; and if I ever disliked a man it was him. He came among us with a perpetual grin, which seemed to say, "Well, ladies, you perceive that I am yet in the market, and I expect to enjoy myself finely while seeing you pull caps for me."[80] But other besides myself now avoided him, and as he had no sister or cousin, to *whom* should he direct his particular attentions but to Jane C., whom he thought he could trifle with as much as he pleased. But he soon found that he had *caught a Tartar,* or rather that a Tartar had caught *him.*[81] How Jane managed the affair I know not, being of course unskilled in such matters; but she kept up the flirtation till it concentrated into a downright courtship, and this finally consolidated into a marriage. The bridegroom looked rather sheepish at first, but he got over that, and also his former faults, which had been merely those of manner, and of which marriage had wrought an entire cure. Jane's upright and useful course of life has made her a respected woman throughout the neighborhood; her pleasant disposition has rendered her husband's home a happy one; her economy and good management have made him as rich as he could have been had he remained single; and now that she wears a cap, collar, and high-necked dress,[82] I am confident she looks as well as half our married women. Her husband, at least, has become so accustomed to her looks, that he appears to be totally unconscious of their lack of beauty; and he is probably now as happy with Jane, as he would have been had he married the *beau ideal*[83] of his youthful fancy.

Betsey.

Recollections of an Old Maid. Number 3

We had in our village one literary lady, poetess, blue-stocking,[84] or whatever else you may please to call her. Sarah D.[85] was always, when a child, considered the best scholar in the district school; and when she grew up, she wrote poetry. Yes,—poetry for the newspapers. I remember well her Address to Spring, Farewell to Melancholy, Ode to Monadnock,[86] and several other very pretty pieces of rhyme. She even sometimes ventured upon what she thought was blank verse, and as there was no one up our way capable of very severe criticism, it passed very well as such.

If any of you had come to our village to see its poetess, you would probably have expected to find her in one of the handsomest houses.— You would have gone straight to the great white house, with a row of poplars before it. But you would not have found her there, for that was 'Squire E's house; and though he had a daughter, yet she was by no means a learned one. The Squire thought that women need not know any thing about book-learning; so he never suffered his daughter to attend school after she could read her Bible, and write her name.

Not finding our poetess there, you perhaps would have directed your course to the yellow dwelling, which stood near the meeting-house; but that was the residence of Mr. F. our minister,[87] who, though he had several daughters, would never suffer[88] them to read novels, nor write poetry.

Then there was Dr. G's house, by far the costliest in the village; but he was an old Bachelor, and no female lived with him but his washer-woman, who said she hated poetry, and all such fantastic[89] stuff.

If you had been told that Sarah did not live in a great two-story house, I think you would have marched directly to the little white cottage with green blinds, and lilac and rose bushes around it. But that was the residence of Miss H, our milliner and mantua-maker;[90] and a blue-stockinged milliner and mantua-maker, is an anomaly which but few places can exhibit, and of which our village certainly afforded no specimen.

Sarah did not reside in the central part of the village, but in a wild rocky place at the north part of the town, where the land was so rough, and the farmers so poor, that it was called Hard-Scrabble. Her father's house was a small unpainted building, near one of those beautiful New Hampshire ponds, which in Old England would be called lakes.

Mr. D. was a tall, gaunt looking man, and when seen on a week-day with his frock on, his old hat flapping over his eyes, and his face tanned to an almost Indian hue, a city gentleman might have thought him worthy of as little notice as the oxen with whom he held so much companionship. And perhaps his opinion would not have changed, if he had looked at him as I have often done, when he entered the meeting-house on the holy Sabbath; for the frock was then exchanged for a suit of very coarse brown, and the Sunday hat was sadly worn. His face, too, was not a shade whiter; but when he seated himself in his pew, and stroked back the thickly clustered hair, a brow was displayed as intellectual as that of Daniel Webster;[91] and I believe that not only Mr. D. but stranger-clergymen would have been as pleased to read sympathy in his expressive eye, as in that of any other man present. He was indeed a true son of the Granite State,[92] and Sarah, his only child, was alike the object of his love and pride. He had early interested himself in her childish studies, and her first lessons in mathematics were taken from him.—Many a long winter evening has she spent in working out the sums which he set for her on the great slate, which usually hung over the fire-place. He afterwards assisted her through Adams's Old Arithmetic;[93] and when she was not more than fourteen years of age, it was customary for the school-master to send the great boys to Sarah D. with their hard sums.

If Mr. O. B. Pierce[94] had flourished in those days, he would have pronounced her an intolerable fool; for she was also an excellent parser,[95] and could see a great deal of wisdom in nouns, pronouns, verbs, adjectives, adverbs, &c.

Sarah did not attend the district school after she was fifteen, but stayed at home and plied the spinning wheel in the day-time, and studied Euclid with her father in the evening; and though "winter winds blew cold and loud,"[96] yet they were totally disregarded by the happy family at Hard-Scrabble.

The following summer, a very joyful event took place for Sarah. An Academy was established in the town just north of ours,[97] and now there was an opportunity for her to study Chemistry, Rhetoric, Logic, and the Languages; and also to take lessons in Painting and Embroidery, and other things which she could not learn at home. Her father had scrabbled together money enough to pay for her books and tuition, and as it was but three miles and a half, she could board at home. Sarah was quite a pedestrian, and so were we all, though we never spun any street-yarn[98]—but we were only prevented from engaging in this exclusively feminine employment, by the impossibility of doing so—for there was not a single street in our village. But we by no means neglected the main road, nor the by-roads, nor the field paths, nor even the fields without paths. The road to the next town was very sandy and rocky, and would have made sad havoc with a pair of nice shoes; but Yankee girls know how to manage such things. Sarah always drew on over her nice white linen stockings a pair of socks, (or footings, as we more commonly called them,) and then put on her cow-hide shoes. Just before she turned the last corner, she took off her thick shoes, and the socks which had preserved her stockings from dust; and then putting on a pair of thin slippers, a foot was displayed which, though not exquisitely small, was neat and pretty enough to please almost any bachelor, young or old. The old shoes and socks were then placed in a recess of the stone wall, and a rock put over them.

It was by management like this that Sarah D. finished her education, and it is in this way that many a New England girl prepares herself to become a teacher in her own Yankee-land, or in the far West, or South.

Sarah would probably have fitted herself to be a Preceptress,[99] but her mother became a paralytic, and she would not leave her. Officious friends told her, that if she went away, she could earn money enough to hire a girl for her mother, and clothe herself handsomely, and perhaps lay up a little fortune besides; but she would not take their advice—and then they said it was a pity that she had spent so much time and money for nothing, and they should think she would wish to have her learning do her some good. She could not but think it was doing her good, for it afforded occupation to a mind which might otherwise have busied itself about her neighbor's concerns, or been sullied by joining in tattling and slander. Her education, though it made her no richer, increased her happiness and her self-respect, and gained for her the esteem of others.

Country people are very apt to talk about those whose ideas of expediency, and of right and wrong, differ from their own; especially if they have the independence to act accordingly. Now, although Sarah was in manner as gentle as a lamb, and in countenance as serene as the lake beside her lowly home, yet her mind was as firm as one of the rocks on her father's farm; so she did not bid adieu[100] to her books because people said they would be of no more use to her, nor do any thing but laugh when some old ladies suspected her of being in love, because she wrote poetry. They were confirmed in their suspicions by her decided refusal of an offer from a rich young farmer, though she gently hinted that his nose was rather florid, and his breath smelled of something worse than tobacco. But this did not account for it to *them,* (for it was before the era of Temperance Societies,)[101] and they said, that if she was not already in love, she must be waiting for some minister, or doctor, or lawyer, or some such *"larned* man." They knew there was none in our village for her; for our minister was married, we had no lawyer, and our doctor (the old bachelor,) was over fifty, and of course past all hope. I think I must sometime give you a description of the doctor, but I cannot stop now. We had a school-master in the central district, a sober, intelligent young man; but Sarah would not have *him,* for he had been engaged for sixteen years.

When Sarah was about twenty-two years of age, Squire E. died. He was supposed to be the richest man in the village, and worth all of five thousand dollars. Besides his farm, he had money at interest, which he had obtained by doing all the law business in the town. He had been Selectman, Town Clerk, Deputy Sheriff, Justice of the Peace, and was considered quite a necessary character. So, after his death, old Mr. I. thought it would be an excellent place for his son, who had just completed his studies, and was strutting about with all the dignity appertaining to a young lawyer, to settle in. Mr. I. was fond of his son, and glad to have him stationed so near him; and although he had expended a great deal upon his education, he exerted himself to build an office, upon which was placed a large sign, inscribed Charles Augustus I., Attorney at Law.

Well, by the time Charles had settled one quarrel, it was absolutely necessary that the women, young and old, should pick him out a wife; and almost every body pitched upon Sarah D, because she was so good, and so learned, and could write poetry. When Sarah heard of it, she felt very sorry for herself, and for *him;* for she thought their future intercourse would not be so pleasant and unrestrained; she even once resolved never to speak kindly to him again, but then she made the very sensible reflection, that he was not to blame for what people said, and that as an old playmate, and now an educated young man, he was entitled to as much attention as any one else. But the lawyer had heard the same things, and fearing that matters were to be taken out of his hands, which he had rather manage himself, he began to avoid Sarah, and could hardly look civil in the room where she was. But he had plenty of smiles for the daughter whom Squire E. had left sole heir to his five thousand dollars.

Nancy E. was pretty, good tempered, and industrious. True, she had but little education; but that was her father's fault, and the young lawyer thought he had enough for himself and a wife. I knew all the contents of Nancy's library, for I saw it often. Upon the bureau in her chamber was a Bible, Hymn Book, Assembly's Catechism, English Reader, and Webster's Spelling Book.[102] She had also a singing book, called Village Harmony, and the three popular novels of the day, Eliza Wharton, Charlotte Temple, and Dorcasina Sheldon; also a little book entitled "Louisa the lovely Orphan, or the cottage on the Moor."[103] She had, besides, a whole file of the only annual which was then much patronized in New Hampshire, and which went by the name of "Thomas's Almanac."[104]

I once lent her the Arabian Nights Entertainment, but she returned it without reading it at all, saying, that she did not believe a word of it was true. I then wished her to read a little book called Alonzo and Melissa, which had exceedingly interested me, and about which I thought she would not be so incredulous; but she never read it, for she said it scared her so that she could not sleep for a week. I was too much provoked to tell her how nicely it all came out, and she probably now shudders at the name of Melissa.[105]

But though Nancy had not a great mind, she had a great farm, which a great many people think a great deal better; and the lawyer concluded to take her for better and for worse. Nobody doubted that he was in love; but some ill natured people thought he loved the farm as well as he did Nancy. But I never blamed him so much as other people did. As he was determined to marry, and had no fortune of his own, I do not think he could have done better than to take the heiress of our village.

I have sometimes been grieved, and as often amused, at the struggles of a poor professional young man, when he enters the connubial state. Pride and public opinion say that appearances must be kept up; and then the "little purse grows light." Yes, so very light, that he cannot "sleep so sweet at night."[106] Madam thinks she must have a maid in her kitchen, and a few more silk gowns than the neighboring farmers' wives, though they are possessed of twice her income; and the poor, perplexed, care-worn husband, reminds me of the hero of one of my nursery songs, (not a very wise one, for they did not write so sensibly for children in my young days as now)—but persons as old as I am, no doubt will recollect it. It commenced,

> "Peter, Peter, pumpkin eater,
> Had a wife, and could not keep her."

But Peter had a resource of which husbands cannot avail themselves in these better times; for the song continues,

> "He put her in a pumpkin shell,
> And there he kept her very well."[107]

A woman would not stay long in a pumpkin shell now, unless indeed, like that of Cinderilla,[108] it should turn into a fine coach, and then, truly, she would like it *very well.*

But as I do not like rich people any better than I do poor people, I will leave Squire I. and his lady, and return to Sarah D.

Whether Sarah became disgusted with literary men, or whether she actually *fell in love,* I do not know; but soon after Nancy I's marriage, she was wedded to a smart, enterprizing young butcher, who carried her off to a neighboring town. I visited her a short time since, after a separation of many years. Her children were about her, and I could at first hear of nothing but cutting teeth, the rash, the measles, and whooping cough; and I thought my old friend was entirely lost to me. But after all the little folks had retired for the night, except the babe which slept beside us in its cradle, I found, in a little quiet conversation, that Sarah had not lost her former tone of mind, nor her relish for mental improvement.

"But pray," said I, "is your learning now of any practical benefit to you?" Her answer was so characteristic, that I must give it in her own words.

"When my husband comes to me for my opinion on every subject, that interests him, and I feel qualified to advise and counsel him, not on account of superior talent, but of superior education; when I see him spending more time and money on books and papers than his neighbors will, and know that I enjoy more of his company and conversation than their wives do, I feel that my learning is of practical benefit. When my children come to me, and ask about the wonders of earth and sky, and I see their eyes glisten, as I point out the beauty and order which exist throughout creation; and when I see that they are not less dutiful, because they can respect as well as love their mother, then I feel that my learning is of practical benefit. And when my little one lies sleeping in my arms, and I have a few moments for undisturbed reflection, I fix my thoughts upon higher subjects than my neighbor's household concerns, or the scandal of the day, and feel that my learning is of practical benefit. And it is my belief, that there is no lot so low, no station of life so obscure and toilsome, but that woman, *even there,* may find a cultivated mind to be of practical benefit."

Betsey.

Witchcraft

It may not, perhaps, be generally known that a belief in witchcraft still prevails, to a great extent, in some parts of New England. Whether this is owing to the effect of early impressions on the mind, or to some defect in the physical organization of the human system, is not for me to say; my present purpose being only to relate, in as concise a manner as may be, some few things which have transpired within a quarter of a century; all of which happened in the immediate neighborhood of my early home, and among people with whom I was well acquainted.

My only apology for so doing is, that I feel desirous to transmit to posterity something which may give them an idea of the superstition of the present age—hoping that when they look back upon its dark page, they will feel a spirit of thankfulness that they live in more enlightened times, and continue the work of mental illumination, till the mists of error entirely vanish before the light of all-conquering truth.

In a little glen between the mountains, in the township of B.,[109] stands a cottage, which, almost from time immemorial, has been noted as the residence of some one of those ill-fated beings, who are said to take delight in sending their spirits abroad to torment the children of men. These beings, it is said, purchase their art of his satanic majesty—the price, their immortal souls; and when satan calls for his due, the mantle of the witch is transferred to another mortal, who, for the sake of exercising the art for a brief space of time, makes over the soul to perdition.

The mother of the present occupant of this cottage, lived to a very advanced age; and for a long series of years, all the mishaps within many miles were laid to her spiritual agency; and many were the expedients resorted to, to rid the neighborhood of so great a pest. But the old woman, spite of all exertions to the contrary, lived on, till she died of sheer old age.

It was some little time before it was ascertained who inherited her mantle; but at length it was believed to be a matter of fact, that her daughter Molly was duly authorized to exercise all the prerogatives of a witch; and so firmly was this belief established, that it even gained credence with her youngest brother; and after she was married, and had removed to a distant part of the country, a calf of his, that had some strange actions, was pronounced by the *knowing ones* to be bewitched; and this inhuman monster chained his calf in the fire-place of his cooper-shop,[110] and burned it to death—hoping thereby to kill his sister, whose spirit was supposed to be in the body of the calf.

For several years it went current that Molly fell into the fire, and was burned to death, at the same time in which the calf was burned. But she at length refuted this, by making her brother a visit, and spending some little time in the neighborhood.

Some nineteen or twenty years since, two men, with whom I was well acquainted, had an action pending in the Superior Court, and it was supposed that the testimony of the widow Goodwin, in favor of the plaintiff, would bear hard upon the defendant. A short time previous to the sitting of the Court, a man by the name of James Doe offered himself as an evidence for the defendant, to destroy the testimony of the widow Goodwin, by defaming her character. Doe said that he was willing to testify that the widow Goodwin was a witch—he knew it to be a fact; for, once on a time she came to his bed-side, and flung a bridle over his head, and he was instantly metamorphosed[111] into a horse. The widow then mounted, and rode him nearly forty miles; she stopped at a tavern, which he named, dismounted, tied him to the sign-post, and left him. After an absence of several hours, she returned, mounted, and rode him home; and at the bed-side took off the bridle, when he re-assumed his natural form.

No one acquainted with Doe, thought that he meant to deviate from the truth. Those naturally superstitious thought that the widow Goodwin was in reality a witch; but the more enlightened believed that their neighbor Doe was under the influence of spirituous liquor when he went to bed; and that, whatever might be the scene presented to his imagination, it was owing to false vision, occasioned by derangement in his upper story; and they really felt a sympathy for him, knowing that he belonged to a family who were subject to mental aberration.

A scene which I witnessed in part, in the autumn of 1822, shall close my chapter on witchcraft. It was between the hours of nine and ten in the morning, that a stout-built, ruddy-faced man confined one of his cows, by means of bows and iron chains, to an apple-tree, and then beat her till she dropped dead—saying that the cow was bewitched, and that he was determined to kill the witch. His mother and some of the neighbors witnessed this cruel act without opposing him, so infatuated were they with a belief in witchcraft.

I might enlarge upon this scene—but the recollection of what then took place, recalls so many disagreeable sensations, that I forbear. Let it suffice to state, that the cow was suffering in consequence of having eaten a large quantity of potatoes from a heap that was exposed in the field where she was grazing.

Tabitha.

THREE

"Our Town": Village Sketches

The Black Glove

AT THE CLOSE of a beautiful summer-day, in the year 1799, on the door-step of a neat little cottage sat a man of venerable appearance, whose broad-brimmed hat bespoke him a member of the Society of Friends. He was busily engaged in reading the Life of George Fox,[112] when the tramp of a horse's hoof called his attention to an approaching traveller. The cottage, being a full half mile from the main road, was seldom visited, save by some of the Society to which the owner belonged; and it was not surprising that a stranger, riding at full speed, should call the attention of the inmates. Arriving at the cottage door, the stranger stopped short, and enquired for Friend B.[113]

"If thy business is with friend B.," said the venerable old man, rising upon his feet, "he stands before thee."

"Your son-in-law," said the stranger, "sent me here to employ your wife to knit a black silk glove for Mr. A.,[114] who is to be ordained to the work of the ministry in the first parish in this town, on the morrow. The glove is wanted by nine o'clock; and Mr. N. said there was no doubt his mother would knit it."

"Hannah, can thee knit the glove?" said the Quaker, turning to his wife. "I will try," said she, "but I fear I shall hardly accomplish the task by nine o'clock."

The stranger then told friend B., that if he would hasten to the meeting-house with the glove as soon as it was done, he should receive a dollar for the service; and if it arrived in season to secure the parsonage lot[115] to Mr. A., his wife should receive the present of a new dress. The honest Quaker could not imagine how a black glove could secure the parsonage lot, and the stranger did not stop to explain.

In the course of an hour, Mr. N. called in, and from him they learned that, by a vote of the town of W.,[116] the parsonage lot was to be given to the first preacher who should be ordained in the town; and that there were to be two candidates for the ministry ordained on the morrow. Mr. A., having but one hand, and that an uncommonly large one, no glove could be found to fit it; and a black glove being an indispensible article, it was thought expedient to hire one knit.

Mrs. B. knit diligently through the whole night, but it was after nine o'clock in the morning before the glove was finished; and friend B. was soon on his way toward the meeting house, which was distant about four miles from the cottage of the Quaker.

We will now leave the cottage, and hasten to the meeting-house. The people were all assembled by nine o'clock, but the glove had not arrived. The ministering brethren concluded that the glove might be dispensed with, until the ceremony of giving the right hand of fellowship.[117] The services accordingly commenced, and proceeded as far as was thought prudent, without the glove. They had waited some minutes in anxious suspense; large drops of perspiration stood upon the face of Mr. A., and he was upon the point of thinking that the parsonage lot was lost, when friend B. bolted into the door of the meeting-house, and with as little ceremony as one of the worthy Society of Friends was ever known to use, strode across the broad aisle, and up the pulpit stairs, with the exclamation, "Neighbor A., here is thy glove!"

The glove was put on, and the services proceeded with all possible despatch. Vain repetitions[118] were dispensed with in the closing prayer, for it was simply the Lord's prayer. The services being concluded a courier was sent to the other parish; and it was ascertained that the ordination of Mr. A. was concluded four minutes sooner than that of Mr. F. Of course the parsonage lot belonged to Mr. A., and Mrs. B. had a new dress for knitting the glove.

Mr. A. soon gathered a church, and it prospered well for a number of years. But in process of time, there was a bitter quarrel between Mrs. A. and the wife of the physician, which ran so high that the church took the matter in hand. After investigating the quarrel, Mr. A. discovered that he *could not* turn the physician's wife out of the church—and his own wife he *would not;* and in a fit of holy anger, he made a solemn promise, without any *proviso,* that he would never administer the sacrament of the Lord's supper to his church again!

This rite was held in the greatest veneration by the most of the church, and they often spoke of the sweet seasons which they had enjoyed together, while commemorating the love of the dying Savior. But now these sweet seasons were at an end—for what the minister said was *law,* and the people had to submit.

Several years after this, the physician, having a prospect of bettering his condition, removed to a distant part of the country. The Sunday after he left town, Mr. A., at the close of the afternoon services, gave notice that there would be a church meeting on Thursday afternoon, preparatory to the administration of the Lord's supper, which sacrament he intended to administer the ensuing Sabbath. The people were astonished, to think that their minister thought of breaking a vow so solemn; and they had strange forebodings of some dreadful calamity which was about to befall them.

After meeting, Mr. A. hastened home. He appeared very gloomy, and soon complained of great distress. Before night, he took his bed, from which he never arose. Before morning, his eyes were closed in death.

Tabitha.

Christmas

I was always taught to regard Christmas-day as the best day in the whole year; but it is not my intention at this time to relate the effect which this instruction has had upon my mind. I will merely say, that Christmas has its present joys, and it also brings to remembrance scenes of "by-gone days"—one of which, (a reminiscence of auld lang syne,) I will proceed to narrate.

I was at that time living in a small manufacturing village, where there was quite a number of English and Scotch families.[119] It was my fortune to live in a cottage of two tenements, one of which was occupied by a Scot who had married an American girl of my acquaintance. With this family I lived on terms of intimate friendship. This naturally introduced me to a number of persons who spent their early years in countries where the manners, customs, and general state of society, differed from those of New England.

My Scotch and English neighbors appeared like one family. The fact that they were so far from the home of their early years, and in the midst of a people who were more than willing to treat them as strangers, increased their affection for each other. They frequently met at my Scotch friend's, to talk of the happy days they had spent in "merry Old England," and in "the land o' cakes,"[120] killing time (as they called it,) by living over their happiest days. These good people often insisted that I should be one of their number at these friendly and social parties; and being naturally social myself, I frequently spent an hour with them, and I have no cause to regret my acquaintance with them—for the tales of "other days and far away," to which I then listened, were not only instructive, but many of them really amusing; and the remembrance of them has since cheered many an hour which would otherwise have been spent in gloomy sadness.

On Christmas Eve, my Scotch friend inquired if I should be frightened if I heard any uncommon noise in the night—at the same time remarking, that his friends intended to spend the night somewhat after the fashion of their own country. I assured him that they would not disturb me, and wished him and his friends a happy night.

I had engaged to finish a piece of needle-work that evening, and it was nearly twelve o'clock before I completed my task. I had extinguished my light, and sat looking at a handful of embers on the hearth, having sent my thoughts on a Christmas excursion. Soon after twelve, my reverie was disturbed by a noise in the entry, which resembled the bleating of sheep, the barking of dogs, and the confusion of human voices. The noise soon ceased, and the following conversation took place:

"Who watches the cote[121] to-night?" "Hugh, Allek and Peter." "Peter cannot watch, for he is in love." "Well, how do you know that?"—"Because he has been making rhymes all day." "And is that a sign that he is in love?" "Why, he has composed a whole love song, and I have gotten it away from him; Ay, here is the new song, which Peter singeth to the once admired, but now old fashioned tune of the Lass of Richmond Hill."[122]

"Who will help me sing it?" "I will."—"And I will."—"And I."—were the answers.—"Well, begin. Listen to Peter's song." Several voices then joined in singing the following song:

1. In yonder grape-bemantled bower,—
   Close by the sloping green,
   At evening's mild and moon-lit hour,
   The village belle is seen.

Chorus. This nymph so fair, so debonair,
    With silent magic art,
As gay and vain I passed the plain,
    Entranced my vagrant heart.

2. Her auburn hair in tresses flows
    Adown her ivory neck,
Her cheek with beauteous crimson glows,
    Her eyes divinely speak.
Chorus. This nymph so fair, &c.

3. With majesty she moves along,
    The pride of every swain;
For her each shepherd tunes his song,
    And pipes the rural strain.
Chorus. The nymph so fair, &c.

4. Such is her unaffected way,
    She charms where'er she moves;
And all with willing mind obey
    The nymph whom virtue loves.
Chorus. The nymph so fair, &c.

5. Discretion marks her even course,
    While reason lights her soul;
And mild persuasion's winning force
    O'er passions bears control.
Chorus. This nymph so fair, &c.

6. Grant me, kind fate, with her to share
    The remnant of my days;
And holy paeans I'll prepare,
    Of gratitude and praise.

Chorus. Since she's so fair, so debonair,
    With silent magic art;
As gay and vain, I passed the plain—

Here the singing ceased, or rather it appeared to be drowned in a shrill cry of horror. Then the sound, as of a heavy weight falling on the floor, was succeeded by groans, and then all was silent.

Scarcely a minute passed ere I heard the clear, musical voice of my Scotch friend, singing the following hymn:

1. "Shepherds, rejoice! lift up your eyes,
   And send your fears away;
   News from the regions of the skies,
   Salvation's born to-day.

2. Jesus, the Lord, whom angels fear,
   Has come to dwell with you;
   To-day he makes his entrance here,
   But not as mortals do.

3. No gold, nor purple swaddling bands,
   Nor royal shining things,
   A manger for the cradle stands,
   And holds the King of kings.

4. Go, shepherds, where the infant lies,
   And see his humble throne;
   With tears of joy in all your eyes,
   Go, shepherds, kiss the son."[123]

Here there was a moment's pause,—then more than a dozen voices broke out, singing,

"Glory to God in the highest, and on earth peace, good will toward men."[124]

The people in the entry now marched out of doors, and across the street to perform the same ceremony at another house. As soon as they had departed, two young ladies who boarded with me, and slept in an adjoining room, ran out, half frightened out of their wits; and catching hold of me, eagerly inquired the cause of the noise they had heard. I bade them not be frightened, but go with me to the window, and hear the *Christmas serenade,* at neighbor Hall's door. I raised the sash a little, and it being a still night, we could distinctly hear the whole performance. The young ladies agreed with me, that our neighbors appeared very devotional, although they had rather a rude way of performing their religious exercises. Having no disposition to sleep, we seated ourselves around the hearth, to talk over the affair. The serenade, rude as it was, had given our feelings a truly devotional turn,—and our thoughts wandered back to that auspicious morn which gave birth to the Messiah. And we followed him in imagination from the manger to the cross;—stopping by the way, at each striking incident, to examine its beauty and the instruction which it contained. And then we traced the progress of the Christian religion, from the days of the apostles to the time then present; and we were astonished to think that its march was so slow, until we examined our own hearts, and there we found a clue to the cause. And we resolved, that from that time we would make it a part of our daily employment, to study the life of the Prince of Peace;[125] and endeavor to fashion our lives according to the perfect pattern of righteousness which he has furnished, not only in precept, but also in example. How far these resolves were brought into practice with regard to my companions, I cannot say—for time and distance have made us strangers to each other. As for myself, I always find that it is much less difficult to make resolves than it is to put them into practice. But if my life has not been in strict accordance with what I purposed at that time, the impressions made upon my mind are not erased; and each returning Christmas reminds me of them, and also of my Scotch friends.

Tabitha.

The First Dish of Tea

Tea holds a conspicuous place in the history of our country; but it is no part of my business to offer comments, or to make any remarks upon the spirit of olden time, which prompted those patriotic defenders of their country's rights to destroy so much tea, to express their indignation at the oppression of their fellow citizens.[126] I only intend to inform the readers of the Lowell Offering, that the first dish of tea which was ever made in Portsmouth, N. H., was made by Abigail Van Dame, my great-great-grandmother.[127]

Abigail was early in life left an orphan, and the care of her tender years devolved upon her aunt Townsend, to whose store fate had never added any of the smiling blessings of Providence; and as a thing in course, Abigail became not only the adopted, but also the well-beloved child of her uncle and aunt Townsend. They gave her every advantage for an education which the town of Portsmouth afforded; and at the age of seventeen, she was acknowledged to be the most accomplished young lady in Portsmouth.

Many were the worshipers who bowed at the shrine of beauty and learning, at the domicil[128] of Alphonzo Townsend; but his lovely niece was unmoved by their petitions, much to the perplexity of her aunt, who often charged Abigail with carrying an obdurate heart in her bosom. In vain did Mrs. Townsend urge her niece to accept the offers of a young student of law; and equally vain were her efforts to gain a clue to the cause of the refusal, until, by the return of an East India merchantman,[129] Mr. Townsend received a small package for his niece, and a letter from Capt. Lowd, asking his consent to their union, which he wished might take place the following year, when he should return to Portsmouth.

Abigail's package contained a Chinese silk hat, the crown of which was full of Bohea tea.[130] A letter informed her that the contents of the hat was the ingredient which, boiled in water, made what was called the "Chinese soup."

Abigail, anxious to ascertain the flavor of a beverage of which she had heard much, put the brass skillet over the coals, poured in two quarts of water, and added thereto a pint bason full of tea and a gill of molasses, and let it simmer an hour.[131] She then strained it through a linen cloth, and in some pewter basons set it around the supper table, in lieu of bean-porridge, which was the favorite supper of the epicures of the olden time.

Uncle, aunt and Abigail seated themselves around the little table, and after crumbling some brown bread into their basons, commenced eating the Chinese soup. The first spoonful set their faces awry, but the second was past endurance; and Mrs. Townsend screamed with fright, for she imagined that she had tasted poison. The doctor was sent for, who administered a powerful emetic; and the careful aunt persuaded her niece to consign her hat and its contents to the vault of an out building.[132]

When Capt. Lowd returned to Portsmouth, he brought with him a chest of tea, a China tea-set, and a copper tea-kettle, and instructed Abigail in the art of tea-making and tea-drinking, to the great annoyance of her aunt Townsend, who could never believe that Chinese soup was half so good as bean-porridge.

The *first dish of tea* afforded a fund of amusement for Captain Lowd and lady; and I hope that the narrative will be acceptable to modern tea-drinkers.

Tabitha.

The First Wedding in Salmagundi

I have often heard this remark: "If their friends can give them nothing else, they will surely give them a wedding." As I have nothing else to present at this time, I hope my friends will not complain if I give them an account of the first wedding in our town. The ceremony of marriage being performed by His Excellence the Governor, it would not be amiss to introduce him first of all.

Let me then introduce John Wentworth, (the last Governor of New Hampshire while the colonies were subject to the crown of Great Britain,) whose country-seat was in Salmagundi.[133] The wedding which I am about to describe was celebrated on a romantic spot by the side of Lake Winnipiseogee. All the neighbors within ten miles were invited, and it was understood that all who came were expected to bring with them some implements of husbandry, such as ploughs, harrows, yokes, bows, wheelbarrows, hods, scythe-snaths, rakes, goads, hay-hooks, bar-pins, &c. These articles were for a fair, the product of which was to defray the expenses of the wedding, and also to fit out the bride with some household furniture. All these implements, and a thousand and one besides, being wanted on the farm of Wentworth, he was to employ persons to buy them for his own especial use.

Johnny O'Lara,[134] an old man, who used to chop wood at my father's door, related the particulars of the wedding one evening, while I sat on a block in the chimney-corner, (the usual place for the greatest rogue in the family,) plying my knitting needles, and every now and then, when the eyes of my step-mother were turned another way, playing slyly with the cat. And once, when we younkers went upon a whortleberry[135] excursion, with O'Lara for our pilot, he showed us the spot where the wedding took place, and described it as it was at the time. On the right was a grove of birches; on the left a grove of bushy pines with recesses for the cows and sheep to retire from the noonday sun. The back ground was a forest of tall pines and hemlocks, and in front were the limpid waters of the "Smile of the Great Spirit."[136] These encircled about three acres of level grass-land, with here and

there a scattering oak. "Under yonder oak," said O'Lara, "the ceremony was performed; and here, on this flat rock was the rude oven
constructed, where the good wives baked the lamb; and there is the
place where crotched stakes were driven to support a pole, upon which
hung two huge iron kettles, in which they boiled their peas." "And on
this very ground," said O'Lara, "in days of yore, the elfs and fairies
used to meet, and, far from mortal ken, have their midnight gambols."

The wedding was on a fine evening in the latter part of the month
of July, at a time when the moon was above the horizon for the whole
night. The company were all assembled, with the exception of the
Governor and his retinue. To while away the time just as the sun was
sinking behind the opposite mountains, they commenced singing an
ode to sunset. They had sung,

> "The sunset is calm on the face of the deep,
>   And bright is the last look of Sol in the west;
> And broad do the beams of his parting glance sweep,
>   Like the path that conducts to the land of the blest"—[137]

when the blowing of a horn announced the approach of the Governor,
whose barge was soon seen turning a point of land. The company gave
a salute of nineteen guns, which was returned from the barge, gun for
gun. The Governor and retinue soon landed, and the fair was quickly
over. The company being seated on rude benches prepared for the
occasion, the blowing of a horn announced that it was time for the
ceremony to commence; and, being answered by a whistle, all eyes
were turned towards the right, and issuing from the birchen grove
were seen three musicians, with a bagpipe, fife, and a Scotch fiddle,
upon which they were playing with more good nature than skill. They
were followed by the bridegroom and grooms-man, and in the rear
were a number of young men in their holyday clothes. These having
taken their places, soft music was heard from the left; and from a
recess in the pines three maidens in white, with baskets of wild flowers
on the left arm, came forth, strewing the flowers on the ground, and
singing a song, of which I remember only the chorus:

> "Lead the bride to Hymen's bowers,
> Strew her path with choicest flowers."

The bride and bridesmaid followed, and after them came several lasses in gala dresses. These having taken their places, the father of the bride arose, and taking his daughter's hand and placing it in that of Clifford, gave them his blessing. The Governor soon united them in the bonds of holy matrimony, and as he ended the ceremony with saying "what God hath joined let no man put asunder," he heartily saluted the bride.[138] Clifford followed his example, and after him she was saluted by every gentleman in the company. As a compensation for this "rifling of sweets," Clifford had the privilege of kissing every lady present, and beginning with Madam Wentworth,[139] he saluted them all, from the gray-headed matron to the infant in its mother's arms.

The cake and wine were then passed round. Being a present from Madam Wentworth, they were no doubt excellent. After this refreshment, and while the good matrons were cooking their peas and making other preparations, the young folks spent the time in playing "blind-man's-buff" and "hide and go seek," and in singing Jemmy and Nancy, Barbara Allen, The Friar with orders gray, The Lass of Richmond Hill, Gilderoy, and other songs which they thought were appropriate to the occasion.[140]

At length the ringing of a bell announced that dinner was ready. "What, dinner at that time of night?" perhaps some will say. But let me tell you, good friends, (in Johnny O'Lara's words,) that "the best time for a wedding dinner is when it is well cooked, and the guests are ready to eat it." The company were soon arranged around the rude tables, which were rough boards, laid across poles, that were supported by crotched stakes, driven into the ground. But it matters not what the tables were, as they were covered with cloth, white as the driven snow, and well loaded with plum puddings, baked lamb, and green peas, with all necessary accompaniments for a well ordered dinner, which the guests complimented in the best possible manner, that is, by making a hearty meal.

Dinner being ended, while the matrons were putting all things to rights, the young people made preparation for dancing; and a joyous time they had. The music and amusement continued until the "blushing morn" reminded the good people that it was time to separate. The rising sun had gilded the sides of the opposite mountains, which were sending up their exhalations, before the company were all on their way to their respective homes. Long did they remember the first wedding in our town. Even after the frosts of seventy winters had whitened the heads of those who were then boys, they delighted to dwell on the merry scenes of that joyous night; and from that time to the present, weddings have been fashionable in Salmagundi, although they are not always celebrated in quite so romantic a manner.

Tabitha.

The Husking

"Farewell the merry husking-night,
  Its pleasant after-scenes,
When Indian puddings smoked beside
  The giant pot of beans."[141]

Yes, farewell to the happy scenes of by-gone, youthful days. But though I bid you farewell, memory, true to her trust, will often, as harvest-time draws near, remind me of the many happy and joyful hours of the afternoon and evening husking-parties,[142] which, in other days and far away, I have spent with my youthful companions.

Of all the huskings which were made by the good people of Salmagundi, none afforded more pleasure than did those which were made by the Friends[143]—more especially those of friend Paul. Friend Paul was a jolly, good-natured sort of a man; who, were it not for his broad-brimmed hat, and plain drab-colored clothes, would never have been suspected of being one of the disciples of George Fox. His wife was as jolly as himself; and they were never happier than when they were surrounded by a whole bevy of young people, whenever they had an invitation to a quilting, husking, apple-bee, or any other merry-making which friend Paul and his wife chose to make.

One bright moon-lit evening, all the lads and lasses in the neighborhood were at the domicil of friend Paul, seated around a huge pile of corn, and with all imaginable nimbleness were trying to forward the hour of the harvest supper—which is always as soon after the corn is all husked as the huskers can wash their hands, and seat themselves around the tables. The jest and repartee had given place to singing, (for friend Paul and his wife loved to hear the rustic songs of olden time,) and many were the songs of woman's love, and woman's woes, and of knight-errants' chivalrous exploits, that were sung. And frequently would the singing cease in the middle of a song, when some lucky swain would claim the usual reward for finding a crimson ear.

Louisa was the fairest girl present. She was an orphan, and had from early childhood been loved with more than a brother's affection by one to whom she was on the point of being united for life. The marriage bans[144] had been proclaimed, and it was rumored that she was to be married at friend Paul's house. This appeared quite probable, as Louisa had lived for some little time in the family, and was a great favorite of Mrs. P's. Louisa was seated near the back door, hard-by which there was a thick copse.[145] The huskers were singing a song which friend Paul said was a favorite of his, and though it was not very poetical, and like many of the old-fashioned songs, not very well rhymed, they sung it with a pathos truly touching. It gave an account of a husking party, where a lady was present who was betrothed. Her lover was going the rounds, with a crimson ear, claiming as his due a kiss from every pretty cheek. As he approached his intended bride, to claim a kiss from her, "the harvest spirit"[146] rushed in at a door, near which the lady sat, and seizing her around the waist, bore her off, and she was never seen more. Her lover pursued them, fell off from a bridge, and was drowned.

The company at friend Paul's were singing

> "The spirit rushed in at the door,
> All on that husking night;
> He seized the lady"——

The lover of Louisa was approaching her, with a crimson ear. He was about to kiss her cheek, when a tall figure, enveloped in white, with an ugly, misshapen head, rushed in at the door, seized Louisa, and departed instantly. Quick as thought, her lover followed them; but before any of the company could so far recover from their surprise as to follow, they were out of sight.

It was proposed to surround the copse, but friend Paul said that he was sure he knew the rogue well, and also where to find him; and to be sure of proceeding according to law, they had better run to the village, (which was hard by) and have a Justice of the Peace on the ground with all haste. "The constable," he said, "being present, there would be little trouble in putting some people where they would have to remain for life." The company looked incredulous, nay, some who delighted in the marvellous, had their superstitious feelings so much excited, that they firmly declared their belief in the reality of a "harvest spirit," and said, that they really believed he had come and "carried Louisa off bodily."

The messenger who had been despatched to the village soon returned, accompanied by a Justice, when all hands repaired to the new house of friend Paul. Here, in the spacious parlor, some sitting, some standing, and all trying to raise their voices so as to be heard by the 'Squire; while each was giving his or her own peculiar opinion of the marvellous incidents of the evening, was this motley group. A closet door opened, and to the no small astonishment of the company, out came Louisa and her lover, preceded by a bridesmaid and groomsman! The 'Squire soon performed the marriage ceremony, confining the rogues for life, without the aid of constable, jury, or judge. After an ablution[147] of hands, the company seated themselves around a table of smoking-hot Indian pudding[148] and baked beans, and of every delicacy which constitutes a first-rate wedding supper.

Tabitha.

La Brainard

Early in the afternoon of a beautiful summer day, the children of the lower school district in South W.[149] were assembled at the house of an opulent farmer, to celebrate the birth-day of little Frances.

"Issadore," said Frances, speaking to her elder sister, who was ever ready to assist the little ones in their pastimes, "will you make us some wreaths for our heads, if we gather the roses? Mama's rose-bush is in full bloom, and I know that she is willing for us to have the roses."

"Don't be so sure of that, my little sister," said Issadore, "for I heard your mama say that she intended to make some rose-water this season. But I will tell you what you can do. You can gather your roses from the long string of wild rose-bushes, the other side of the orchard; and you can find plenty of violets near by the rose-bushes; and I will make you as many wreaths as you want."

Away ran the children in high glee, to gather their wild flowers. But Frances soon returned. "Oh, Issadore," said she, "will you not come out with us, and sit on the bench under the great oak, to make our wreaths? La Brainard is coming over yonder hill, and the children say that they shall not be afraid if you are with us." Issadore took her sister by the hand, and they hastened to the oak.

La Brainard was a harmless mad-man, who had been for nearly forty years promenading round Lake Winnipisiogee, and through the towns in the neighborhood of the lake, subsisting all the while upon charity. Many were the stories respecting the cause of La Brainard's mental derangement, but nothing was known for a certainty. It was evident that he had been liberally educated; and at times his manners told that he had been conversant with refined society. The father of Issadore had taught his children to be kind to the "unfortunate;" and at his house, La Brainard was always sure of a welcome reception. But there were many who treated him with contempt; and "Old Brainard" was the bug-bear with which they frightened their children to obedience.

La Brainard drew near, and when opposite the rose-bushes he stopped, gazed at the children, and appeared to be quite delighted. After a few minutes spent in looking at the children, he took down the bars, and came into the field, bending his steps toward the oak.

"Monsieur La Brainard," said Issadore, "I am glad to see you. Have you found any dinner to-day?"

"Yes," said he, "I have had a good dinner."

"So much the better," said Issadore, "for now you have nothing to do, but to sit down by me, and help wreathe some garlands for these children; and tell me the story which you have so many times promised."

La Brainard took up his cane, and counted the notches.—"See!" said he, "I have commenced upon the last week of the last month of the fortieth year of my wanderings. Yes, I will tell you the story,—I may not have another chance.

"You will find," said La Brainard, "that I am the hero of the story which I have promised you. But I shall be brief with the narrative of my early days. Suffice it to say, that the first twenty years of my life were spent under the immediate eye of my parents, and a private tutor. At the age of twenty, I was sent to Paris, to complete my education. My father had an estate of two thousand louis d'ors[150] per annum. He resided in a chateau, a few miles from Marseilles.[151] My mother was an English lady; and the day before I left home for Paris, she sailed for England. The voyage was prescribed by her physician—her health having been on the decline for some time previously. She died at Portsmouth about eight months after, as she was on the point of sailing for France. After this, my father took up his residence in a convent of Capuchins[152] at Marseilles.

"I had been in Paris nearly two years, when a circumstance took place, which made it absolutely necessary that I should not only quit Paris, but also France, with all possible despatch. I had become attached to, or to tell the truth, I was deeply in love with mademoiselle Le Rose, the daughter of a shop-keeper in the Rue St. Dennis.[153] All my leisure time was devoted to the lovely Marie. I often hired a hackney coach, and took Marie with me to Nanterre.[154] Here we would alight, and spend an hour in promenading around the quarries. One day, as we were sauntering along the road, happening to be several roods behind Marie, a man rushed out from one of the openings, and seizing her around the waist, was dragging her into the opening, when I rushed to her rescue, and plunging a dagger into his breast, laid him dead upon the spot. As he fell, he looked me in the face, and faintly articulated, 'Oh, La Brainard, you have murdered your friend!' Words cannot express my astonishment in beholding de Montesson, my bosom friend, dead at my feet,—murdered by my own hand!

"There was no time to reflect. Quick as thought, I dragged the dead body into the opening, and then bore Marie, fainting, to the coach. It was well for me that it was twilight; otherwise the coachman might have suspected some foul play. It was dark and had begun to rain, before we reached the Rue St. Dennis. I dismissed the coach, and by an unfrequented route, sought the convent of Carmelites.[155] The Prior[156] was my father's brother. I told him my sad story, and he advised me to leave France, as de Montesson belonged to a powerful family, and a discovery would bring me to a disgraceful death. My uncle provided me with a mask; it had a shorn crown, and a long white beard. In this disguise, and habited like a Carmelite, I walked to Marseilles. My father gave me three thousand louis d'ors, and a promise of more, when he had an opportunity.

"A few days after, I went on board a merchant vessel bound to America. Marie accompanied me, having first given me a husband's right to protect her. It was not long after my arrival in America, before I purchased a farm, in a beautifully sequestered place; and had come to the resolution of spending my days in the New World. After the Declaration of Independence, (my heart being on the side of the Americans,)

I enlisted in the cause of liberty; and I continued in the service, until the taking of Fort Griswold by the British.

"You will find, by reading the narrative of that event, that after the fort was carried, Col. Ledyard had his sword plunged into his own bosom, by the British officer to whom he presented it; and also that there was a general massacre, not only of those who resisted, but also of those who surrendered, which continued until all the garrison were either killed or wounded.[157] I was among the wounded. A blow on the head from a sword, deprived me of sense. How long I remained in this situation, I know not; but the first that I remember, a surgeon was dressing my head. After I had, in a measure, recovered from my wounds, I was discharged on parole. I returned to the place which I had chosen for my future home. It was late at night when I arrived at my journey's end; and where I expected to rest from the toils of war, and in the sweet society of my Marie, find that peace, which only could be an antidote for the past. Warily did I enter the dwelling, intending not to disturb its sleeping inhabitants, or have my arrival known until morning. A candle was burning in the room where Marie used to sleep; the door was ajar; I entered the room, when, oh horrid to relate! I found Marie not only locked in the embraces of sleep, but also in the arms of a rival. This sight overcame me. I gave a scream, and fell senseless on the floor.

"Weeks, and months, I was confined to the bed of sickness; and when I did at length recover from sickness, I left my home in despair. How long I wandered, I know not. But stopping one night, by the side of the Winnipisiogee, I fell asleep. De Montesson haunted my dreams; he stood before me; the blood was streaming from the wound in his breast. 'See,' said he, 'the work of thy hand. This was done to avenge a perfidious woman. To expiate thy crime, for forty years shalt thou be a wanderer around this lake; and I will be thy constant companion.'

"When I awoke, the phantom was by my side; and summer or winter, it has ever been with me; and though I know it to be but the effect of a disordered imagination, I cannot drive it from me. Last night I again dreamed of conversing with it. At the close of our conversation, de Montesson said, 'La Brainard, thy crime is expiated; thy pilgrimage will soon be ended, and I forgive thee.' To-day I have felt calm; for the phantom no longer frowns upon me; but on the contrary, he smiles, and we have walked arm in arm, as we used to do in the public gardens of Paris."

La Brainard here ended his narrative, and expressed a wish to take a nap under the oak; "for," said he, "the moon will rise a little past eight, and then I must continue my journey."

Issadore ran to the house, and brought a pillow to put under the old man's head, bidding him when he awoke, to come to the house for his supper; and then taking his provision sack to replenish, left him to repose.

Early in the evening, while Issadore and her father were conversing about La Brainard, the old man entered the room. He appeared quite rational, and conversed with great affability for nearly an hour. After partaking of supper, which had been delayed on his account, La Brainard rose to depart. Issadore brought him his provision sack; he slung it around his neck, and raised his hands to invoke a blessing upon the head of Issadore, who, crossing her arms upon her breast, knelt before him—a thing which she often did, because it gratified La Brainard; and his invocations, being rather of a ludicrous character, afforded a fund of amusement for her father. "Holy Virgin," said La Brainard, "let thy blessings descend upon St. Issadore; and when she has no home but the wide world, may she find friends who will treat her with that kindness which she has ever manifested toward La Brainard; and, O God, do Thou protect the orphan."

After this ceremony, La Brainard took his cane in his right hand, and reached out his left, as if in the act of taking some one by the hand, at the same time saying, "let us go," he took his departure.

"Well," said Issadore's father, "La Brainard is as crazy as ever; the poor man's imagination has only taken another turn; but, as my Issadore is canonized, as completely as if the business had been done by the pope, I hope she will be our guardian tonight, by seeing that the fire is safe, the lights put out, and the doors closed. Good night, St. Issadore."

A few days after this, La Brainard was found dead by the high-way side, some forty miles from W.[158] His head was resting on a knoll, his hands upon his breast, and clasping a wooden crucifix.

Several years after La Brainard's death, a young physician came to W. to reside. His wife and Issadore were soon on terms of intimacy. One day, after they had been speaking of La Brainard, Issadore was invited into the physician's study. The doctor drew aside a green curtain which hung in one corner of the room, and asked Issadore, if she would like to see an old acquaintance. "The skeleton of La Brainard, ladies," said the doctor. "Impious wretch!" said Issadore, "what right have you to those bones?" The doctor smiled, and entered into an argument to show the utility of having a skeleton; he closed his remarks by saying, "we prefer having those who have no friends to grieve for them; and besides, La Brainard was crazy." "He was nevertheless a man," said Issadore, "and suffered enough for the freedom of America, to entitle his bones to a resting-place beneath her soil." "But it is otherwise decreed," said the doctor.

Issadore was silent, but not convinced that it was right to have the bones of La Brainard thus rudely handled. She even mentally wished the doctor might live to feel his own bones rot. Whether the Scottish gift of second sight[159] gave rise to this wish, cannot be ascertained. But the doctor lived to find it accomplished, for his bones were so defected,[160] that several of his ribs crumbled to pieces before his death.

I will close my story by expressing a wish, that science may yet bring to light some remedy for diseases of the brain; hoping that the time is not far distant, when all who are afflicted with mental derangement will meet with the sympathy which was due to the unfortunate La Brainard.

Tabitha.

The Old Farm-House

Ay, well do I remember the old farm-house—its spacious halls, its drawing-rooms, dining-rooms, and every room, from the attic to the cellar—not one of which had not a story connected with it of ghosts, hobgoblins, or something of the kind.

This house was built by Governor Wentworth, (the last Colonial Governor of New-Hampshire,) for a country residence, and was the largest house in the whole township. It was situated hard-by a beautiful pond of water, which covered some hundreds of acres, and contained a number of islands which added much to its beauty. In this pond, tradition says, the young wife of the old gray-haired Governor[161] once made her spouse believe that she had thrown herself, after being refused admittance to the house upon her return from a moon-light frolic and ramble, which had kept her from home through the greater part of the night. The Governor, hearing a splash in the water, rushed out in his night-clothes to rescue his wife from a watery grave, when she in her turn took possession of the house, and refused her husband admittance; and he (poor soul!) had to spend the remainder of the night in the stable, wrapped in horse-blankets—a circumstance which Johnny O'Lara said proved "beyond demonstration," that the Governor's wife was his better half.

The large farm of the Governor had not only its garden, orchard, and mowing, pasturage, tillage and wood-lands, but also its park, lawn, shady walks, and many other embellishments, which are now remembered among the things which "were, and are not." The lawn was on the right hand from the house, the park on the left—the distance from the extreme part of the one to that of the other, might be three-fourths of a mile. The lawn is memorable as the place for dancing by moon-light, a custom which was fashionable in the day of Governor Wentworth, and which was highly approved of by his youthful partner, who made it a point of duty to honor by her presence all the merry-makings of her rustic neighbors. A narrow strip of dark growth, such as pine, hemlock, spruce and fir, was left standing when the land was cleared. This strip was called "the green ribbon," and commenced at the extreme part of the lawn, and extended a mile and a half to an eminence, called Mount Delight.[162] It wound over the mouth, making a double bow, and then extended to the extreme part of the park. Here it terminated, and a white-washed, picket-fenced lane led to the house. A beautiful park through the green ribbon made it a delightful walk, either at blazing noon, or by the mild light of night's silver queen. It was from a ramble through the green ribbon, after a frolic on the lawn, that Madam Wentworth had returned, on the memorable night, when, by stratagem, she took possession of the farm-house, to the great discomfiture of the good Governor.

Upon the breaking out of the Revolutionary war, Governor Wentworth (who was a patriot at heart, and could not in conscience join with the British, and believing the cause of American independence to be a hopeless one, dared not join with the Americans) fled the country; and the farm-house, with all its appendages, fell into other hands.[163] It had various owners from time to time; and at the period when I first became acquainted with it, it was owned by a Mrs. Raynard, a native of Yorkshire, England.[164] Our whole township being destitute of public buildings, with the exception of one meeting-house, Mrs. Raynard's hall was the chosen place for all the Thanksgiving, Christmas, New-Year, and Washington balls. This made the old farm-house a place dear to the hearts of all the young ones who delighted in the innocent pastimes of youth. And thrice dear was the old farm-house in the memory of many; for there many an acquaintance commenced, that ended in friendship; and there, within its mouldering walls, many a friendship commenced which ripened into a pure and holy love. And when, tired of dancing, the young people would promenade through the house, while the attention of the rest was engaged in listening to some legendary tale of the spirits which had been known to haunt the house ever since the day on which Governor Wentworth left America, some bashful swain would muster courage to "pop the question" to his "beloved"—while she, from fancying herself in the midst of ghosts and hobgoblins, would so sensibly feel the need of a protector, that "I will be thine, and only thine," came with less hesitation from her trembling lips.

If the young people could have been the sole arbiter of the fate of the old farm-house, it would have stood the test of time—so much did they prize it. But it was made of perishable materials, and doomed to fire. Whether it was fired accidentally, or by an incendiary, is a question in the minds of many, which without doubt will ever remain unanswered. Mrs. Raynard, at the time it was burned, was on the point of being married to a neighboring widower, whose children were very much opposed to the match, for fear that Mrs. R. would bring their father to poverty; and report said that they often expressed a wish that the old woman would take fire and burn up. Mrs. R. was taken into the family of the gentleman to whom she was to have been married, who, upon better acquaintance, concluded not to marry her. The gentleman's children have not prospered so well as it was expected they would; and the "wise ones," when conversing of these things, often think of retribution, and the old farm-house.

Revered building! a small tribute is due thee, in memory of the many scenes of joy and sorrow which have been witnessed within thy walls! Many of these have long been buried in oblivion, and many are still green spots in memory! But *they*, too, will pass away, and thou also wilt be forgotten. Peace to thy ashes!

Tabitha.

Our Town: How It Looked

How beautifully has Miss Mitford delineated to us the scenes and events of Our Village. The English collection of cottage and castle, of hut and hall, of park and patch, of lawn and lane, of field and forest, of grove and garden, of mead and morass, of hill and hollow, and of shine and shade. With these has she intermingled the more interesting scenery of the heart, and made all other pictures but scene-curtains to its simple dramas,—its every-day tragedy and comedy. She has portrayed love and laughter, smiles and sorrows, hope and fear, early life and long-awaited death; and we weep and rejoice, because our own hearts tell us that she has pictured truly.[165]

And why, then, may we not portray Our Town; the six-miles-square collection of hill and field, of pond and plain, of dense, dark wood and winding river? "Our Town;" so duly set off by State commissioners, within the memory of "the oldest inhabitant," encircled by the imaginary line drawn by the surveyor, and peopled, in the very first instance, by "a happy and glorious posterity." "Our Town;" baptized long ago, according to records kept carefully by the town-clerk, as Windham or Pelham, or some other *ham;* or Newton or Burlington, or some other *ton;* or Craftsbury or Tewksbury, or some other *bury;* as Peterboro' or Marlboro', or some other *boro';* and faithfully delineated upon the Governor's chart, long before any two houses stood within sight of each other. "Our Town;" with its legends of struggle with the Red man, and warfare with bears, wild-cats, wolves, and raccoons; and of wild adventures with snow-storms, winds, and floods. "Our Town;" to which the great statesman looks back as the cradle of his genius; and whose humble homes are the brightest spots in the memory of the distant emigrant, the roving traveller, the bustling citizen, and the sea-tossed mariner. "Our Town;" every home in it has its tale and legend, for every heart has had its life-long drama.

"Our Town;" it needs no very particular description, but looks somewhat like an italic *Q,* the quirl being the pond.[166] It has, of course, its meetinghouse, its schoolhouses, and its hearsehouse. These constitute its public buildings; for I now speak of one of the humblest of *"our towns."* There is not even an enginehouse, in all its length and breadth; and the meetinghouse does duty as town hall and vestry.[167] "Our Town" has a main road, running like a great artery through its system; and numerous extra roads and lanes, like lesser veins, circulate around. There is the East Road and the Back Road, and the Pond Hill Road and the Smith Road. Then there is Love Lane and Pleasant Lane, and Briery Lane and Horse Lane; to say nothing of the little nameless lanes, which might not inappropriately be called Cow Lane or Sheep Lane, if the accommodation of those travellers was of sufficient importance.

Then there were hills; Centre Hill, on which stood the meeting-house, like the crown over all; and there was Bear Hill, and Stag Hill, and Sugar Hill, and Blackberry Hill, and Pond Hill, and who knows how many more? And there were rocks, great ledges of them, stretching like a strong backbone along many a well-improved and productive farm; and huge single rocks, which rounded their hard backs up from the green earth, like a petrified tortoise of the primeval time; when the mastodon strode the forest, and there were nought but "giants in those days."[168] Then there were heaps of rocks in every field and orchard; loose stones, lying one upon the other, the monuments of the oft-repeated victories of General Industry,—a warrior who had his enthusiastic admirers and adherents in every family of "Our Town." A few patches of woodland were marked off, perhaps, by a "Virgini' fence,"[169] or a circlet of colossal roots, but, in general, a stone wall was hedge, fence, and ditch. Then "Our Town" has its little ponds; bright eyes, looking up to heaven from among the hills and rocks, and sending back the sun or star light, mirrored in their liquid depths. Ponds, fringed with the beautiful blue-flag and tall, broad grasses, and on which the lily floated and gazed up into the day; and "Our Town" had a part of Big Pond.[170]

"Our Town" had its woods,—its groves of maples; where, in spring, the sugar-makers hoarded their sweets,—and its forests of oak and of pine. Then there were the walnut, the chestnut, and the butternut; renowned among the juveniles for many an expedition, when they went, like the squirrel, to lay up food for winter.

Such were the natural lineaments of "Our Town," with its many lovely landscapes and skyscapes; for the blue heavens arched over it, as over all towns, and gave us a shifting and often gorgeous scene of sunsets and sunrisings; of clouds and clear blue depths; of smiling moon and glittering stars, and of brilliant Aurorean lights.[171]

Man had done nothing great, nor wonderful, for "Our Town;" but still, he had wrought a change in what his fathers called "the howling wilderness;"[172] and another time, we will tell of the human beings who lived, and loved,—who thought, and felt, and acted,—in "Our Town."

Betsey.

Lowell.

Our Town. No. 2. Our Meeting-House (Continued from Vol. 6)

Our meeting-house was of course the principal public building in *our town*. Like true descendants of the Puritans, the townsfolk were a go-to-meeting people. The fervor and punctuality with which this duty was practised, was in truth the chief test of character. It was the place to which the failing footsteps tended last, and the little child was early taught to turn its face toward the house of God. It was the place, also, where public business of a secular kind was attended to, and perhaps subdued and hallowed in a degree, that often disgracefully clamorous assemblage, "a town-meeting." Being one of the unprivileged sex, I can, of course, describe none of the political manœuvres, nor "Timon" like draw any of the portraits of the orators of our town.[173] Of the rites at the inner temple of freedom I know nothing. But I know that, if there was any snow upon the ground at that time in March, the best sleigh and handsomest horse in town were sent for the minister, who prayed with and I trust for them, though to have availed himself of a farther privilege, would have neutralized all past and future efforts for other good. I know that little clubs met nightly in advance of the eventful day, at the village tavern, and that, occasionally, the sober face of a squire or selectman, joined the more boisterous and unselect group. But these worthies more usually satisfied themselves with a call in the edge of the evening at each other's houses, or a conversation at the road-side, or a casual meeting in the woods or fields. I know that there was a time when the successful candidate to the State Legislature always testified his gratitude to those who had so kindly elected him, by an invitation to the bar-room of that tavern. I know that, spite of minister and prayers, and a general sober deportment, there was drunkenness and quarrelling on that day, more than on any other:

> "But things like this we know must be,
> Wherever there is—*liberty;*"

at least such was the usual salvo to the consciences[174] of our townsmen.

But on the Sabbath our meeting-house was the focus at which all the population centred, and I can describe it as we saw it then. Outwardly, it was an unassuming structure, crowning a gentle elevation about halfway between the northern and southern boundaries, on the main road. It had once been painted, but the rain and the snow had now denuded it of all such outward varnishment, and without any spire or porch, it was simple enough in its exterior for a Quaker tabernacle. Indeed, the irreverent wags[175] as often called it the "Lord's barn," as the "Lord's house," and were at times but refractory creatures, when shut up there upon the holy day. The door still retained some unmistakable tokens that it had once been of a cream color, and upon it were posted the notices of impending marriages, with other documents of like public importance.

It was equally plain within—the simple whitewashed ceiling was only variegated by a few weather stains, which seemed to indicate a suspicious state of affairs among the shingles on the roof. The pews were unpainted and unvarnished, there were no carpets nor cushions, and every thing *plainly* indicated that Sabbath worship was not to be made an easy thing. Along the broad aisle were the principal pews; Colonel Smith's, and 'Squire White's, and Deacon Johnson's, and Major Brown's, upon the right hand, and as many more of the aristocracy upon the left. Colonel Smith's pew had three crickets,[176] a spit-box, a book-rack, and a little swing shelf of pine at the head of the pew, for the colonel to rest his arm upon.

At the right hand of the pulpit, was the minister's pew, and in due order with it, a succession of square pews around the walls of the house—these pews were a step higher than those in the body of the house, and those of them that had windows were not considered inferior to those in the broad aisle.

The side pews had often a high-backed flag-bottomed chair[177] in the middle of them, for the "grand ma'am" of the family, and some of these carved oaken antiques would now be a treasure in many a city parlor.

One of the pews was noted as being made of two by the abstraction of the intervening partition. This was for Ensign Brewer's family, which was the largest family collection in the church. The window to his pew was shaded by a green blind, which was quite a conspicuous badge upon the exterior. There were no curtains nor shutters; indeed nothing of the superfluous, save a row of little carved trunnels[178] at the tops of the pews, which, sometimes, twisted in the hands of a restless child, sent forth a shrill squeak to the annoyance of the preacher, the disturbance of the congregation, and the dire dismay of the witless culprit, who shrank aghast from the frowns and starings and head-shakings of its awful guardians.

The floors and seats were white and clean, it being a matter of habit with the good house-wives to go once a year and "clean up the pew," though Mrs. Ensign Brewer, and Mrs. Colonel Smith, and such ladies, sometimes employed Peggy Ceasar, a colored woman, as their deputy. Peggy's pew was in the gallery, and she was the only woman, save those in the choir, that went up stairs to sit. Perhaps she has one of the highest seats in heaven.[179]

The rest of the gallery was occupied by outlaw boys, a few crazy men and idiots, with a sprinkling of old bachelors, who, in our town were classed with negro women, fools, and children.

The fixtures of the choir were merely the seats; for the bass-viol, the violin, and the singing books were usually brought and taken upon the Sabbath. The last mentioned instruments were of late introduction into the meeting-house, and the innovation had caused much discussion and some displeasure. Ensign Brewer had threatened to leave if they were brought, and, one sabbath, went with his two wagon-loads of folk over to the Methodist meeting, by the pond, in the edge of the next town; but all the next week, he was "Brother Brewer" to every poor humble Whitfieldian, and the Ensign, who *was* a bit of an aristocrat in his way, concluded to go back to the old meeting-house.[180]

Old 'Squire White favored the instruments, because his son, Captain White, the leader of the choir, and a great teacher of singing schools, was for the *improvement;* and Colonel Smith was very acquiescent, "for a raison that he had." The other opponents after awhile gave up. The colonel's reason was this: it was quite a matter of ambition with the young women in our town, to rise in the world, at least to the singing seats; and, as Captain White wished to make as few enemies as possible, and be popular among his pupils, he took as many as he could, and more than he should, into the choir, enjoining it upon them very earnestly to *"sing softly,"* which meant *to make as little noise as possible.* But it was a rebellious company at best; and, if I write the full history of this choir, no one will wonder that the captain died in the prime of life of a disease of the heart.

Colonel Smith had a grand-daughter, Julia, who was a great favorite in his family. Now Miss Julia wished very much to lift up her voice in the Sabbath praises, but Captain White had never invited her into the seats; he knew very well that she was not at all backward at the singing schools, and singing meetings, and doubtless understood her desire to assist him in the church psalmody;[181] but none of Miss Julia's hints and attentions had availed her aught. Now, for one of Colonel Smith's family to sit quietly in his pew every Sabbath, while Mary Foster, one of the poorest girls in town, and her father a drunkard, as it was called then, led the first treble—this was too much for the colonel to bear. So one Sabbath he waited upon Miss Julia into the seats, as though he were doing the captain the greatest favor in the world. The damsel availed herself of her position, and such shrill screams and shriekings as went up that day, seemed premonitions of the death of the choir. The captain saw her during the week and invited her politely to take herself away—aware as he was that this might be the commencement of a feud between all the Whites and the Smiths, which would only be comparable to those of the Guelphs and the Ghibbelines, the Montagues and Capulets.[182] Probably no Smith would ever have gone to the captain's singing school again, and a new singing master might have been introduced into the town by the manœvrings of Mrs. John Junior, as the younger Mrs. Smith the mother of Miss Julia was called, had not a peace been conquered. Mrs. Colonel and Mrs. John Junior were remarkably peaceable when the violin and clarionet were introduced into the choir, and even the colonel thought instrumental music no more objectionable than the singing of non-professors (of religion). The cause of this unexpected acquiescence was soon understood. The colonel found a time and place to tell the captain, that Miss Julia had improved very much in singing since she had studied some books he had purchased for her, and he wanted her to have a chance in the seats again. Miss Julia *had* learned something, and improved in the art of keeping still; at all events, she could not rival the instruments.

But I have almost done with our meeting-house. In later days it had a stove, with an abundance of funnel,[183] which ran around behind the posts, but previously it had been warmed by the foot-stoves, and soap-stones, and heated bricks, carried by the old ladies.

Our congregation well-befitted such a house. They came to meeting on foot, if they lived within walking distance, and if not they rode in a wagon, filled with seats and stools, and folks, according to the size of the family. There was a row of stalls and a horse-block[184] in the rear of the church for their accommodation. All looked well, for they wore their best, and some were really quite dignified in appearance. Colonel Smith walked erect as a grenadier,[185] though his hair was thin and silvery, and his cane seemed more for grandeur than support. Mrs. Colonel wore a black silk gown and a leghorn bonnet, and in winter a broad-cloth cloak.[186] Mrs. Captain White led the fashions, and was duly stared at every Sabbath. The poorest old lady carried a "posie," consisting at least of some spicy pinks, and a sprig of caraway or lavender.[187] The young gentlemen always formed a group around the door, before the services commenced, and the pretty girls blushed, and were perhaps all the more careful in their toilet, on account of their scrutinizing observations. On a windy day these were very annoying, but looked upon as much a "necessary evil," as the rattling of the windows.

Our Town. No. 3. Our Pulpit

If our meeting-house deserves a whole chapter by itself, our pulpit should at least have a separate paragraph. Its location was opposite the front door, and up about half way between the floor and gallery. The deacons' seat was in front of it, on a level with the first step. Here sat two white-headed patriarchs, Deacon Smith, and Deacon Carter. They were men who differed widely in looks, character, and influence; albeit in office and week-day calling alike. Deacon Smith was brother to the Colonel, and like him a fine portly figure. There was more of pride than of humility in his look and bearing, though he professed to be a very humble Christian. In his youth, it was said he had been a reprobate; worldly, reckless, and profane; denying God and contemning[188] man. Of course he did not prosper. His betrothed forsook him; his relatives denied him; his neighbors avoided him; and all feared him.

For years he was like an Ishmaelite, his hand against every man, and every man's hand against him.[189] At length he came out with a confession of a dream, which was very much like the vision of Saul, of Tarsus; only that there was no one with him to see the light, or hear the sound of the heavenly voice; but no one doubted the statement, for he who had once been a scoffer, sat penitent and stricken at the feet of the godly.[190] From this time the world went well with him. He married his choice, was admitted church member, and indeed became one of the pillars of the church; was then made a deacon, and no one had more zeal and influence than he. He kept strict watch over the parson, and would have seen the slightest misstep towards hetoradoxy;[191] he was at the head of the committees upon psalmody, and the minister's tax; officiated with the pastor at the monthly concert, and Friday evening prayer-meeting; and had an oversight with regard to religious affairs in general; saw that the Bible was duly read in the town schools, and that the teachers were religiously disposed men or women; that they attended church, and took classes in the Sabbath School, with other matters of like importance; and, indeed, it seemed as though the fear of the deacon's reproof tended greatly towards the strengthening of the outworks of Zion.

Yet still the deacon was a hard taskmaster, severe in his family, and an extortioner in his dealings. But, as a portion of his gains was given to the Lord, these short comings were forgiven him.

Deacon Carter was quite another man. From his childhood he had feared God, and kept his commandments, and loved and respected his fellow man. Yet trials grievous had come upon him. His wife and children died; his house was burned by lightning from heaven; his cattle sickened and wasted away; his crops failed, it seemed, more often than his neighbors' did. Yet never was there a murmur at his heart, and his lips said, "It is the Lord, let Him do as seemeth good unto him."[192] His life was a lesson of patience and submission; and his words, though few, were those of a Christian; spare in frame, humble in aspect, deferential in word and manner, there was little in him to *command* respect, yet he possessed the regard and esteem of all who knew him. "Deacon Carter is a Christian" said even the Infidel; and in him was honored his Lord and Master.

Our pulpit was very humble; it was uncurtained and uncarpeted. Even the stairs were unpainted, and only when the great elm, in the rear threw its shadow across the window, was it shaded. That window larger than the others, and arched at the top, was distinguished from them all, within and without, aside from its position, which was at the inner corners of two above and two below.

The green velvet cushion, on which lay the time worn Bible, was faded and worn; and the two tassels which depended therefrom, before the eyes of the congregation, were ravelled and rusty. The inner portion of it, too, was evidently decaying, and resolving into dust. And whenever some young preacher exchanged with our good pastor, who had more zeal in his head than grace in his heart, and, fearing failure in his attempts to impress his sentiments upon his audience, determined, at least, to thump them into the cushion; when he lifted up his voice and dashed down his hands, such clouds, not of incense but of dust, would arise, such hosts of rebel atoms come up before him, that he generally desisted from the attempt.

But, as time passed on, the necessity of new pulpit trimming was discovered, and many were the plans laid to accomplish the desired object. Mrs. Deacon Smith, a little, thin, abject looking woman, who could n't speak three words without coughing, started with a subscription paper, but she soon wearied and gave it up. Then a sewing society was talked of; but as everybody did their own sewing at home, there was nobody in our town to sew for. The singers volunteered a concert; but very little was gained by that, as they got into a quarrel and broke their lamps, which were borrowed and must be replaced; and injured the bass-viol, which must be repaired. At length, another subscription was agreed upon and half a dozen young ladies chosen to canvass the town. This last was successful; and, when the materials were purchased, the ladies collected at Mrs. Deacon Smith's, and transformed them into sacred garniture. And what a transformation in our pulpit? Instead of one green cushion, there was crimson damask for the whole pulpit-top, at the sides as well as front of the preacher, edged with a splendid tasseled gimp;[193] and the curtain behind, looped, and festooned, and tasseled to match, threw its ruddy hue over the preacher and his congregation. A new japan[194] spit-box was provided in lieu of the old wooden one, and new steps replaced the blocks with which the speakers graduated their height in the desk, a strip of carpeting for the stairs, and a new Bible exhausted the funds; leaving, as the religious duty of another generation, the replenishing of the communion service.

Lowell.

Prayer in a Sick-Room

Our Physician was a praying man. "Many a time and oft" was he known to retire from his study after he had returned from visiting his patients, and there on his bended knees, give vent to the feelings of his heart in audible prayer—beseeching the Father of mercies and the Giver of every good and perfect gift, to have compassion on the sick, and to give him all of that wisdom which was necessary for one who professed the healing art.[195] And he would often, when a patient was very sick or in great distress, retire from the sick room, and in another apartment pour out his soul to God in prayer, in behalf of the sick and the distressed.

But he was entirely averse to praying in a sick-room. He was often heard to say that he never but once, in the whole course of forty years' practice, knew prayer in a sick-room to do any good; and then, he believed that it was the means of saving life.

Our Physician said, that once he had a patient by the name of Nute, who was afflicted with a swelling in the throat. It had come to a crisis, and for several days Capt. Nute, (as he was called,)[196] had taken nothing as nourishment, excepting what he had received by wetting his mouth with a feather dipped in milk and water. It was early in the morning, and the Physician sat by the bed-side of the apparently dying man. In one hand, he held his watch; in the other, the wrist of his patient. Pulsation was nearly gone; and momentarily was the grim messenger expected to make his appearance. The door opened, and Pompey, a colored man who lived hard by, entered the room. He approached the bed with the inquiry, "How Cap'n Noot du?"

"Oh," said the Physician, "he is a dying man!"

"Why you no sabe um?" said Pompey.

"I have done every thing which I can, in the line of my profession," said the Physician, "and if my prayers could be answered, the Captain would be saved; but I have lost my influence at the Throne of Grace.[197] Pompey, nothing but prayer can save our friend; the Lord may save him in answer to your prayers. And now, even this moment, pray that the Lord may spare him, and let not his blood be upon your head because you shrank from duty."[198]

Pompey fell upon his knees, clasped his hands, rolled his white eyes up into his head, and thus commenced: "Oh Lord, please spare Cap'n Noot!" He then raised himself up to see what effect it had upon the Capt.; then fell upon his knees again, saying, "Oh Lord, please spare Cap'n Noot—he good man—he build berry good cider-mill!"—Again Pompey raised himself up, and looked upon the Captain. Seeing his face of a dark crimson, while he appeared to be struggling with the agonies of death, the negro's indignation was aroused against his

Maker. He stamped with his foot, smote his fists, and (while his whole frame trembled with violent emotion) exclaimed, "You *can* spare him *jes well's not,* if you ony *mine* to!"

This had the desired effect. The Captain's risible muscles gave way, and he burst into a laugh. The Physician raised his patient, to prevent him from strangling while discharging the corrupt matter from his throat; and when the Captain was again laid back upon his bed, he called Pompey to him, and putting a five dollar note in his hand, said, "There, my good fellow, accept that. You have by your prayers caused the swelling in the Captain's throat to break, and thereby saved his life—for which we all owe you much."

Pompey called every morning to inquire for "Cap'n Noot;" and one morning, when the Captain was so far recovered as to be able to walk by leaning upon the shoulder of Pompey, they took a walk to the barn-yard, where Pompey had his choice of one of five cows. The tears trickled down the dark visage of the honest negro—he thanked the Captain a thousand times, and promised that he would daily remember him in his prayers.

Our Physician often said, he feared that the mirth which Pompey's prayer occasioned, might lead some to suppose that he ridiculed sacred things; but he comforted himself by reflecting, that the end justified the means which were used to save a fellow being from the jaws of death.

Jemima.

Recollections of My Childhood

CHAPTER I

I was very happy when a child; and I love now to do all in my power to promote the happiness of childhood. Yet my pleasures were all of my own creation; and I believe those children are generally the happiest, who are left to seek their own amusements. When the little grandchild of the Empress Josephine,[199] had received from his royal relatives many rich birth-day gifts, and was still observed to look dissatisfied and unhappy, he replied, in answer to their questions, "I wish you would let me go out and play in that beautiful little puddle." When I was a child, I was allowed to play in all the puddles, beautiful and not beautiful. I waded the pond for lilies, and the brooks for minnows; I roamed the fields for berries, and the meadows for flowers; I wandered in the woods for ivy-plums, and picked ising-glass[200] from the rocks; I watched the robins that built for many years their nest in the chestnut tree; and nursed, with truly motherly care, the early lambs and chickens.

I had also my dairy, where the fruit of the mallows[201] was my make-believe cheese; and my mimic store, where the shelves for china were filled with broken bits of glass and crockery-ware, and those for English goods were filled with the skins of variegated beans, in imitation of calicoes, while those of white beans were my cotton cloth. Then there was my baby-house, the tenants of which never numbered less than a dozen, made of rags, and all of the female gender.

These were my summer pleasures. In the winter, we had no time for amusement but in the evening, and then we got together and enjoyed ourselves finely. Our kitchen was a long, low one, with a great beam in the middle of the ceiling, from which depended festoons of dried apples, and bundles of herbs. In the window-corners hung strings of red peppers, and over the fireplace were our crook-necked squashes. The fire-place itself was a very wide one; and in one corner was stationed our blue-pot;[202] and in the other, the kettle in which we boiled potatoes for the cattle, and which was as big as a witch's caldron.

When there were enough of us, we played whirl-the-plate,[203] blind-man's-buff, and hurly-burly—together with many other good old-fashioned games; and our refreshments were nuts and apples, the seeds of which we exerted our skill in snapping at each other. If our number was smaller, we parched corn in the ashes; and it was fine sport to see the white kernels pop out of their warm place; or we played checkers, on a board crossed off with a coal, and with red and yellow kernels of corn for our men. Sometimes we repeated the old stories of Blue-beard, Cinderilla, Catskin, King Lab, and Jack and his bean-stalk, of which we had among us about a dozen different versions.[204]

But it was a great treat to me to listen to the queer stories of Old Bill, who had once been a sailor, and seen many different countries. The boys called him "the wandering Jew," and "my man Friday," because he had no home, but stayed with any one who would give him board and lodging for his labor.[205] If he had been as fond of working as of talking, he would have been a very profitable hand upon a farm; still he was willing to cut wood, shell corn, fodder the cattle, and do many other chores—and he was excellent company.

I was always willing to go and draw cider, as an inducement for him to stay and talk with us; and I listened with gaping mouth and eyes to his marvellous tales of Spaniards, Frenchmen, Indians, and Negroes; and though I presume they were mostly true, they appeared as wonderful to me as so many fairy tales.

But the scene of many of my youthful pleasures, was the district school-house. And now while I think of her, I must tell you about our school-ma'am, who was a spinster. She professed to hate the whole race of man-kind, and averred that she was an old maid from choice, and not from necessity; but I am sure if she had wished to marry, no one would have had her. She was so long, and sharp, and skinny, and cross, that the old folks disliked her almost as much as the young people did. She was always grumbling and growling about something or other, and was in fact one of those who take a great deal of comfort in being miserable—and in making other people so too. She was said to be the cause of many of the family quarrels in the neighborhood; had broken off a number of matches; and had been several times brought before the church for falsehood, though she was one of the most active members of all the female societies. Nevertheless, she was thought a most admirable school-mistress, because she was so *strict.* In those days, teachers were valued according to their skill in using the rod and ferula;[206] and according to this standard of excellence, Miss Prudence K. was all perfection.

I remember how she whipped me one Monday morning, because I did not courtesy to her when she passed me on her way to meeting; and one day, when she saw me looking over on the boys' side at my two cousins, she said that I must go and sit between the two boys.[207] I had observed that she saw me, and was expecting as a punishment to have to stand an hour on a crack in the floor, or stoop down and hold my finger on a nail, until it seemed as though my blood had settled in my brain, or sit on the peaked rack till the girls went out, or be soundly whipped with the long birch stick—so when I heard my sentence, I thought it by no means a severe one; but I looked as miserable as possible, for fear she would find out my real feelings; and the fear that the long face would slip off, was the only thing which kept it on.[208]

I often hear teachers lament that *they* cannot *educate* the children placed under their care. Their instructions are neutralized by the influences of home and companions; and if all teachers were what they should be, this would indeed be cause for deep regret. But I should have been a stiff, formal, selfish, unhappy being, if Miss Prudence could have changed me to what she wished me to become. If I was subdued while under her eye, when I was released there was for me a regenerating influence in the voices of my brothers, sisters and school-mates; in the songs of the birds and the hum of the bees; in the bleating of the lambs, and the cooing of the doves; and the bright sun-shine alone could make my young heart leap for joy.

CHAPTER 2

My school enjoyments did not consist in spelling long words, and doing hard sums, but in getting through with these tasks as speedily as possible; and then it was a pleasure merely to be with my little friends. I used also to amuse myself with drawing on my slate,—though my pictures were like those of very ancient times, totally desti-tute of back-ground and perspective. My houses were always in ruins, for they never stood upright, and if I made a tower, it was sure to be in imitation of the leaning one.[209] My cows always had crooked horns, and my horses looked like mules; my carriages appeared as if the in-mates would tumble out; and my men and women had longer noses, larger eyes, wider mouths, and sharper chins, than ever belonged to the heads of human beings.

But when I first mentioned our school-house, my recollections were of the happy evenings I had passed in it. It was there that we had our spelling-schools, and there the singing-schools always met. I generally attended the latter, though I was not a singer. I went as *spectator*—for my eyes were full as active as my ears.

It was not from want of inclination, that I did not use my voice. I had a pretty good ear, but there was some deficiency in my lungs, or throat, or something else. I once made a most heroic resolution to overcome the difficulty, if possible. So I took the singing book, and went out into the hay-loft, where no one could hear me. I began *fa, sol, la, fa,* (that was before the discovery of *do, ra*)—and there I stopped. However, I began again; *fa, sol, la, fa, sol*—but the *sol* was a dreadful squeak. I tried the third time; for I thought if I could only get over the top of the gamut, I could come down very respectably on the other side—but it was all in vain; and after that attempt, I gave up all hopes of ever sitting in the singing seats. But I continued to attend the school, for we had few amusements, and the girls never had to pay any thing. If they found candles, they were welcome to their instruction—and for candle-sticks, we had little square blocks of wood, with holes bored in them.

Besides the evening schools, the boys sometimes had exhibitions, as they called them—that is, they met to speak dialogues, such as Damon and Pythias, and Money makes the mare go, &c.[210] Occasionally, an overgrown lad, who looked old enough to attend town meeting, would get up and shout forth,

> "You'd scarce expect one of my age,
> To speak in public on the stage,"—[211]

and then some little six-year-older would faintly drawl out,

> "I am monarch of all I survey,
> My right there is none to dispute;
> From the centre all round to the sea,
> I am lord of the fowl and the brute."[212]

And then some bashful, white-headed fellow would get up, and, with a hysterical smile, giggle out,

> "Pity the sorrows of a poor old man,
> Whose trembling limbs have borne him to your door,"
> &c.[213]

Our fathers usually attended these *exhibitions*, and enjoyed them as much as a city beau does the theatre; but our mothers always stayed at home. Country women almost invariably confine their pleasures to their own hearths. Their hearts are in their homes, and New-England women are generally patterns of domestic excellence.

But I must not omit to notice our debating societies; for our young men used to meet at the school-house, and discuss the questions, Is deception justifiable in any case whatever? Are all mankind descended from one common parent? Is party spirit justifiable? Would a dissolution of the Union be beneficial? Ought females to be allowed the right of suffrage? I have no doubt, that if these learned worthies had submitted their decisions and the chains of reasoning which led to them, to the public, these knotty questions would have been forever set at rest.

That old school-house, the scene of so many of my youthful recollections, has been taken down, and the new one does not stand in the same place. This was done several years ago; and as I was then at home, I will tell you about it. When the district was first measured to find the central point for the school-house, it was found to be exactly at the top of a hill. So the building was erected there, and stood for many years, to exercise the climbing faculties of all the children in the district. But when it was found necessary to rebuild it, the wish prevailed that it should be placed either upon the north or south side of the hill, and not upon the top of it. The reasons were, that it was a very bleak site for a house, and wood had become more scarce and valuable.

So it was unanimously agreed that the new school-house should be under the hill; and then the question was warmly discussed, Upon which side? The people on the north side, said it should be there; and those upon the south side that it should not; and the whole district was for a time in violent commotion about it. Never did Tariff, Veto, Nullification, or Sub-treasury, produce more of a sensation in the great world beyond us, than did this important question in the little world around us. The people on the north side justly thought, that as there were more children *there,* the school-house should be built to accommodate them; but those on the south side argued, that as there were more young families there, the proportion of the school-going population which soon be in their favor.

At last it was decided to leave it to the Doctor, who was the richest man in the district, and who, on account of his great learning and active benevolence, was possessed of much influence. He had no family of his own; so it was thought he would be an impartial umpire—and as he lived on the south side, the people there thought he would decide in their favor. But the Doctor, like a kind-hearted man as he was, decided in favor of the youngsters on the north side; and the old maids, who had not before given him up as irreclaimable, now looked very blue; for they saw plainly that, it was not the Doctor's intention that any little feet should ever start from *his* house, to climb over the bleak hill.

These recollections may have been tedious, but those of you who have never lived in the country, will observe, that simple incidents can draw forth the good and evil passions of the heart, and that country villages may be the scene of much real happiness or misery. Yet I think that, in general, a rural life is most favorable to morals, and of course to happiness; and when I hear of the vice and corruption of some of our larger cities, and tremble for a moment for our liberties and institutions, I fix my thoughts on the many country homes, which are still the abodes of sterling worth and principle; and I feel that from *them* are to come the regenerating influences which are still to bless and sustain us.

Betsey.

The Whortleberry Excursion: A True Narrative

About a dozen of us, lads and lasses, had promised friend H. that on the first lowery day, we would meet him and his family, on the top of Moose Mountain, for the purpose of picking whortleberries, and of taking a view of the country around.[214] We had provided the customary complement of baskets, pails, dippers, &c.; and one morning, which promised a suitable day for our excursion, we piled ourselves into a couple of wagons, and rode to the foot of the mountain, and commenced climbing it on foot. A beaten path and spotted trees were our guides. A toilsome way we found it—some places being so steep that we were obliged to hold by the twigs, to prevent us from falling.

Three-quarters of an hour after we left our horses, we found ourselves on the whortleberry ground—some of us singing, some chatting, and all trying to see who could pick the most berries. Friend H. went from place to place among the young people, and with his social conversation gave new life to the party—while his chubby boys and rosy girls, by their nimbleness plainly told that they did not intend that any one should beat them in picking berries.

Towards noon, friend H. conducted us to a spring, where we made some lemonade, having taken care to bring plenty of lemons and sugar with us, and also bread and cheese for a lunch. Seated beneath a wide-spreading oak, we partook of our homely repast; and never in princely hall were the choicest viands eaten with a keener relish. After resting awhile, we recommenced picking berries, and in a brief space our pails and baskets were all full.

About this time, the clouds cleared away, the sun shone out in all the splendour imaginable, and bright and beautiful was the prospect. Far as the eye could reach, in a north and north-easterly direction, were to be seen fields of corn and grain, with new-mown grass-land, and potatoe plats, farm-houses, barns, and orchards—together with a suitable proportion of wood-land, all beautifully interspersed; and a number of ponds of water, in different places, and of different forms and sizes—some of them containing small islands, which added to the beauty of the scenery. The little village of Wakefield corner, which was about three miles distant, seemed to be almost under our feet;[215] and with friend H.'s spy-glass, we could see the people at work in their gardens, weeding vegetables, picking cherries, gathering flowers, &c. But not one of our number had the faculty that the old lady possessed, who, in the time of the Revolution, in looking through a spy-glass at the French fleet, brought the French-men so near, that she could hear them chatter; so we had to be content with ignorance of their conversation.

South-westerly might be seen Cropple-crown Mountain; and beyond it, Merry-meeting Pond, where, I have been told, Elder Randall, the father of the Free-will Baptist denomination, first administered the ordinance of baptism.[216] West, might be seen Tumble-down-dick Mountain;[217] and north, the Ossipee Mountains; and far north, might be seen the White Mountains of New-Hampshire, whose snow-covered summits seemed to reach the very skies.

The prospect in the other directions, was not so grand, although it was beautiful—so I will leave it, and take the shortest route, with my companions, with their baskets and pails of berries, to the house of friend H. On our way, we stopped to view the lot of rock maples, which, with some little labor, afforded a sufficient supply of sugar, for the family of friend H., and we promised that, in the season of sugar-making the next spring, we would make it convenient to visit the place, and witness the process of making maple sugar.

Our descent from the mountain was by a different path—our friends having assured us, that although our route would be farther, we should find it more pleasant; and truly we did—for the path-way was not so rough as the one in which we travelled in the morning. And besides, we had the pleasure of walking over the farm of the good Quaker, and of hearing from his own lips many interesting circumstances of his life.

The country, he told us, was quite a wilderness when he first took up his abode on the mountain; and bears, he said, were as plenty[218] as woodchucks, and destroyed much of his corn. He was a bachelor, and lived alone for a number of years after he first engaged in clearing his land. His habitation was between two huge rocks, at about seventy rods from the place where he afterwards built his house. He showed us this ancient abode of his; it was in the midst of an old orchard. It appeared as if the rocks had been originally one; but by some convulsion of nature it had been sundered, mid-way, from top to bottom. The back part of this dwelling, was a rock wall, in which there was a fire-place and an oven. The front was built of logs, with an aperture for a door-way; and the roof was made of saplings and bark. In this rude dwelling, friend H. dressed his food, and ate it; and here, on a bed of straw, he spent his lonely nights. A small window in the rock wall, admitted the light, by day; and by night, his solitary dwelling was illuminated with a pitch-pine torch.

On being interrogated respecting the cause of his living alone so long as he did, he made answer, by giving us to understand, that if he was called "the bear," he was not so much of a brute as to marry until he could give his wife a comfortable maintenance; "and moreover, I was resolved," said he, "that Hannah should never have the least cause to repent of the ready decision which she made in my favor."[219] "Then," said one of our company, "your wife was not afraid to trust herself with the bear?" "She did not hesitate in the least," said friend H.; "for when I 'popped the question,' by saying, 'Hannah, will thee have me?' she readily answered, 'Yes, To—;' she would have said 'Tobias, I will;' but the words died on her lips; and her face, which blushed like the rose, became deadly pale; and she would have fallen on the floor, had I not caught her in my arms. After Hannah got over her faintness, I told her that we had better not marry, until I was in a better way of living; to which she also agreed. And," said he, "before I brought home my bird, I had built yonder cage;" pointing to his house; "and now, neighbors, let us hasten to it; for Hannah will have her tea ready, by the time we get there." When we arrived at the house, we found that tea was ready; and the amiable Mrs. H., the wife of the good Quaker, was waiting for us, with all imaginable patience.

The room in which we took tea, was remarkably neat. The white floor was nicely sanded, and the fire-place, filled with pine tops and rose-bushes; and vases of roses were standing on the mantel-piece.[220] The table was covered with a cloth of snowy whiteness, and loaded with delicacies; and here and there stood a little China vase, filled with white and damask roses.

"So-ho!" said the saucy Henry L., upon entering the room; "I thought that you Quakers were averse to every species of decoration; but see! here is a whole flower garden!" Friend H. smiled and said, "the rose is a favorite with Hannah; and then it is like her, with one exception." "And what is that exception?" said Henry. "Oh," said our friend, "Hannah has no thorns to wound."[221] Mrs. H's heightened color and smile, plainly told us, that praise from her husband was "music to her ear." After tea, we had the pleasure of promenading through the house; and Mrs. H. showed us many articles of domestic manufacture, being the work of her own, and her daughters' hands. The articles consisted of sheets, pillow-cases, bed-quilts, coverlets of various colors, and woven in different in patterns,—such as chariot wheels, rose-of-sharon, ladies'-delight, federal constitution—and other patterns, the names of which I have forgotten. The white bed-spreads and the table covers, which were inspected by us, were equal, if not superior to those of English manufacture; in short, all that we saw, proclaimed that order and industry had an abiding place in the house of friend H.

Mrs. H. and myself seated ourselves by a window, which overlooked a young and thrifty orchard. A flock of sheep were grazing among the trees, and their lambs were gamboling from place to place. "This orchard is more beautiful than your other," said I; "but I do not suppose it contains any thing so dear to the memory of friend H., as is his old habitation." She pointed to a knoll, where was a small enclosure,[222] and which I had not before observed. "There," said she, "is a spot more dear to Tobias; for there sleep our children." "Your cup has then been mingled with sorrow?" said I. "But," replied she, "we do not sorrow without hope; for their departure was calm as the setting of yonder sun, which is just sinking from sight; and we trust that we shall meet them in a fairer world, never to part." A tear trickled down the cheek of Mrs. H., but she hastily wiped it away, and changed the conversation. Friend H. came and took a seat beside us, and joined in the conversation, which, with his assistance, became animated and amusing.

Here, thought I, dwell a couple, happily united. Friend H., though rough in his exterior, nevertheless possesses a kindly, affectionate heart; and he has a wife, whose price is above rubies.[223]

The saucy Henry soon came to the door, and bawled out, "The stage[224] is ready." We obeyed the summons, and found that Henry and friend H.'s son had been for our vehicles. We were again piled into the wagons—pails, baskets, whortleberries, and all; and with many hearty shakes of the hand, and many kind farewells, we bade adieu to the family of friend H.—but not without renewing the promise, that in the next sugar-making season, we would re-visit Moose Mountain.

Jemima.

The Sugar-Making Excursion

It was on a beautiful morning in the month of March, (one of those mornings so exhilarating that they make even age and decrepitude long for a ramble,) that friend H. called to invite me to visit his sugar-lot—as he called it—in company with the party which, in the preceding summer, visited Moose Mountain upon the whortleberry excursion.[225] It was with the pleasure generally experienced in revisiting former scenes, in quest of novelty and to revive impressions and friendships, that our party set out for this second visit to Moose Mountain.

A pleasant sleigh-ride of four or five miles brought us safely to the domicile of friend H., who had reached home an hour previously, and was prepared to pilot us to his sugar camp. "Before we go," said he, "you must one and all step within doors, and warm your stomachs with some gingered cider." We complied with his request, and after a little social chat with Mrs. H., who welcomed us with a cordiality not to be surpassed, and expressed many a kind wish that we might spend the day agreeably, we made for the sugar camp, preceded by friend H., who walked by the side of his sleigh, which appeared to be well loaded, and which he steadied with the greatest care at every uneven place in the path.

Arrived at the camp, we found two huge iron kettles suspended on a pole, which was supported by crotched stakes driven in the ground, and each half full of boiling syrup. This was made by boiling down the sap, which was gathered from troughs that were placed under spouts which were driven into rock-maple trees, an incision being first made in the tree with an auger.[226] Friend H. told us that it had taken more than two barrels of sap to make what syrup each kettle contained. A steady fire of oak bark was burning underneath the kettles, and the boys and girls, friend H.'s sons and daughters, were busily engaged in stirring the syrup, replenishing the fire, &c.

Abigail, the eldest daughter, went to her father's sleigh, and taking out a large rundlet, which might contain two or three gallons, poured the contents into a couple of pails.[227] This we perceived was milk, and as she raised one of the pails to empty the contents into the kettles, her father called out, "Ho, Abigail! has thee strained the milk?" "Yes, father," said Abigail.

"Well," said friend H., with a chuckle, "Abigail understands what she is about, as well as her mother would; and I'll warrant Hannah to make better maple sugar than any other woman in New England, or in the whole United States—and you will agree with me in that, after that sugar is turned off and cooled." Abigail turned to her work, emptied her milk into the kettles, and then stirred their contents well together, and put some bark on the fire.

"Come, Jemima,"[228] said Henry L., "let us try to assist Abigail a little, and perhaps we shall learn to make sugar ourselves; and who knows but what she will give us a 'gob' to carry home, as a specimen to show our friends; and besides, it is possible that we may have to make sugar ourselves at some time or other; and even if we do not, it will never do us any harm to know how the thing is done." Abigail furnished us each with a large brass scummer,[229] and instructed us to take off the scum as it arose, and put it into the pails; and Henry called two others of our party to come and hold the pails.

"But tell me, Abigail," said Henry, with a roguish leer, "was that milk really intended for whitening the sugar?"

"Yes," said Abigail, with all the simplicity of a Quakeress, "for thee must know that the milk will all rise in a scum, and with it every particle of dirt or dust which may have found its way into the kettles."

Abigail made a second visit to her father's sleigh, accompanied by her little brother, and brought from thence a large tin baker,[230] and placed it before the fire. Her brother brought a peck measure two-thirds full of potatoes, which Abigail put into the baker, and leaving them to their fate, returned to the sleigh, and with her brother's assistance carried several parcels, neatly done up in white napkins, into a little log hut of some fifteen feet square, with a shed roof made of slabs.[231] We began to fancy that we were to have an Irish lunch. Henry took a sly peep into the hut when we first arrived, and he declared that there was nothing inside, save some squared logs, which were placed back against the walls, and which he supposed were intended for seats. But he was mistaken in thinking that seats were every convenience which the building contained,—as will presently be shown.

Abigail and her brother had been absent something like half an hour, and friend H. had in the mean time busied himself in gathering sap, and putting it in some barrels hard by. The kettles were clear from scum, and their contents were bubbling like soap. The fire was burning cheerfully, the company all chatting merrily, and a peep into the baker told that the potatoes were cooked.

Abigail and her brother came and taking up the baker carried it inside the building, but soon returned, and placed it again before the fire. Then she called to her father, who came and invited us to go and take dinner.

We obeyed the summons; but how were we surprised, when we saw how neatly arranged was every thing. The walls of the building were ceiled[232] around with boards, and side tables fastened to them, which could be raised or let down at pleasure, being but pieces of boards fastened with leather hinges and a prop underneath. The tables were covered with napkins, white as the driven snow, and loaded with cold ham, neat's[233] tongue, pickles, bread, apple-sauce, preserves, doughnuts, butter, cheese, and *potatoes*—without which a yankee dinner is never complete. For beverage, there was chocolate, which was made over a fire in the building—there being a rock chimney in one corner. "Now, neighbors," said friend H., "if you will but seat yourselves on these squared logs, and put up with these rude accommodations, you will do me a favor. We might have had our dinner at the house, but I thought that it would be a novelty, and afford more amusement to have it in this little hut, which I built to shelter us from what stormy weather we might have in the season of making sugar."

We arranged ourselves around the room, and right merry were we, for friend H.'s lively chat did not suffer us to be otherwise. He recapitulated to us the manner of his life while a bachelor; the many bear-fights which he had had; told us how many bears he had killed; how a she-bear denned in his rock-dwelling the first winter he commenced clearing his land—he having returned home to his father's to attend school; how, when he returned in the spring, he killed her two cubs, and afterwards the old bear, and made his Hannah a present of their skins to make a muff and tippet; also his courtship, marriage, &c.

In the midst of dinner, Abigail came in with some hot mince pies, which had been heating in the baker before the fire out of doors, and which said much in praise of Mrs. H.'s cookery.

We had finished eating, and were chatting as merrily as might be, when one of the little boys called from without, "Father, the sugar has grained." We immediately went out, and found one of the boys stirring some sugar in a bowl, to cool it. The fire was raked from beneath the kettles, and Abigail and her eldest brother were stirring their contents with all haste. Friend H. put a pole within the bail[234] of one of the kettles, and raised it up, which enabled two of the company to take the other down, and having placed it in the snow, they assisted friend H. to take down the other; and while we lent a helping hand to stir and cool the sugar, friend H.'s children ate their dinners, cleared away the tables, put what fragments were left into their father's sleigh, together with the dinner dishes, tin baker, rundlet, and the pails of scum, which were to be carried home for the swine. A firkin[235] was also put into the sleigh; and after the sugar was sufficiently cool, it was put into the firkin, and covered up with great care.

After this we spent a short time promenading around the rock-maple grove, if leafless trees can be called a grove. A large sap-trough, which was very neatly made, struck my fancy, and friend H. said he would make me a present of it for a cradle. This afforded a subject for mirth. Friend H. said that we must not ridicule the idea of having sap-troughs for cradles; for that was touching quality, as his eldest child had been rocked many an hour in a sap-trough, beneath the shade of a tree, while his wife sat beside it knitting, and he was hard by, hoeing corn.

Soon we were on our way to friend H.'s house, which we all reached in safety; and where we spent an agreeable evening, eating maple sugar, apples, beech-nuts, &c. We also had tea about eight o'clock, which was accompanied by every desirable luxury—after which we started for home.

As we were about taking leave, Abigail made each of us a present of a cake of sugar, which was cooled in a tin heart.—"Heigh ho!" said Henry L., "how lucky! We have had an agreeable visit, a bountiful feast—have learned how to make sugar, and have all got sweet-hearts!"

We went home, blessing our stars and the hospitality of our Quaker friends.

I cannot close without telling the reader, that the sugar which was made that day, was nearly as white as loaf-sugar, and tasted much better.

Jemima.

Tribute to Salmagundi

Salmagundi, it appears, has excited the curiosity of very many people; and many are desirous to know something of the general character of the place. To gratify, in some measure, the curious, inquiring mind, this little tribute is offered.

The "old settlers," as the first white inhabitants were called, were a hardy, industrious people; with a fair amount of general benevolence, and self-esteem; qualities which are inherited by their descendants, and form leading traits in their characters. The misfortunes of one are, in a measure, felt by all; and they take an honest pride in performing all those little acts of kindness which, when done in a spirit of fraternity, endear the members of a community to each other.

In olden time, paupers were known only by name in Salmagundi; and I believe it would have been thought by the good people, an impeachment of their moral character, to have one of their town's-men supported at public expense. The first application for assistance from the town, is within my own remembrance. The applicant was a poor shingle-maker, who was so unfortunate as to put his shoulder out of place, and was for several months unable to work.

The first select-man of Salmagundi had long been a dealer in dry goods,[236] groceries, and all other articles usually kept in the store of a country village; and was well acquainted with the pecuniary circum- stances, and also the benevolent feelings of every one of his customers. To this man Mr. Griffin made his wants known, who, after he had heard his tale of distress, pretended to make an entry on the town books, and then supplying him with things necessary for his present comfort, told him to call again when any thing more was needed.

Saturday evening, according to their usual custom, the gentlemen of our village assembled at the grocery to talk over their affairs, and consult with each other in laying plans for the future. Some of the most wealthy and benevolent were called aside, and made acquainted with the necessities of Mr. Griffin; and, after a brief consultation, they came to the conclusion that they should not suffer so much in purse, by jointly supporting him for a short time, as they should in character by having his name on the town books as a pauper. Accordingly the grocer was authorized to supply Mr. Griffin with all things needful, at their expense.

Mr. Griffin's mortification, in consequence of being under the necessity of asking for help, together with the pain occasioned by his hurts, threw him into a fever which threatened to run high; but when he was made acquainted with the kindness of his neighbors, which was entirely unlooked for, it proved to be a more valuable restorative than medicine, and he soon became convalescent. And, what was still better, from being some given to intemperate habits, he became remarkable for his soberness.

It was a number of years after this circumstance took place, before Salmagundi had any paupers; but in process of time, through the mismanagement of his children, the farm of the old gentleman who was the bridegroom in "The first wedding of Salmagundi," was offered for sale; and its ancient owner, who still lived upon it, was thrown penniless upon the world.

The "old settlers" could not bear to see this worthy pilgrim houseless, and through their influence the town purchased the farm; thereby providing means for their friend to remain comfortable for life in his old home; and also providing a home for many others.

These things will give a more favorable impression of Salmagundi, when the fact is known, that, till within a few years, (and for aught I know to the contrary perhaps up to the present time,) paupers in the neighboring townships were set up at auction, and, not like slaves,[237] struck off to the highest bidder—but struck off to him who will keep them for the least pay—an inhuman practice, which ought to be deprecated by all who have any claims to humanity.

The people of Salmagundi are remarkable for their sobriety, general intelligence, and morality; also, for the attention paid to the education of their children, who are first of all, fitted for the common every-day affairs of life—the useful, never being neglected for the ornamental branches of education.

As a general rule, they endeavor to educate their children in the best possible manner, consistent with their circumstances and prospects,—wisely considering, that a good education is of more value than a splendid patrimony.

Some of the descendants of the "old settlers" are respected in the literary world; others are ornaments to the Bench, and Bar. Of this, Salmagundi is honestly proud, as well she may be.

The above hasty production may give some idea of the general character of Salmagundi. What exceptions there are to this character, it is no part of my business to delineate.

Tabitha.

A Winter Evening

It was one of those beautiful winter evenings, when night's silver queen[238] sheds her soft lustre on crusted snow and glittering ice, that the merry peals of laughter were heard throughout our little village; and at every door, with heart-felt glee, was sung the old ballad,—

> "Come, boys and girls, come out to play,
> The moon is a-shining as bright as day.
> Come with a whoop, and come at a call;
> Come with a good will, or not at all."[239]

The boys and girls responded to this invitation, by a simultaneous rush into the street, and with a sufficient number of hand-sleds, made all possible haste to a steep snow-bank, near the shore of a small pond, whose icy fetters were of the smoothest polish. Then commenced the delightful sport of sliding down hill, seated on a hand-sled—the boys on the front part, and the girls on the hinder part. "Hurrah!" and with the velocity of a steam-engine, down went the sleds to the foot of the hill, nor stopped until they reached the shore of the pond, and had slid no little distance over its glass-like surface.

After a while, the fatigue of climbing up hill was thought not to be sufficiently compensated by the pleasure of sliding down; and it was proposed that they should slide across the pond, and call at Dr. W.'s[240] on the opposite side. All agreed to this proposal, for right sure they were, not only of a kindly greeting, a social chat, and much good counsel, but also of apples and cider in great plenty. It was agreed upon to slide around the shore of the pond, in order to enjoy the delightful scenery of a lot of beech and maple trees, with here and there a tall hemlock and a dwarf spruce, all richly clad in a drapery of jeweled ice, which, glittering in moon-beams, seemed to vie in splendor with the spangled firmament above.

While admiring the splendor of the scene, a dark substance in a path which lay through the wood, attracted attention; and some of the younkers, upon going to ascertain what it might be, found that it was the body of a poor day laborer, who, having taken a drop too much of the "O be joyful," his usual remedy for the evils of "smoky house, and scolding wife," had sat down to soliloquize upon the delights of "home, sweet home;" and, giving way to a drowsy sensation, would no doubt have slept the sleep of death, but for the timely assistance of this playful company.

"Halloa! uncle Levi!" shouted the boys at the top of their voices. "Wake up, wake up, and help us trap a racoon,"—at the same time shaking him with all their might.

"Coon in the wood-pile," at length hiccuped the poor inebriate.

The girls took off their aprons, and lashed two of the hand-sleds together with them; then spread some of their cloaks upon the sleds, upon which the boys placed uncle Levi, (as they called him,) and wrapping him up in cloaks, made all possible haste to the hospitable mansion of Dr. W.

The good doctor thought it a fine frolic, when, *sans ceremonie,*[241] his door flew open, and some half-dozen boys entered, dragging in "uncle Levi," and followed by all the boys and girls belonging to our village; but when he learned in what a sad state "uncle Levi" was found, he administered all needful restoratives, and the boys and girls experienced the heart-felt pleasure of knowing of a truth, that with the assistance of Dr. W., they had not only saved the life of a fellow creature, but had been instrumental in reclaiming an inebriate—for "uncle Levi" from that time tasted not *strong drink.*

After seeing "uncle Levi" comfortable, and partaking of some refreshments, the young people started for home. The doctor, with true country politeness, accompanied them half way; and when he stopped to view the forest trees, all glistening in their jeweled winter-robes, he confessed that his eyes scarce saw a lovelier sight. "But," said he, musing, "Heaven beheld a lovelier sight, when so many young hearts and hands, on this very spot, were actively engaged in doing good; and surely some blessing will attend the work."

B. C.

Appendix A: Pedigree Chart

Betsey Guppy
b 29 Dec. 1797; Wolfeboro, N.H.
d 24 Sept. 1886; Wayne, Ill.
bur St. Charles, Ill.
m1 30 June 1820; Wakefield, N.H.

Spouses:
Josiah Chamberlain
Thomas Wright
Charles Boutwell
I. A. Horn

William Guppy
b 1770; Brookfield, N.H.
d 20 Aug. 1828; Wolfeboro, N.H.
bur Wolfeboro, N.H.
m unknown

Comfort Meserve
b 10 Sept. 1772; Dover, N.H.
d 14 Feb. 1802; Wolfeboro, N.H.
bur probably Wolfeboro, N.H.

Joshua Guppy
b Nov. 1739?; Beverly, Mass.
d 1806; Brookfield, N.H.
bur Brookfield, N.H.
m 1767?

Sarah Loud
b Portsmouth, N.H.
d 1822; prob. Brookfield, N.H.

Stephen Meserve
b 1750?
d 26 June 1792; Rochester, N.H.
m ca. 1795

Mary (Molly) Yeaton
b 28 Sept. 1753; Dover, N.H.
d 1 June 1849

Joshua Guppy
b unknown
d Nov. or Dec. 1739; R.I.
m 27 Jan. 1731; Beverly, Mass.
Mrs. Margaret Deveraux

Margaret Shattuck
b 22 June 1707; Salem, Mass.
d unknown

Solomon Loud
b 30 Sept. 1713
d 1762; Portsmouth, N.H.
m 7 March 1735

Abigail Dam/e
bp 22 Jan. 1717; Newington, N.H.
d unknown

Clement Meserve (Lt.)
b 1716
d 23 July 1800: Dover, N.H.

Abigail Ham
b unknown
d unknown

Samuel Yeaton
b ca. 1726; New Castle, Isles of Shoals, N.H.
d after 1765; Rochester, N.H.
m 1752

Patience
b unknown
d unknown

Joshua Guppy

Michael Bacon

Margaret Shattuck
b ca. 1674; Salem, Mass.

William Loud (1686–1708/9)
b Portsmouth, N.H.

Abigail Abbott (ca. 1680–1763)
b Portsmouth, N.H.

Moses Dam/e (1673–1754)
b Newington, N.H.

Abigail Huntress
b Bloody Point, N.H.

Daniel Meserve (1678–1756?)
b Portsmouth, N.H.

Deborah Merrow (b. 1677)
b Oyster River, N.H.

John Ham (1699–1763)
b

Abigail
d 4 Jan. 1797

Richard Yeaton (b. ca. 1698)
b New Castle, Isles of Shoals, N.H.

Hannah (Davis?) (b. ca. 1702)
b Isles of Shoals, N.H.

---

b = birthdate and place
bp = date and place of baptism
d = death date and place
m = marriage date and place
bur = burial place

Appendix B: Brief Chronology of Betsey Guppy Chamberlain's Life

1797 Born Brookfield, N.H., 29 December, the second child of William Guppy and Comfort Meserve.

1798 In June the family moves to Wolfeboro, N.H.

1802 On 14 February Comfort Meserve Guppy dies.

1803 On 7 November William Guppy remarries: Sally Marden of Wolfeboro.

1808 William Guppy briefly jailed and tried for theft; found not guilty.

1819 Betsey teaches school during summer session, Brookfield, N.H.

1820 On 25 June marries Colonel Josiah Chamberlain, a Brookfield, N.H., widower with three children.

1820–23 Two children born (precise birthdates unknown) to Josiah and Betsey.

1823 On 19 July Josiah Chamberlain dies. Betsey appointed administratrix of the estate.

1828 On 14 February successfully sues her father to recover her dower. William Guppy dies 20 August.

1830 In the federal census, Betsey recorded as a Brookfield, N.H., "free white" female head of a family, aged thirty to forty, with a boy and a girl between five and ten years old.

1831–39 On 6 March 1831, "Mrs. Betsy Chamberlin" joins the First Congregational Church, Lowell, Mass. From 1831 to 1839, with sister Harriet Guppy, works in mills in Newmarket, N.H., and Lowell, Mass. May have worked in the cloth-room and as a boardinghouse keeper. On 12 April 1834, the marriage "In Lowell, [of] Mr. Thomas Wright to Mrs. Betsey Chamberlain." The couple apparently separated.

1840–43 From October 1840 to January 1843, her writings appear in the *Lowell Offering*. On 26 March 1843, Betsey Chamberlain and Charles Boutwell, a widower, are married in Du Page County, Ill.

1848–50 From December 1848 to February 1850, Betsey lives in Lowell and contributes writings to *The New England Offering*. After February 1850, returns to Illinois to live with her husband. Recorded in federal census taken 15 October 1850 in Wayne Township, Du Page County, Ill., as the fifty-three-year-old wife of Charles Boutwell, a farmer aged fifty-eight.

1860 On 8 August recorded in federal census as a sixty-two-year-old female living in Wayne Station, Du Page County, Ill., with Charles Boutwell, a seventy-year-old farmer.

1863 Charles Boutwell dies 30 October. Betsey named administratrix of the estate.

1866 In March, signs indenture with Daniel Dunham of Wayne to recover her widow's dower. On 21 November marries I. A. Horn of Kentucky.

1870 On 11 August recorded in federal census as "Boutwell, Betsey," a seventy-three-year-old female sharing a house with forty-seven-year-old Comfort Chamberlain.

1880 Recorded in federal census taken 4 June as Betsey Boutwell, a widow and housekeeper aged eighty-two, living in Wayne Township, Du Page County, Ill., with her fifty-seven-year-old widowed daughter, Comfort Barnum.

1886 Dies 24 September in Wayne Station, Ill. Buried in unmarked grave in Little Woods Cemetery, St. Charles, Ill.

Appendix C. Chronological Listing of Writings

1840

Betsey. "A Letter about Old Maids." *Lowell Offering* Ser. 1, no. 1 (October): 4–5.

Betsey. "Recollections of an Old Maid. Number 1." *Lowell Offering* Ser. 1, no. 1 (October): 5–7.

Betsey. "Recollections of an Old Maid. Number 2." *Lowell Offering* Ser. 1, no. 2 (December): 21–22.

Tabitha. "Old Maids and Old Bachelors. Their Relative Value in Society." *Lowell Offering* Ser. 1, no. 2 (December): 30–31.

1841

Tabitha. "Christmas." *Lowell Offering* Ser. 1, no. 3 (February): 40–42.

Betsey. "Recollections of an Old Maid. Number 3." *Lowell Offering* Ser. 1, no. 4 (March): 49–52.

Tabitha. "The Last Witch of Salmagundi." *Lowell Offering* Ser. 1, no. 4 (March): 55–57.

Tabitha. "The First Wedding in Salmagundi." *Lowell Offering* 1, no. 1 (April): 16–19.

Tabitha. "A Vision of Truth." *Lowell Offering* 1, no. 2 (May): 44–45.

Jemima. "Our Physician." *Lowell Offering* 1, no. 3 (June): 70–72.

Betsey. "Recollections of My Childhood." *Lowell Offering* 1, no. 3 (June): 78–84.

Tabitha. "The Black Glove." *Lowell Offering* 1, no. 4 (July): 114–16.

Tabitha. "Origin of Small Talk." *Lowell Offering* 1, no. 5 (July 15): 159–60.

Jemima. "The Whortleberry Excursion: A True Narrative." *Lowell Offering* 1, no. 6 (August): 177–81.

Tabitha. "A New Society." *Lowell Offering* 1, no. 6 (August): 191–92.

Tabitha. "La Brainard." *Lowell Offering* 1, no. 7 (September): 203–9.

Jemima. "The Sugar-Making Excursion." *Lowell Offering* 1, no. 8 (October): 225–29.

Tabitha. "Fortune-Telling. A Narrative of Salmagundi." *Lowell Offering* 1, no. 9 (November): 257–61.

Tabitha. "The Husking." *Lowell Offering* 1, no. 10–11 (December): 292–94.

Tabitha. "The Old Farm-House." *Lowell Offering* 1, no. 12 (December 15): 362–64.

1842

B. C. "Visit to a Grave-Yard." *Lowell Offering* 2, no. 2 (February): 58–59.

Tabitha. "A Legend of the Olden Time." *Lowell Offering* 2, no. 4 (April): 102–10.

B. C. "A Winter Evening." *Lowell Offering* 2, no. 4 (April): 115–17.

Tabitha. "The First Dish of Tea." *Lowell Offering* 2, no. 5–6 (May): 143–44.

Tabitha. "Sabbath Morning." *Lowell Offering* 2, no. 7 (June): 207–8.
Tabitha. "The Indian Pledge." *Lowell Offering* 2, no. 7 (June): 215–17.
Jemima. "Prayer in a Sick-Room." *Lowell Offering* 2, no. 8–9 (July): 262–63.
Tabitha. "A Fire-Side Scene." *Lowell Offering* 2, no. 8–9 (July): 274–75.
Tabitha. "Tribute to Salmagundi." *Lowell Offering* 2, no. 8–9 (July): 285–87.
B. C. "A Reverie." *Lowell Offering* 2, no. 10 (July 15): 318–19.
Tabitha. "Witchcraft." *Lowell Offering* 2, no. 11–12 (August): 335–37.
B. C. "The Delusion of the Heart." *Lowell Offering* 2, no. 11–12 (August): 337–48.

1843
Betsey. "Cousin Mary." *Lowell Offering* 3, no. 4 (January): 89–95.

1848
Betsey, Lowell. "Our Town: How It Looked." *New England Offering* 6, no. 9 (December): 203–4.

1849
"Our Town. Number 2. Our Meeting-House" (continued from vol. 6). *New England Offering* 7, no. 8 (August): 183–86.
Lowell. "Our Town. Number 3. Our Pulpit." *New England Offering* 7, no. 9 (September): 210–11.

1850
Betsey. "Aunt 'Dear Soul.'" *New England Offering* 8, no. 2 (February): 29–31.

Notes

Preface

1. Harriet Hanson Robinson, *Loom and Spindle; or, Life among the Early Mill Girls*, rev. ed. (1898; reprint, Kailua, Hawaii: Pacifica Press, 1976), 86.
2. Harriet Hanson Robinson, "Names and *Noms de Plume* of the Writers in *The Lowell Offering*" (1902), in Judith A. Ranta, *Women and Children of the Mills: An Annotated Guide to Nineteenth-Century American Textile Factory Literature* (Westport, Conn.: Greenwood Press, 1999), 299.

Biographical and Critical Introduction

1. Betsey Chamberlain, "Recollections of an Old Maid. Number 1," p. 164; subsequent page references from Chamberlain's writings will appear in parentheses. The page numbers refer to this volume.
2. Robinson, *Loom and Spindle*, 86.
3. Nancy Lecompte, "Molly Ockett: Abenaki Healing Woman," *Ne-Do-Ba*, online, Internet, available: http://www.avcnet.org/ne-do-ba/bio_moly.html (28 July 2002); Trudy Ann Parker, *Aunt Sarah, Woman of the Dawnland: The 108 Winters of an Abenaki Healing Woman* (Lancaster, N.H.: Dawnland Publications, 1994), 5, 28–29; Robinson, *Loom and Spindle*, 86.
4. Robinson, *Loom and Spindle*, 75.
5. Claudia L. Bushman, *"A Good Poor Man's Wife": Being a Chronicle of Harriet Hanson Robinson and Her Family in Nineteenth Century New England* (Hanover, N.H.: University Press of New England, 1981); Bernice Selden, *The Mill Girls: Lucy Larcom, Harriet Hanson Robinson, Sarah G. Bagley* (New York: Atheneum, 1983); Shirley Marchalonis, *The Worlds of Lucy Larcom, 1824–1893* (Athens: University of Georgia Press, 1989).
6. Harriet Farley, *Shells from the Strand of the Sea of Genius* (Boston: James Munroe, 1847); Harriot F. Curtis, *S.S.S. Philosophy* (Lowell: Merrill and Heywood, 1847); Lucy Larcom, *The Poetical Works of Lucy Larcom* (Boston: Houghton, Mifflin, 1884); Abba A. Goddard, *Gleanings. Some Wheat—Some Chaff* (New York: D. Appleton, 1856).
7. Massachusetts, Commissioners to Examine into the Condition of the Indians in the Commonwealth, *Report of the Commissioners Relating to the Condition of the Indians in Massachusetts* (Boston: n.p., 1849).
8. Colin G. Calloway, "Introduction: Surviving the Dark Ages," in *After King Philip's War: Presence and Persistence in Indian New England* (Hanover, N.H.: University Press of New England, 1997), 8. See also Laurel Thatcher Ulrich, *The Age of Homespun: Objects and Stories in the Creation of an American Myth* (New York: Knopf, 2001), 354.
9. Calloway, "Introduction: Surviving the Dark Ages," 7–8.
10. Karen L. Kilcup, "Writing 'The Red Woman's America': An Introduction to Writing by Earlier Native American Women," in *Native American Women's Writing, 1800–1924:*

An *Anthology* (Oxford: Blackwell, 2000), 2–3; Kenneth M. Roemer, introduction to *Native American Writers of the United States* (Detroit: Gale, 1997), xii; Robinson, *Loom and Spindle*, 86. Nicholas Guppy, "Genealogy of the Guppy Family," unpublished typescript held by the Dover, N.H., Public Library, 1990, records that Joshua Guppy married "Sarah, an Abenaki Indian woman." See also Guppy family correspondence in the possession of Jill Cresey-Gross, Westford, Mass., March 2000.

11. "Ne-Do-Ba (Friends)," online, Internet, available: http://avcnet.bates.edu/ne-do-ba/ (28 July 2002); Roemer, Introduction, xii; Robinson, *Loom and Spindle*, 86.

12. Roemer, introduction, xii.

13. Evan T. Pritchard (Micmac), *No Word for Time: The Way of the Algonquin People* (Tulsa, Okla.: Council Oak Books, 1997), 106.

14. On New England Native women's dispossession, see Jean M. O'Brien, "'Divorced' from the Land: Resistance and Survival of Indian Women in Eighteenth-Century New England," in Calloway, *After King Philip's War*, 144–61; Calloway, "Introduction: Surviving the Dark Ages," 9.

15. Harriet Hanson Robinson and Harriette Lucy Robinson Shattuck, Papers, 1833–1937, Schlesinger Library, Radcliffe College, 29:19.

16. Frank B. Sanborn, *New Hampshire: An Epitome of Popular Government* (Boston: Houghton, Mifflin, 1904), 138–39.

17. In "Cousin Mary," Chamberlain's narrator-self comments, "I felt my own more turbulent spirit rebuked by the meekness of [Mary]" (p. 147), and in "Christmas," the narrator discloses her vulnerability to "gloomy sadness" (p. 182).

18. Benjamin F. Parker, *History of the Town of Wolfeborough, New Hampshire* (1901; reprint, Wolfeboro, N.H.: Wolfeboro Historical Society, 1988), 300.

19. Parker, *History of the Town of Wolfeborough*, 107; Charles T. Libby, *The Libby Family in America: 1602–1881* (1882; reprint, Salem, Mass.: Higginson Books, 1991), 128. This wedding story seems to have been more legend than fact. According to John R. Ham's *Dover, New Hampshire, Marriages, 1623–1823* (Dover, N.H., 1904), 136, Reuben Libbey and Sarah Goss were married by Rev. Joseph Adams in Dover on 1 July 1754.

20. Henry Lorne Masta, *Abenaki Indian Legends, Grammar and Place Names* (Victoriaville, P.Q.: La Voix des boisfrancs, 1932), 101; Parker *History of the Town of Wolfeborough*, 43. See, for instance, "Our Physician," in which Chamberlain's narrator recalls that when the town "physician was an old man, . . . I was quite a child" ("Our Physician," *Lowell Offering* 1, no. 3 [June 1841]: 70), and "Recollections of My Childhood," describing early childhood experiences. See also Q. David Bowers, *History of Wolfeboro, New Hampshire, 1770–1994*, 2 vols. (Wolfeboro, N.H.: Wolfeboro Historical Society, 1996), 1:33.

21. George M. Bodge, *Soldiers in King Philip's War* (1906; reprint, Baltimore: Genealogical Publishing Company, 1967), 295; Calloway, "Introduction: Surviving the Dark Ages," 13.

22. Robert S. Canney, *The Early Marriages of Strafford County, New Hampshire, 1630–1850*, 2 vols. (Bowie, Md.: Heritage Books, 1995), 1:213; New Hampshire, *Provincial and State Papers*, 40 vols. (Concord, N.H.: Published by authority of the legislature of New Hampshire, 1867–1942), 11:508–9; Jay Mack Holbrook, *New Hampshire 1732 Census* (Oxford, Mass.: Holbrook Research Institute, 1981), 40; Mary P. Thompson, *Landmarks in Ancient Dover, New Hampshire*, complete ed. (1892; reprint, Durham, N.H.: Durham Historic Association, 1964), 93; Walter Bryent, "Walter Bryent's Winnipesaukee Journal,

1747," *The New-England Historical and Genealogical Register* 32 (1878): 301. See Colin G. Calloway, *Dawnland Encounters: Indians and Europeans in Northern New England* (Hanover, N.H.: University Press of New England, 1991), 217–18.

23. Bowers, *History of Wolfeboro*, 1:36–44.

24. John Greenleaf Whittier, "To the National Era," 1853, in *The Letters of John Greenleaf Whittier*, ed. John B. Pickard (Cambridge, Mass.: Belknap Press of Harvard University, 1975), 2 (1846–60): 228.

25. Canney, *The Early Marriages of Strafford County, New Hampshire*, 1:129; John S. Fipphen, *Cemetery Inscriptions, Wolfeboro, New Hampshire* (Bowie, Md.: Heritage Books, 1993), 166; Albert D. Rust, *Record of the Rust Family* (Waco, Tex.: A. Rust, 1891), 96.

26. Brookfield (N.H.) Town Record Book, 1:148 (1797), 1:152 (1798); Canney, *The Early Marriages of Strafford County*, 1:130.

27. Wolfeboro (N.H.) Town Records, 1:363 (7 November 1803), 371 (11 June 1802).

28. See Bowers, *History of Wolfeboro*, 1:34, and Parker, *History of the Town of Wolfeborough*, 43–44.

29. Howard Parker Moore, *A Genealogy of the First Five Generations in America of the Lang Family* (Rutland, Vt.: Tuttle Co., 1935), 72; Joshua Guppy's birth is recorded in *Vital Records of Beverly, Massachusetts* (Topsfield, Mass.: Topsfield Historical Society, 1906), 1:160. Joshua, the son of Joshua (d. 1739?) and Margaret Bacon Devereux Guppy, was baptized in the First Parish Unitarian Church, Beverly, on 4 November 1739, so he was probably born not long before that. According to Beverly, Mass., death records, Joshua Sr. died in Rhode Island between 16 November and 10 December 1739. Since Rhode Island was the home of the Narragansett, whose religious beliefs Betsey Chamberlain represented in "The Indian Pledge" and "Visit to a Grave-Yard," Joshua Sr.'s death in Rhode Island suggests he may have had some connection with the Narragansett ("A List of Deaths in Beverly, Made by Col. Robert Hale," *Essex Institute Historical Collections* 5 [1863]: 21). The vital records of Marblehead, Mass., include the marriage of John Devereux and Margaret Bacon on 25 April 1726 (*Vital Records of Marblehead, Massachusetts* [Salem, Mass.: Essex Institute, 1903–1908], 2:117). By 1729, Margaret "Devoreux" was a Salem widow (*Essex Institute Historical Collections*, 16:15). The Bond of Administration of Estate of Joshua Guppy Late of Beverly [Mass.] Deceased, 15 April 1740 (#11984), is signed by Margaret Guppy (her mark), Michael Bacon, and Robert Smith. Margaret Bacon, born 22 June 1707 in Salem, Mass., had a brother Michael, born 30 September 1705 in Salem. Based on this evidence, I think that the widow, Margaret Bacon Devereux, became Joshua Guppy Sr.'s wife on 27 January 1731.

30. Clarence E. Dame, "Descendants of Dea. John Dam of Dover, N.H.," *The New England Historical and Genealogical Register* 111 (1957): 45–55. Dame notes that Abigail Dam, the daughter of Moses Dam and Abigail Huntress Dam, was born in Dover, N.H., and baptized on 22 January 1716.

31. Carolyn D. Chase, John E. Bowker, and Ann Bailey Pinkham, *Our Yesterdays: The Story of Brookfield, New Hampshire* (Brookfield: Queen's Bay Publishing, 1999), 33, 108, 413; Donna-Belle Garvin and James L. Garvin, *On the Road North of Boston: New Hampshire Taverns and Turnpikes, 1700–1900* (Concord, N.H.: New Hampshire Historical Society, 1988), 112–13.

32. Parker, *History of the Town of Wolfeborough*, 523; Harrison Moore, Wolfeboro Historical Society, conversation with author, Wolfeboro, N.H., 19 July 1999.

33. John S. Fipphen, *1798 Direct Tax, New Hampshire District #13* (Bowie, Md.: Heritage Books, 1989), 26–27; Wolfeboro (N.H.) Town Records, 1:376; Strafford County (N.H.) Probate Records, William Guppy's Will (24 November 1826), 39:109–16; Parker, *History of the Town of Wolfeborough*, 137, 403, 413–14.

34. Stearns, Ezra S., ed. *Genealogical and Family History of the State of New Hampshire* (1908; reprint, West Jordan, Utah: Stemmons Publishing, 1990), 2:782.

35. At the New Hampshire Bureau of Vital Records in Concord, there is no marriage on record for a Joshua Guppy in the 1700s, but early records are incomplete.

36. Lowds, Guppys, Evans, and Smith to Walden, Strafford County (N.H.) Registry of Deeds (17 October 1779), 3:427.

37. Moore, *A Genealogy of the First Five Generations*, 72; Portsmouth (N.H.) Town Records, 16:633, 17:4, 152, 224, 292; Chase, Bowker, and Pinkham, *Our Yesterdays*, 33, 48, 413; Brookfield (N.H.) Town Records, unpublished (New Hampshire State Library, Concord), 1:323–24, 442, 2:19, 124, 216, 268, 33, 49–50.

38. Wolfeboro (N.H.) Town Records, 1:371 (11 June 1802).

39. Church of Jesus Christ of Latter-day Saints, *Family Search International Genealogical Index*, online, Internet, available: http://www.familysearch.org (8 August 2002), film 458306, IGI record: Comfort Meserve. Although Canney's *Early Marriages of Strafford County* records that Stephen Meserve (b. 1750), the son of Lt. Clement Meserve, married Abigail Yeaton (2:363), probate documents identify his wife as "Molly," a nickname for Mary (Strafford County [N.H.] Probate Registry, Division of Stephen Meserve's Estate, 5:387); Helen F. Evans, *Abstracts of the Probate Records of Strafford County, N.H., 1771–1799* (Bedford, N.H.: H. F. Evans, 1983), 186–87; "Yeaton. Mary Yeaton," *Boston Transcript Genealogical Columns* 7719 (10 October 1928); Martin E. Hollick, personal communication with author, 17 May 2000.

40. Stearns, *Genealogical and Family History*, 2:644–45; Bowers, *History of Wolfeboro*, 1:35; Franklin McDuffee, *History of the Town of Rochester, New Hampshire, from 1722 to 1890* (Manchester, N.H.: J. B. Clarke Co., 1892), 2:611; Strafford County (N.H.) Registry of Deeds, Hopley Meserve (20 March 1829), 138:54; Strafford County (N.H.) Probate Registry, Inventory of Stephen Meserve's Estate (27 September 1792), 3:440.

41. Strafford County (N.H.) Probate Registry, Clement Meserve's Will (9 March 1793), 6:189; One passage of Abigail Meserve's will reads: "I give and bequeath to my beloved daughter, Abigail Pinkham, the wife of James Pinkham, a certain tract or parcel of land lying in Dover and Madbury [N.H.], containing twenty-nine acres, with the dwelling house and buildings thereon, and which fell to me by heirship from my mother Abigail Ham." Strafford County (N.H.) Probate Records, Abigail Meserve's Last Will and Testament (4 November 1826), 6:467; Ham, *Dover New Hampshire Marriages*, 83. In *Vital Records of Dover, New Hampshire* (1894; reprint, Bowie, Md.: Heritage Books, 1977), records appear for Abigail Ham, mother and daughter. On 16 June 1728, "Abigail, Wife of John Ham, & their Child'n, Elizabeth & Abigail" were baptized by Rev. Jonathan Cushing, First Church, Dover, N.H. (138).

42. See "The Meserve Family" for Daniel Meserve's forebears. See *Vital Records of Dover, New Hampshire*, 49, 139, 202, and *passim*.

43. Brookfield (N.H.) Town Record Book, 1 (1797):148; 1 (1798):152.

44. Guppy v. Hanson & al., New Hampshire, Superior Court of Judicature (Strafford County), Court Records, 5 (1799–1803): 365–66.

45. Guppy v. Rust, New Hampshire, Superior Court of Judicature (Strafford County), Court Records, 8 (1808): 244–45.

46. State v. Guppy, New Hampshire, Superior Court of Judicature (Strafford County), Court Records, 8 (1808): 325–27.

47. Guppy v. Mason, New Hampshire, Superior Court of Judicature (Strafford County), Court Records, 9 (1811): 128–35; Guppy v. Mason, New Hampshire, Superior Court of Judicature (Strafford County), Court Records, 9 (1813): 405–13.

48. Seavey v. Guppy, New Hampshire, Superior Court of Judicature (Strafford County), Court Records, 12 (1820): 4–8.

49. State v. Guppy, New Hampshire, Superior Court of Judicature (Strafford County), Court Records, 17 (1823): 366–67; Drew & Ux. v. Guppy, New Hampshire, Superior Court of Judicature (Strafford County), Court Records, 22 (1828): 437–38.

50. Richards v. Guppy, New Hampshire, Superior Court of Judicature (Strafford County), Court Records, 22 (1826): 43–44; Richards v. Guppy, New Hampshire, Superior Court of Judicature (Strafford County), Court Records, 22 (1826): 54.

51. Richards v. Guppy, New Hampshire, Superior Court of Judicature (Strafford County), Court Records, 22 (1826–27): 150–52; Strafford County (N.H.), Probate Records, William Guppy's Will (24 November 1826), 39:110; Chase, Bowker, and Pinkham, *Our Yesterdays*, 189.

52. Guppy & ux. v. Guppy, New Hampshire, Superior Court of Judicature (Strafford County), Court Records 22 (1827): 228–29; Guppy v. Guppy, New Hampshire, Superior Court of Judicature (Strafford County), Court Records, 22 (1827–28): 241.

53. Drew & Ux. v. Guppy, New Hampshire, Superior Court of Judicature (Strafford County), Court Records, 22 (1828): 437–38; Chamberlin v. Guppy, New Hampshire, Superior Court of Judicature (Strafford County), Court Records, 22 (1828): 443–44; Langley v. Guppy, New Hampshire, Superior Court of Judicature (Strafford County), Court Records, 22 (1828): 444–45.

54. File on schoolteachers, Brookfield (N.H.) Town Records, 1819.

55. Harriet Farley, "Editorial," *Lowell Offering* 5, no. 8 (August 1845): 188. For other factory women's unfavorable schoolteaching experiences, see Eliza Jane Cate, "Lights and Shadows of Factory Life in New England: Emma Hale," *The New World*, extra series 51, no. 2.27 (February 1843): 7–24; Lura, "Myra, the Factory Girl," *The Operatives' Magazine* 2 (July–August 1842): 69–71, 81–87; and Matilda, "Ann and Myself: No Fiction," *Lowell Offering* 1, no. 3 (June 1841): 74–78.

56. Wolfeboro (N.H.) Town Records, 1:713; Canney, *The Early Marriages of Strafford County*, 1:130; Wakefield (N.H.) Town Records, 1:630; Marjorie G. H. Banks, *Through the Open Doors of the First Congregational Church, Wakefield, New Hampshire* (Wakefield, N.H.: M. G. H. Banks, 1985), 143; Charles Burleigh, *The Genealogy of the Burley or Burleigh Family* (Portland, Maine: B. Thurston & Co., 1880), 29; Craig F. Evans, Brookfield (N.H.) Town Archivist, personal communication with author, 22 March 2000; *New Hampshire 1830 Federal Census*, Strafford County, reel 78, p. 430; Chandler E. Potter, *The Military History of the State of New Hampshire, 1623–1861*, 2 vols. in 1 (Baltimore: Genealogical Publishing Company, 1972), 2:253; Craig F. Evans, Brookfield (N.H.) Town Archivist, personal communication with author, 22 March 2000.

57. Strafford County (N.H.) Registry of Deeds, 109:404; Strafford County (N.H.) Probate Records, Administration, 29 December 1820; Chase, Bowker, and Pinkham, *Our Yesterdays*, 109, 408.

58. Craig F. Evans, Brookfield (N.H.) Town Archivist, personal communication with author, 19 March 2000; Strafford County (N.H.) Probate Records, Administration, 5 September 1823; Brookfield (N.H.) Town Records, 2:406.

59. Strafford County (N.H.) Probate Records, Inventory of Josiah Chamberlain's Estate, 31:76 (13 October 1823); Strafford County (N.H.) Probate Records, Administration Account, Josiah Chamberlain's Estate, 25 May 1824.

60. Strafford County (N.H.) Probate Records, William Guppy's Will (24 November 1826), 39:113–14.

61. Chamberlin v. Guppy, New Hampshire, Superior Court of Judicature (Strafford County), Court Records, 22 (1828): 443–44; Strafford County (N.H.), Probate Records, Inventory William Guppy's Estate, 38 (16 October 1828): 176.

62. Marylynn Salmon, *Women and the Law of Property in Early America* (Chapel Hill: University of North Carolina Press, 1986), 141, 143; Langley v. Guppy, New Hampshire. Superior Court of Judicature (Strafford County), Court Records, 22 (1828): 444–45; "Marriages and Deaths: Wakefield, N.H., 1784–1834," unpublished typescript microfilmed by the Genealogical Society (Salt Lake City, Utah, 1952): 36.

63. Strafford County (N.H.) Probate Records, William Guppy's Will, 39:109 (4 November 1826), and Administration Account.

64. *New Hampshire 1830 Federal Census*, Strafford County, reel 78, p. 430.

65. See "Native American Genealogy," State Historical Society of Missouri, online, Internet, available: http://www.system.missouri.edu/shs/nativeam.html (28 July 2002).

66. See Strafford County (N.H.) Registry of Deeds records.

67. Chase, Bowker, and Pinkham, *Our Yesterdays*, 39.

68. Brookfield (N.H.) Tax Assessment Books, March 1832 and March 1833.

69. Strafford County (N.H.) Registry of Deeds, 151:527, 164:109, 174:459. Joseph L. Beckett, *The Exeter, New Market, and South New Market Directory* (Boston: D. Dudley, 1872), 100; Nellie Palmer George, *Old Newmarket, New Hampshire: Historical Sketches* (Exeter, N.H.: News-Letter Press, 1932), 83; Sylvia Fitts Getchell, *The Tide Turns on the Lamprey: Vignettes in the Life of a River: A History of Newmarket, N.H.* (Newmarket: S. F. Getchell, 1984), 67; Strafford County (N.H.) Registry of Deeds, 164:109, 174:459.

70. George, *Old Newmarket, New Hampshire*, 68, 72–76, 88, 64; "Lines for Newmarket," *The Gleaner* (Manchester, N.H.), 8 February 1845, lines 21–24; B. C., "A Reverie," p. 131.

71. Robinson, *Loom and Spindle*, 86.

72. L. T. H., "A Letter to Cousin Lucy," *Lowell Offering* 5, no. 5 (May 1845): 109.

73. Thanks to Nancy Lecompte for first suggesting this idea.

74. Lucy Larcom, *A New England Girlhood: Outlined from Memory* (1889; reprint, Boston: Northeastern University Press, 1986), 165; Harriet Farley, "Scenes on the Merrimac," in *Shells from the Strand*, 220; Robinson, *Loom and Spindle*, 22–23.

75. *Lowell Directory* (1845), 23; *Hand-Book for the Visiter to Lowell* (Lowell, Mass.: D. Bixby and Co., 1848), 8, 36.

76. For this information I am indebted to Barbara F. Reed, Church Historian, Christ Church United in Lowell, Mass.

77. "Marriages," *Columbian Centinel* (Boston), 18 April 1834. According to the Office

of the City Clerk, Lowell, Massachusetts, they were married on 12 April 1834. "Married," *Lowell Mercury* (Lowell, Mass.), 18 April 1834.

78. Robinson, *Loom and Spindle*, 75, 86.

79. William Richard Cutter, comp., *New England Families, Genealogical and Memorial*, 4 vols. (Baltimore: Clearfield Co., 1994), 4:2290; Parker, *History of the Town of Wolfeborough*, 394.

80. Benjamin Floyd, *Supplement to the Lowell Directory: Containing the Names of the Females Employed* (Lowell, Mass.: Leonard Huntress, 1836), 172; *Massachusetts 1840 Federal Census*, Middlesex County, reel 187, p. 88.

81. "New England Items: New Hampshire," *Boston Morning Journal*, 18 December 1877, 4; Harriet B. Guppy Kelley, Carroll County (Ossipee, N.H.) Probate 2916, 1878–1885; *New Hampshire 1860 Federal Census*, Carroll County, reel 667, p. 493.

82. *Hand-Book for the Visiter to Lowell*, 20–21; Larcom, *New England Girlhood*, 228–31, 233.

83. *Massachusetts 1840 Federal Census*, Middlesex County, reel 187, p. 88.

84. Robinson, *Loom and Spindle*, 86; Craig F. Evans, Brookfield (N.H.) Town Archivist, personal communication with author, 19 March 2000; Georgia Drew Merrill, ed., *History of Carroll County, New Hampshire* (Boston: W. A. Fergusson & Co., 1889), 459.

85. "The Death-List of a Day. An Eminent New York Journalist Is Dead," *New York Times*, 10 March 1881, 5; "Obituary. Ivory Chamberlain, Journalist," *New York Herald*, 10 March 1881; "Obituary. Ivory Chamberlain," *New-York Daily Tribune*, 10 March 1881.

86. "Obituary. Ivory Chamberlain, Journalist," *New York Herald*, 10 March 1881. Although Thomas Chamberlain is identified in his family's probate records as a "Capt.," according to United States military records Thomas Chamberlain (1758–1815) served two years (1777–79) as a private in the Revolution (National Archives and Records Service, Revolutionary War Pension and Bounty-Land-Warrant Application File, Thomas Chamberlain [of Brookfield, N.H.] Pension File). No reference to Capt. Ivory Chamberlain could be found in National Archives and Records Service Revolutionary War records.

87. See Chase, Bowker, and Pinkham, *Our Yesterdays*, 433; "Miss Esther M. Meserve. 40392," National Society of the Daughters of the American Revolution, *Lineage Book*, Mary Ellis Augsbury, Historian General (Washington, D.C., 1915), 41:150.

88. Some genealogy for Ivory Chamberlain's family has been recovered. Ivory married Mary Diana Ingalls of Cooperstown, N.Y., on 29 November 1849. They had two children, Samuel Selwyn (1851–1916) and Elizabeth (d. 1936 in Chappaqua, N.Y.). Samuel married Mary T. Munson in 1873. See James S. Featherston, "Samuel S. Chamberlain (25 Sept 1851–25 January 1916)," in *American Newspaper Journalists, 1901–1925*, ed. Perry J. Ashley (Detroit: Gale Research Co., 1984), 38–42.

89. In the 1840 census for Kane County, Illinois, Charles Boutwell, a farmer between 50 and 60 years of age, was the head of a household of six younger people, aged 1 to 30. If his age is noted correctly, Charles Boutwell would have been born before 1792. See *Illinois 1840 Federal Census*, Kane County, reel 62, p. 2. In the 1820 census, a free white farmer, Charles Boutwell, aged 27–45, is recorded as living in Concord, New York, with one free white female aged 16–26 and one free white female child under age 10. Since Betsey's husband was born in 1792, he would have been 28 in 1820, so the Concord farmer could be her husband. See *New York 1820 Federal Census*, Niagara County, reel 69, p. 128; "Obituary. Ivory Chamberlain, Journalist," *New York Herald*, 10 March 1881; Ruth

Flesher Robb, "1850 Du Page County, Illinois, Federal Census" (typescript, November 1976), 190; *War of 1812 Muster Rolls*, roll 21.

90. *Lowell Offering* 5, no. 12 (December 1845): inside back cover; Robinson, *Loom and Spindle*, 68; also 92–114; Marchalonis, *The Worlds of Lucy Larcom*, 11.

91. Du Page County Courthouse (Wheaton, Ill.), Marriage license no. 116, vol. ooA; Harriet B. Guppy Kelley, Carroll County (Ossipee, N.H.), Probate 2916, 1878–1885; "Illinois Public Land Purchase Records," 685:209 (12 July 1844); Deed, Grantee: Charles Boutwell, Grantor: Solomon Dunham, Du Page County (Ill.) Recorder's Office (26 April 1843), 20:336; Deed, Grantee: Charles Boutwell, Grantor: Solomon Dunham, Du Page County (Ill.) Recorder's Office (29 November 1845), 20:338; Deed, Grantee: Charles Boutwell, Grantor: James Littlewood, Du Page County (Ill.) Recorder's Office (1849), 20:338; Tannisse T. Blatchford, *An Honorable Heritage: A Biography of Wayne Township, Illinois, 1834–1984* (Wayne, Ill.: Wayne Community Association, 1984), 18.

92. Hattie G. Glos and Frederick S. Weiser, *Wayne Community and Township History*, rev. and enl. ed. ([Glen Ellyn?] Ill.: Priv. print., 1953), 20–23.

93. Robinson and Shattuck, Papers, 29:16.

94. Daniel D. Addison, *Lucy Larcom: Life, Letters, and Diary* (Boston: Houghton, Mifflin, 1895), 21–27.

95. Glos and Weiser, *Wayne Community and Township History*, 15.

96. *Illinois 1860 Federal Census*, Du Page County, reel 175, p. 374; Frederick S. Weiser, ed., *Genealogical and Historical Records of Wayne Township, Volume 1, Genealogical* (Wayne, Ill.: Wayne Township, 1953), 60.

97. Marriage license no. 116, Du Page County (Ill.), Charles Boutwell and Betsey Chamberlain (26 March 1843); Glos and Weiser, *Wayne Community and Township History*, 35; Marriage license no. 4386, Du Page County (Ill.), I. A. Horn and Betsey Boutwell, 20 November 1866.

98. Glos and Weiser, *Wayne Community and Township History*, 7–9, 41; Blatchford, *Honorable Heritage*, 1; Rufus Blanchard, *History of Du Page County, Illinois* (Chicago: O. L. Baskin, 1882), 271.

99. Blatchford, *Honorable Heritage*, 6–8; Du Page County (Ill.) Recorder's Office, Warranty deed no. 18625 (3 January 1854), Grantor: Charles Boutwell, Grantee: Jona B. Haviland, book 28, p. 557; C. W. Richmond, *A History of the County of Du Page, Illinois* (1857; reprint, Naperville, Ill.: Naperville Sun, 1974), 170–71; Du Page County (Ill.), County Court, Inventory—Charles Boutwell's Estate (18 January 1864), 9:443.

100. *Illinois 1850 Federal Census*, Wayne Township, Du Page County, reel 105, p. 107; *Illinois 1860 Federal Census*, Wayne Township, Du Page County, reel 175, p. 359.

101. Du Page County (Ill.) Probate Records, Inventory of Charles Boutwell's Estate and Appraiser's Estimate for the Widow (21 January 1864), 10:250.

102. Deed and Agreement. Grantor: Daniel Dunham. Grantee: Betsey Boutwell. Du Page County (Ill.) Recorder's Office, no. 7364 (1866), 29: 582–83.

103. *Illinois 1870 Federal Census*, Wayne Township, Du Page County, reel 217, p. 526.

104. Marriage License, State of Illinois, Du Page County, no. 4386 (21 November 1866); *Illinois 1870 Federal Census*, Wayne Township, Du Page County, reel 217, p. 526.

105. *Illinois 1860 Federal Census*, St. Charles, Kane County, reel 191, p. 238. Austin and Comfort Barnum's children are listed as George H., age eight and born in Illinois; Mary C., age five and born in Illinois; and Allice O., female age nine months and born in

Illinois. The household also includes Josephine Harrison (?), age fifteen and born in Sweden; *Illinois 1880 Federal Census*, Wayne Township, Du Page County, reel 203, p. 178.

106. L. G. Bennett, E. A. Lyons, and H. Brooks, comps., "Map of Du Page County, Illinois" (1862; reprint, Wheaton: Du Page County Historical Society, 19—?); Thompson Brothers & Burr, "Map of Wayne Township," *Combination Atlas Map of Du Page County, Illinois* (1874; reprint, Wheaton: Du Page County Historical Society, 1975), 98–99; "Wayne," *Wheaton Illinoian*, 1 October 1886, [8].

107. *Illinois 1870 Federal Census*, Wayne Township, Du Page County, reel 217, p. 526; *Illinois 1880 Federal Census*, Wayne Township, Du Page County, reel 203, pp. 178–79.

108. "Wayne Center Cemetery. History of Cemetery," unpublished manuscript held at the Wayne (Ill.) Town Building; Blatchford, *Honorable Heritage*, 17.

109. See the following issues of the *Wheaton Illinoian* (Wheaton, Ill.), held by the Wheaton Public Library: 6 March 1885, 13 March 1885, 3 April 1885, 9 October 1885, 16 October 1885, and 28 May 1886.

110. "Wayne," *Wheaton Illinoian*, 1 October 1886, 8; *Illinois 1870 Federal Census*, Wayne Township, Du Page County, reel 217, p. 526; *Illinois 1880 Federal Census*, Wayne Township, Du Page County, reel 203, p. 178–79; Thompson Brothers & Burr, "Map of Wayne Township," 1874; Blatchford, *Honorable Heritage*, 25.

111. St. Charles (Ill.) Township, Cemetery Department, telephone conversation with author, 5 June 2001.

112. Elias Cornelius, *The Little Osage Captive, an Authentic Narrative* (Boston: Samuel T. Armstrong and Crocker & Brewster; New York: John P. Haven, 1822), 91; H. F. [Harriet Farley (m. Dunlevy or Donlevy)], "Editorial: The Factory Girls and Their Magazine," *Lowell Offering* 5, no. 11 (November 1845): 264; Robinson, *Loom and Spindle*, 57.

113. Cornelius, *Little Osage Captive*, 91.

114. Rufus B. Anderson, ed., *Memoir of Catharine Brown, A Christian Indian of the Cherokee Nation* (Philadelphia: American Sunday School Union, 1832), 43, 159–60.

115. Theda Perdue, introduction to *Cherokee Editor: The Writings of Elias Boudinot* (Knoxville: University of Tennessee Press, 1983), 15. In his chapter on Elias Boudinot, Bernd C. Peyer also contends that Boudinot was not *Poor Sarah*'s author: *The Tutor'd Mind: Indian Missionary-Writers in Antebellum America* (Amherst: University of Massachusetts Press, 1997), 222.

116. *Poor Sarah; or, The Indian Woman* (1820; reprint, New York: American Tract Society, [between 1827 and 1833]), 2; Perdue, introduction to *Cherokee Editor*, 6; *Poor Sarah*, 3, 8.

117. *Poor Sarah*, 7, 4–5; William Apess (Pequot), *The Experiences of Five Christian Indians of the Pequot Tribe* (1833) in *On Our Own Ground: The Complete Writings of William Apess, a Pequot*, ed. and with an intro. by Barry O'Connell (Amherst: University of Massachusetts Press, 1992), 119–53.

118. Daniel F. Littlefield Jr. and James W. Parins, *American Indian and Alaska Native Newspapers and Periodicals, 1826–1924* (Westport, Conn.: Greenwood Press, 1984), 265; Kilcup, *Native American Women's Writing*, 57–58; Lowell, Mass., City Library, *Catalogue of the City School Library, Lowell, Mass., Established May 20, 1844* (Lowell, Mass.: Courier Steam Press, 1858), 5.

119. Frances H. Whipple (m. Green, m. McDougall), *Memoirs of Elleanor Eldridge*, 2d ed. (1843; reprint, Salem, N.H.: Ayer, 1971), 14, v–vii, 34, 92.

120. William J. Gilmore, *Reading Becomes a Necessity of Life: Material and Cultural Life in Rural New England, 1780–1835* (Knoxville: University of Tennessee Press, 1989), 19–20.
121. Ibid., 26, 20.
122. Parker, *History of the Town of Wolfeborough*, 413–414; Strafford County (N.H.) Probate Records, William Guppy's Inventory (16 October 1828), 38:175–84. Contents of William Guppy's library were listed as follows: "Josephus works, Holy Bible, Domestic Encyclopedia, Laws of New Hampshire, Common prayer, Paleys Philosophy, Cooks Voyages, Irish Eloquence, Napoleon Bonaparte, Morse Geography, History of United States, Robins Journal, Bells Sermons, History of Vermont, Vilage Curate, History of John Bull, Watts hymns, Sorrows of Werter, Italian Nun, Ela or the Delusion of the heart, French Convert, Robert Boyles Adventures, Constitution of Massachusetts, Hariot Newell, and Devil upon Sticks." Any of these may have been read by Chamberlain and thus could have influenced her writings.
123. Robinson, *Loom and Spindle*, 41; Elfrieda B. McCauley, "The New England Mill Girls: Feminine Influence in the Development of Public Libraries in New England, 1820–1860," Ph.D. diss., Columbia University, 1971.
124. McCauley, "New England Mill Girls," 105.
125. Middlesex Mechanic Association (Lowell, Mass.), *A Catalogue of the Library of the Middlesex Mechanic Association, at Lowell, Mass.* (Lowell, Mass.: Leonard Huntress, 1840), 113, 49, 148–49, 153, *passim*; Larcom, *New England Girlhood*, 230.
126. Lowell, Mass., First Unitarian Society, *Catalogue of Books of the Parish Library* (Lowell, Mass.: S. J. Varney, 1854), 21, 40, 10, 4, *passim*; Robinson, *Loom and Spindle*, 57.
127. D., "Female Education," *The Lady's Pearl* (Lowell, Mass.) 1 (1840), 155; Robinson, *Loom and Spindle*, 57; Lowell Circulating Library, *Catalogue of Books Contained in the Lowell Circulating Library, Connected with the Lowell Bookstore* (Lowell, Mass.: Stevens and Co., 1834), 6, 10, 25, 73.
128. Larcom, *New England Girlhood*, 237, 239; McCauley, "New England Mill Girls," 144.
129. Eliphalet Case, "A Sketch of Lowell," *Star of Bethlehem* (Lowell, Mass., and Manchester, N.H.) 13 March 1841; Susanne M. Robertson, *Programme—Lowell Musicale (1825–1900): A Musical Portrait of the Spindle City* (N.p.: Euterpe Press, 1984), 10–15, 45–47.
130. "Factory Life—Romance and Reality," *The Voice of Industry* 3.21 (3 December 1847); *Lowell Courier* 16 July 1840, 8 October 1836, 7 September 1840, 9 September 1840, 1 November 1836.
131. Bushman, *"A Good Poor Man's Wife,"* 184–85.
132. For instance, see Ella [Harriet Farley], "The Portrait Gallery. No. 1.—Pocahontas," *Lowell Offering* 3, no. 1 (October 1842): 14–20; J. S. W. [Jane S. Welch], "Plea for the Indian," *Lowell Offering* 3, no. 3 (December 1842): 56–57; M. R. G. [Marian R. Green (m. Kimball)], "The Indians," *Lowell Offering* 3, no. 7 (April 1843): 163–64; B. [Josephine L. Baker (m. Choate)], "The Indian," *Lowell Offering* 4, no. 9 (July 1844): 197–98; Frances, "The Indian Maiden," *Lowell Offering* 4, no. 9 (July 1844): 201–2; J. L. B. [Josephine L. Baker (m. Choate)], "The Indian Maiden's Revenge," *Lowell Offering* 4, no. 9 (July 1844): 205–7; and J. L. B. [Josephine L. Baker (m. Choate)], "Nepomiwassit," *Lowell Offering* 5, no. 11 (November 1845): 250–51. The most interesting and empathetic text is Pumen, "The Dark Side," *Lowell Offering* 3, no. 11 (August 1843): 246–47.
133. Lucy Larcom, "Among Lowell Mill-Girls," *Atlantic Monthly*, November 1881, 606.

134. McCauley, "New England Mill Girls," 146; Robinson, *Loom and Spindle*, 60, 98; Larcom, *New England Girlhood*, 169–73.

135. Robinson, *Loom and Spindle*, 62, 75; Editors, "A social meeting . . . ," *Lowell Offering* Ser. 1, no. 2 (December 1840): 19; H. F. [Harriet Farley], "Editorial," *Lowell Offering* 3, no. 2 (December 1843): 47.

136. Abel Charles Thomas, *Autobiography of Rev. Abel C. Thomas* (Boston: J. M. Usher, 1852), 266.

137. Robinson, *Loom and Spindle*, 77; Harriet H. Robinson, "The Life of the Early Mill-Girls," *Journal of Social Science* 16 (December 1882): 137; Abel C. Thomas, "Permanency of the Offering," *Lowell Offering* Ser. 1, no. 4 (March 1841).

138. Philip S. Foner, ed., *The Factory Girls: A Collection of Writings on Life and Struggles in the New England Factories of the 1840s by the Factory Girls Themselves* (Urbana: University of Illinois Press, 1977), 26; Abel C. Thomas, "Things Needful," *Star of Bethlehem* (Lowell, Mass., and Manchester, N.H.), 27 May 1843; Abel C. Thomas, "Editor's Valedictory," *Lowell Offering* 2, no. 11–12 (August 1842): 379–80.

139. H. F. [Harriet Farley], "Editorial," *Lowell Offering* 3, no. 2 (November 1843): 48; J. S. W. [Jane S. Welch], "The Mother and Daughter," *Lowell Offering* 4, no. 6 (April 1844): 126–28; H. F. [Harriet Farley], "Editorial," *Lowell Offering* 3, no. 9 (June 1843): 214.

140. Aleta Feinsod Cane and Susan Alves, "American Women Writers and the Periodical: Creating a Constituency, Opening a Dialogue," in *"The Only Efficient Instrument": American Women Writers and the Periodical, 1837–1916* (Iowa City: University of Iowa Press, 2001), 1.

141. Abel C. Thomas, "Editorial Corner," *Lowell Offering* Ser. 1, no. 1 (October 1840): 16; "Notices," *Lowell Offering* 3, no. 4 (January 1843): inside back cover.

142. Editors, "To Readers and Correspondents," *Lowell Offering* Ser. 1, no. 3 (February 1841); Editors, "We have many excellent articles . . . ," *Lowell Offering* Ser. 1, no. 4 (March 1841): 64; Editors, "The Garland of the Mills," *Lowell Offering* Ser. 1, no 4 (March 1841): 64.

143. *Lowell Offering* Ser. 1, no. 2 (December 1840): 21; *Lowell Offering* Ser. 1, no. 4 (March 1841): 57.

144. Thomas, "Editorial Corner."

145. Editors, "Editorial," *Lowell Offering* Ser. 1, no. 2 (December 1840); Harriet Farley, "Our Introductory," *New England Offering* 7, no. 1 (January 1849): 1.

146. Thomas, *Autobiography*, 266; Abel C. Thomas, "Editorial," *Lowell Offering* 1, no. 6 (August 1841): inside back cover; Thomas, "Editorial Corner"; Larcom, *New England Girlhood*, 221; Robinson, "Life of the Early Mill-Girls," 136–137.

147. Harriet Farley, "Editorial," *Lowell Offering* 3, no. 12 (September 1843): 282; "To Patrons," *Lowell Offering* 3, no. 6 (March 1843): inside front cover.

148. In "A Sketch of Lowell" published in the *Lowell Courier* and reprinted in the *Star of Bethlehem*, Eliphalet Case wrote, "3,200 copies of No. 1 [of the *Lowell Offering*], were printed; 3,750 of No. 2; and 4,500 of No. 3. The first edition of No. 1, was soon exhausted, and a second edition of 2,000 has been published, and will soon be taken up" (*Star of Bethlehem* [Lowell, Mass., and Manchester, N.H.] 1, no. 11 [13 March 1841]).

149. "Biographical Sketch," in Larcom, *The Poetical Works*, iii. See Addison, *Lucy Larcom*,

10. Harriet Farley, "To Readers and Correspondents," *New England Offering* 7, no. 2 (February 1849): 25.

150. Robinson, *Loom and Spindle*, 86.

151. Pritchard, *No Word for Time*, 173.

152. Gordon M. Day and Michael K. Foster, "Oral Literature of the Northeastern Algonquians and the Northern Iroquoians," in *Dictionary of Native American Literature* (New York: Garland, 1994), 74.

153. Jeremy Belknap, *The History of New-Hampshire*, 3 vols. (1784; reprint, Dover, N.H.: Printed for O. Crosby and J. Varney by J. Mann and J. K. Remick, 1812), 1:201–2; Cotton Mather, *Magnalia Christi Americana: or, The Ecclesiastical History of New-England*, 2 vols. (1702; reprint, Hartford: Silas Andrus, 1820), 2:512–13.

154. Roger Williams, *A Key into the Language of America* (1643), excerpted in *The Heath Anthology of American Literature*, 3d ed., Paul Lauter, gen. ed. (Boston: Houghton Mifflin, 1998), 271, 277; Mather, *Magnalia Christi Americana*, 1:505; Lowell, Mass., City Library, *Catalogue* (1858), 126.

155. Mather, *Magnalia Christi Americana*, 1:505; Samuel G. Drake, *Biography and History of the Indians of North America*, 7th ed., rev. and enl. (Boston: Antiquarian Institute, 1837), bk. 1, chap. 2, p. 8.

156. Joseph Bruchac (Abenaki), *Lasting Echoes: An Oral History of Native American People* (New York: Avon Books, 1997), 1–13.

157. Lydia H. Sigourney, *Traits of the Aborigines of America: A Poem* (Cambridge, Mass.: University Press, 1822), Canto 1: lines 17–21; John G. Whittier, "The Indian's Tale," in *Legends of New England* (1831; reprint, Baltimore: Clearfield, 1992), 101: lines 25–31. For Sigourney's less favorable views of Native people, see her characterization of them as "untutor'd tribes" (6) lacking knowledge of Jesus Christ (9, 26–27). Contending that the "Red Man has departed forever," Whittier's narrator describes Native people as heathens and savages (8–9, 11).

158. Nancy Lecompte (Ne-Do-Ba), personal communication with author, 23 April 2000.

159. Apess, *Experiences of Five Christian Indians*, 145, *passim*; Kilcup, "Writing 'The Red Woman's America,'" 8.

160. Kristin Herzog, "Native American Oral Traditions," in Cathy N. Davidson and Linda Wagner-Martin, eds., *Oxford Companion to Women's Writing in the United States* (New York: Oxford University Press, 1995), 607–9.

161. Lydia Maria Child, "Adventure in the Woods" (1826), in Karen L. Kilcup, ed., *Nineteenth-Century American Women Writers: An Anthology* (Oxford: Blackwell, 1997), 65–68.

162. H. J. [Hannah Johnson (m. Noyes)], "The Indian's Faith," *Lowell Offering* 2, no. 2 (February 1842): 44–46.

163. Ibid., 45–46.

164. Ella [Harriet Farley], "The Lessons of Nature," *Lowell Offering* 2, no. 4 (April 1842): 98–99. These lines are derived from Alexander Pope's *An Essay on Man* (1733–34), Epistle 1: 99–100: "Lo! the poor Indian, whose untutor'd mind / Sees God in clouds, or hears him in the wind"; ibid., Epistle 4, line 332.

165. M. R. G. [Marian R. Green (m. Kimball)], "The Indians," *Lowell Offering* 3, no. 11 (August 1843): 264, lines 29–32; Pumen, "The Dark Side," *Lowell Offering* 3, no. 11 (August 1843): 247.

166. J. S. W. [Jane S. Welch], "Plea for the Indian," *Lowell Offering* 3, no. 3 (December 1842): 57; Ella [Harriet Farley], "The Portrait Gallery. No. 1.—Pocahontas," *Lowell Offering* 3, no. 1 (October 1842): 17–18.

167. John W. Hayley, *Tuftonboro, New Hampshire: An Historical Sketch* (Concord, N.H.: Rumford Press, 1923), foreword (n.p.).

168. William Apess, *Eulogy on King Philip* (1836) in *On Our Own Ground: The Complete Writings of William Apess, a Pequot*, ed. and with an intro. by Barry O'Connell (Amherst: University of Massachusetts Press, 1992), 279, 281, *passim*.

169. Ibid., 281.

170. Lydia Maria Child, *The First Settlers of New-England: or, Conquest of the Pequods, Narragansets and Pokanokets. As Related by a Mother to Her Children*, by a Lady of Massachusetts (Boston: Munroe and Francis, 1829), iii–iv, 14.

171. Washington Irving, "Philip of Pokanoket," *The Sketch Book of Geoffrey Crayon, Gent.* (1819–20; reprint, New York: Penguin Books, 1988), 243. See Child, *First Settlers*, 86.

172. Richard Moody, ed., *Dramas from the American Theatre, 1762–1909* (Cleveland: World Publishing, 1966), 199, 203.

173. John Augustus Stone, *Metamora; or, The Last of the Wampanoags* (1829), in Moody, *Dramas from the American Theatre*, 207–8; Calloway, "Introduction: Surviving the Dark Ages," 8; Stone, *Metamora*, 226.

174. B. C., "The Delusion of the Heart," *Lowell Offering* 2, no. 11–12 (August 1842): 347.

175. Ann Plato, "The Natives of America," *Essays Including Biographies and Miscellaneous Pieces, in Prose and Poetry* (1841; reprint, New York: Oxford University Press, 1988), 111: lines 29, 31, 33; Plato, "Decision of Character," *Essays*, 42; William Apess, *A Son of the Forest* (1831), in *On Our Own Ground*, ed. O'Connell, 97, 97n.

176. Apess, *Experiences of Five Christian Indians*, 119–20.

177. The fifteen *Lowell Offering* dream visions with allegorical elements are: Caroline [Emmeline A. Larcom], "Happiness," 1, no. 2 (May 1841): 41–42; Tabitha [Betsey Chamberlain], "A Vision of Truth," 1, no. 2 (May 1841): 44–45; Ellen, "Memory and Hope," 1, no. 6 (August 1841): 175–77; N. S. L., "An Allegory," 2, no. 2 (February 1842): 62–63; Bereaved, "A Reverie," 2, no. 2 (February 1842): 64; Rosaline, "Pleasure and Pain," 2, no. 3 (March 1842): 88–91; Ella [Harriet Farley], "A Dream," 2, no. 5–6 (May 1842): 187–90; Jane [Eliza Jane Cate], "Garden of Life," 2, no. 10 (15 July 1842): 299–300; Isabella [Harriet Lees], "The Poet's Dream," 3, no. 8 (May 1843): 188–90; Ella [Harriet Farley], "Voices of the Night," 4, no. 8 (June 1844): 181–83; Rosina, "A Morning Reverie," 4, no. 9 (July 1844): 211–12; Rotha [Lucy Larcom], "A Flower Dream," 4, no. 10 (August 1844): 217–19; S. T., "An Afternoon Ramble," 5, no. 2 (February 1845): 30–31; R. H. [Rachel Hayes?], "The Feast of Languages," 5, no. 3 (March 1845): 57–58; D. [Eliza Jane Cate], "An Allegory," 5, no. 10 (October 1845): 237. The *Lowell Offering* dream visions lacking allegorical elements are: A. D. T. [Abby D. Turner], "A Spring Phantasy," 1, no. 4 (July 1841): 106–7; Tabitha [Betsey Chamberlain], "A New Society," 1, no. 6 (August 1841): 191–92; Tabitha [Betsey Chamberlain], "Sabbath Morning," 2, no. 7 (June 1842): 207–8; B. C. [Betsey Chamberlain], "A Reverie," 2, no. 10 (15 July 1842): 318–19; M. A. [Mary Anne Spaulding?], "Journey to the Moon," 4, no. 1 (November 1843): 9–12; M. M'W., "A Dream," 5, no. 5 (May 1845): 116–17. The *Lowell Offering* waking vision pieces are: Abigail [Abby D. Turner], "A Merrimack Reverie," Ser. 1, no. 2

(December 1840): 29–30; H., "A Visit from Hope," 1, no. 1 (April 1841): 13; Frances, "Hope and Despair," 1, no. 7 (September 1841): 222–24; H. J. [Hannah Johnson], "Ramble of Imagination," 1, no. 8 (October 1841): 234–37; Orianna [Hannah Johnson], "Unbelief and Faith. An Allegory," 2, no. 5–6 (May 1842): 183–85; M. C., "An Allegory," 4, no. 5 (1844): 101–2; "The Dream-Land," 5, no. 2 (February 1845): 32–33; Rotha [Lucy Larcom], "The Gold-Enslaved," 5, no. 2 (February 1845): 46–47; B. McD., "Evening Fantasies," 5, no. 11 (November 1845): 241–42.

178. N. S. L., "An Allegory," *Lowell Offering* 2, no. 2 (February 1842): 62–63; Jane [Eliza Jane Cate], "Garden of Life," *Lowell Offering* 2, no. 10 (15 July 1842): 299–300.

179. S. T., "An Afternoon Ramble," *Lowell Offering* 5, no. 2 (February 1845): 30–31.

180. Rotha [Lucy Larcom], "A Flower Dream," *Lowell Offering* 4, no. 10 (August 1844): 217, 219.

181. "The Factory Inquisition, or American Bastille," *Working Man's Advocate* (New York), 16 November 1844 (for a synopsis, see Ranta, *Women and Children of the Mills*, 212–13). That *Other* Factory Girl, "A Dream," *Voice of Industry* 1, no. 16 (11 September 1845), exposes social evils (see Ranta, *Women and Children of the Mills*, 226). For two more dream visions published in 1840s labor papers, see "The Pilgrim's Vision," *The Gleaner* (Manchester, N.H.), 4 January 1845, and "The Employer's Family Devotion," *The Mechanic* (Fall River, Mass.), 22 June 1844). These are synopsized in Ranta, *Women and Children of the Mills*, 222–23, 260–61.

182. Andrew Wiget, *Native American Literature* (Boston: Twayne Publishers, 1985), 38.

183. Pritchard, *No Word for Time*, 23, 51.

184. Though not a dream vision, Chamberlain's "A Legend of the Olden Time" (not reproduced here) shares their reformist and idealist qualities. This daring story shows how multicultural harmony can be achieved between two racially different, antagonistic groups when both accept and even embrace each other's differences. The story concludes with several interracial, interfaith marriages—radical concepts for her predominantly white, Christian readers.

185. Wiget, *Native American Literature*, 51; Gretchen M. Bataille and Kathleen Mullins Sands, *American Indian Women: Telling Their Lives* (Lincoln: University of Nebraska Press, 1984), 3; Pritchard, *No Word for Time*, 33.

186. Parker, *History of the Town of Wolfeborough*, 107.

187. John G. Whittier, *Supernaturalism of New England* (1847; reprint, Baltimore: Clearfield, 1993), 3; Whittier, *Legends of New England*, 8, 56–57.

188. Speare, introduction to *New Hampshire Folk Tales*, 9.

189. Ibid.

190. Bataille and Sands, *American Indian Women: Telling Their Lives*, 24, 3, 17.

191. Ibid., 18–19.

192. Judith Fetterley and Marjorie Pryse, introduction to *American Women Regionalists, 1850–1910* (New York: W. W. Norton, 1992), xii.

193. Josephine Donovan, *New England Local Color Literature: A Women's Tradition* (New York: Frederick Ungar, 1983), 143n.

194. Mary Russell Mitford, *Our Village* (1824–32; reprint, London: Macmillan, 1910), 3; Chamberlain, "A Letter about Old Maids," p. 158; "The Lowell Offering," *North American Review* 52, no. 2 (1841): 538.

195. Donovan, *New England Local Color Literature*, 31.

196. Charles Knight, "Introduction by the English Editor," *Mind amongst the Spindles: A Selection from the Lowell Offering, a Miscellany Wholly Composed by the Factory Girls of an American City*, ed. Charles Knight and Harriet Martineau (London: Charles Knight, 1844), xiii.

197. Harriet Hanson Robinson, *Massachusetts in the Woman Suffrage Movement* (Boston: Roberts Brothers, 1881), 203; Patty [Harriet Farley], "The Party," *Lowell Offering* 4, no. 8 (June 1844): 174–77; Kate [Harriot F. Curtis], "First Efforts of Genius," *Lowell Offering* 3, no. 1 (October 1842): 5–9. For *Lowell Offering* imitations of Chamberlain's writings, see Patty [Harriet Farley], "The Husking," 4, no. 4 (January 1844), 63–68; Edith, "The Old Meeting-House," 5, no. 8 (August 1845), 169–71; Elizabeth [Elizabeth D. Perver], "Constancy," 5, no. 8 (August 1845), 173–75; and M. R. G. [Mariam R. Green], "The Paring (or Apple) Bee," 5, no. 12 (December 1845), 268–71.

198. Benjamin B. Thatcher, *Indian Biography* (New York: Harper & Brothers, 1836), 1:305; Lois M. Feister and Bonnie Pulis, "Molly Brant: Her Domestic and Political Roles in Eighteenth-Century New York," in *Northeastern Indian Lives, 1632–1816*, ed. Robert S. Grumet (Amherst: University of Massachusetts Press, 1996), 295–320; Bunny McBride and Harald L. Prins, "Walking the Medicine Line: Molly Ockett, a Pigwacket Doctor," in Grumet, *Northeastern Indian Lives*, 321–47.

199. Ulrich, *Age of Homespun*, 355.

200. Nancy A. Walker, *A Very Serious Thing: Women's Humor and American Culture* (Minneapolis: University of Minnesota Press, 1988), 9.

201. Caroline M. Kirkland, *A New Home—Who'll Follow? or, Glimpses of Western Life, 1839*, excerpted in Katharine M. Rogers, ed., *The Meridian Anthology of Early American Women Writers* (New York: Penguin, 1991), 319–20; Larcom, *New England Girlhood*, 245.

202. Susan Hazen-Hammond, *Spider Woman's Web: Traditional Native American Tales about Women's Power* (New York: Berkley, 1999), 43.

203. William Simmons, *Spirit of the New England Tribes: Indian History and Folklore, 1620–1984* (Hanover, N.H.: University Press of New England, 1986), 98–99.

204. Thatcher, *Indian Biography*, 1:278; Charles Brockden Brown, *Edgar Huntly* (1799; reprint, ed. David Stineback, New Haven, Conn.: New College and University Press, 1973), 194; Stone, *Metamora*, 221; Catharine Maria Sedgwick, *Hope Leslie; or Early Times in the Massachusetts* (1827; reprint, New York: Garrett Press, 1969), 66.

205. Sarah Josepha Hale, "An Old Maid," in *Traits of American Life* (Philadelphia: E. L. Carey & A. Hart, 1835), 256; Catharine Maria Sedgwick, "Old Maids," in *Tales and Sketches* (Philadelphia: Carey, Lea, and Blanchard, 1835), 102.

206. Chamberlain, "A Letter about Old Maids," pp. 157–58; Chamberlain, "Old Maids and Old Bachelors," pp. 159–60; Margaret Fuller, "The Great Lawsuit. Man versus Men. Woman versus Women," July 1843, in *The Feminist Papers: From Adams to de Beauvoir*, ed. Alice S. Rossi (1973; reprint, Boston: Northeastern University Press, 1988), 176–77; Margaret Fuller, *Woman in the Nineteenth Century* (1845; reprint, New York: W. W. Norton, 1971), 96–99.

Notes to Chamberlain's Writings

1. A crucial battle in Native history took place on 20 August 1794: the Battle of Fallen Timbers. At Fort Miami on the Maumee River (in present-day Ohio), Michikinikwa/

Little Turtle (Miami/Mahican), and Weyapiersenwah/Blue Jacket (Shawnee), led a confederation of Miami, Ojibwa, Delaware, Potawatomi, Shawnee, and Ottawa bands against federal troops headed by General "Mad" Anthony Wayne. The Indians' defeat led to their loss of huge portions of the Northwest Territory.

2. "Sartin" is slang for "certain." In 1798, "Independence, a Patriotic Song" (first line, "Hail, Independence, Hail"), written by Mr. Dunham to the tune "Dauphine," was published in Hanover, N.H. (*Connecticut Gazette*, 18 July 1798, 4).

3. "The Land of Steady Habits" is an old Connecticut state motto.

4. Equipped, attired.

5. Spelled variously as "Cantantowwit," "Cautantowwit," or Kawtantowwit," this is the name of the Algonquin, or more specifically the Narragansett, great God thought to dwell in the southwest.

6. From John Dryden's "The Cock and the Fox" (1700), lines 325–32. This epigraph was inserted by the editor, Abel Thomas, not by Chamberlain. See *Lowell Offering* 1, no. 6 (August 1841): inside back cover.

7. The eight-hour workday had been advocated in lectures to Lowell's women workers as early as 1834 by Charles Douglas, editor of the *New England Artisan* (see 3, no. 12 [22 March 1834], and Hannah Josephson, *The Golden Threads: New England's Mill Girls and Magnates* [New York: Duell, Sloan and Pearce, 1949], 255).

8. Luke 10:7: "[F]or the laborer is worthy of his hire." 1 Tim. 5:18: "The laborer *is* worthy of his reward."

9. A kind of paper measuring 11 x 7$\frac{1}{2}$ inches.

10. The building, room, or office where accounts were kept for the Merrimack Corporation.

11. Fairies or nymphs dwelling in lakes, streams, and rivers.

12. Cf. Benjamin Franklin, *Poor Richard Almanack for the Year of Christ 1737* (Barre, Mass.: Imprint Society, 1970), 106: "After crosses and losses men grow humbler & wiser."

13. 1 John 1:7: "But if we walk in the light, as he is in the light, we have fellowship one with another, and the blood of Jesus Christ his Son cleanseth us from all sin."

14. After weaving, cloth was picked, which involved close examination under bright light and removal of imperfections with tweezers. Any undyed spots were retouched with a brush and dye.

15. The Roman goddess of the dawn or early morning.

16. Heb. 13:15: "By him therefore let us offer the sacrifice of praise to God continually."

17. In Greek mythology, Morpheus is the son of sleep and the god of dreams.

18. In the nineteenth century, the term *fancy* was synonymous with *imagination*.

19. This was the nineteenth-century spelling of Lake Winnipesaukee, New Hampshire. Chamberlain's childhood home was located on the lake's shore.

20. A variant spelling of *bobolink*.

21. The ancient Israelites, or perhaps, for Chamberlain, Native people.

22. Ps. 146:1: "Praise the Lord, O my soul."

23. In the 1830s and 1840s, workers' groups called Improvement Circles met in Lowell, Mass., for self-education and cultural enrichment. Activities included public readings and discussion.

24. In this context, "Apocalypse" refers to the New Testament Book of Revelation.

See Rev. 22:2: "In the midst of the street of it, and on either side of the river, *was there* the tree of life, which bare twelve *manner of* fruits, *and* yielded her fruit every month: and the leaves of the tree *were* for the healing of the nations."

25. 1 Kings 19:12: "And after the earthquake a fire; *but* the Lord *was* not in the fire: and after the fire a still small voice."

26. Cf. Gen. 9:12–13: "And God said, . . . I do set my bow in the cloud, and it shall be for a token of a covenant between me and the earth."

27. Cottage.

28. Andirons.

29. From William Shakespeare, *As You Like It*, 2:7: "Then the whining schoolboy, with his satchel / And shining morning face, creeping like snail / Unwillingly to school" (lines 145–47).

30. The English actress Sarah Kemble Siddons (1755–1831).

31. The New Testament records that Mary and Martha lived with their brother Lazarus at Bethany, a village not far from Jerusalem. On one occasion, when Jesus and His disciples were their guests (Luke 10:38–42), Mary sat at Jesus' feet and listened to Him while her sister Martha busied herself with preparing food and waiting on the guests; when Martha complained, Jesus said that Mary had chosen the better part. Saint Mary Magdalene was an early follower of Christ as recorded in the New Testament, e.g., John 20 and Mark 16.

32. William Cowper (1731–1800) and George Gordon Byron (1788–1824) were English poets, and Robert Burns (1759–96) was a Scottish poet. Robert Burns's song-poem, "Highland Mary" (1792), was well known. "Lament for Mary," which has not been identified, may be Robert Burns's "Lament of Mary, Queen of Scots" (1791).

33. "Polly" was a nickname for "Mary."

34. *Sine qua non* is a Latin phrase denoting something essential or indispensable.

35. An ancient Greek mathematician, Euclid was important for his work in geometry.

36. In the Old Testament, Job was a wealthy landowner who suffered great losses and tribulation. Thus, "Job's Troubles" was the name for a particularly difficult quilt design.

37. A variant spelling of *coverlet,* an outer bed covering, quilt, or counterpane.

38. A chip hat is made from thin wooden strips. A tippet is a scarf-like fur or woolen garment worn about the shoulders or the neck and shoulders.

39. A vandyke was a wide linen or lace collar or neckerchief. Morocco leather, made from sheepskin or lambskin, was used primarily in shoemaking.

40. A cravat is a men's garment worn about the neck, such as a scarf. Pomatum was a scented ointment used as a perfume or hairdressing. Day & Martin was probably a brand of boot and shoe polish.

41. Satan, the devil.

42. Interpretation.

43. Hannah Gould Flagg (1789–1865), "The Bridemaid" (1839): "That every string had snapped so silently, / Quivered and bled unseen" (lines 11–12).

44. In the nineteenth century, *consumption* signified a wasting illness, especially phthisis (tuberculosis of the lungs).

45. In spite of.

46. "Turning cups" is an old method of telling fortunes. After drinking tea or coffee, one turns the cup upside down on the saucer and waits for it to cool. Then the cups are

turned upright, and the fortune-teller tries to read the cup's patterns to predict future events.

47. "Salmagundi," the name for a salad of chopped meat, anchovies or pickled herring, and onions dressed with lemon juice and oil, was also chosen as the title for a well-known early nineteenth-century literary periodical, *Salmagundi; or, the Whim-Whams and Opinions of Launcelot Langstaff, Esq. and Others* (1807–08), written by Washington and William Irving and James K. Paulding.

48. Besides denoting Black Bartholomew, the "black man" was also an epithet for the devil or Satan.

49. The woman had borne Salter's child out of wedlock.

50. An illegitimate child.

51. An allusion to the serpent who tempted Eve to her fall in the Garden of Eden. See Gen. 3.

52. "To give the mitten to" is a colloquial expression meaning to dismiss someone as a lover.

53. A bar or shop where alcoholic beverages are sold in small quantities.

54. The time when the ground becomes cold and snowy enough to ride or drive a sleigh upon.

55. Rough fibers of flax or hemp, tow was typically spun by poor women for meager payment.

56. Drunkard.

57. In colonial America, a parish designated a subdivision of a county, often having its own church and clergy.

58. Befell.

59. Probably a trough for collecting the sap from maple trees to make syrup and sugar.

60. Close by, very near to.

61. A pair of oxen.

62. "Squire" is a diminution of "esquire," a title often granted to lawyers and the wealthiest townsmen.

63. Alcoholic beverage.

64. A large pot for burning vegetables to produce the lye commonly used in making soap.

65. In New England towns, selectmen (usually three to nine) are still elected today to serve as the chief public officials overseeing town governance.

66. In Greek mythology, the boatman Charon ferried the spirits of the dead across the river Styx to the Elysian fields.

67. A newspaper.

68. Cf. Job 11:12: "For vain man would be wise, though man be born *like* a wild ass's colt."

69. Stanza five of Robert Burns's "Green Grow the Rashes" (1783). In *A New England Girlhood: Outlined from Memory*, Lucy Larcom recalls that the "songs of Burns were in the air" in the 1830s and 1840s when she worked in Lowell (239).

70. According to Gen. 1–3, Adam and Eve were the first human beings created by God.

71. Name.

72. Indigestion.

73. Nathaniel P. Willis's "Saturday Afternoon" (1831): "I am willing to die when my time shall come, / And I shall be glad to go; / For the world, at best, is a weary place, / And my pulse is getting low" (lines 25–28).

74. Luke 16:3: "I can not dig; to beg I am ashamed."

75. Rev. 12:3: "[B]ehold a great red dragon, having seven heads and ten horns." Rev. 13:1: "And I stood upon the sand of the sea, and saw a beast rise up out of the sea, having seven heads and ten horns." Rev. 17:3: "I saw a woman sit upon a scarlet-colored beast . . . having seven heads and ten horns."

76. Examining or exploring (a geographic region, etc.).

77. A charitable, religious organization.

78. Victoria (1819–1901), queen of Great Britain and Ireland from 1837 to 1901, and empress of India.

79. The Jew's harp is a small musical instrument played by holding it against the teeth or lips and plucking with the fingers.

80. "To pull caps for" means for women to bicker and quarrel noisily, especially over a man.

81. "To catch a tartar" is a colloquialism meaning to lay hold of, or meet, a person who proves too strong for oneself.

82. The modest attire of a married woman.

83. Someone worthy of imitation, an ideal or model.

84. A female intellectual.

85. Possibly Sarah H. Dearborn (b. 1806?) of Wakefield, N.H.

86. Monadnock is a mountain in southern New Hampshire.

87. Probably Elder Mark Fernald, pastor of the First Christian Church in Wolfeboro from 1812 to 1838 (Parker, *History of the Town of Wolfeborough*, 317–18).

88. Allow.

89. Fanciful, unreal.

90. One who makes dresses, cloaks, etc., for women; a dressmaker.

91. Daniel Webster (1782–1852), an American politician beloved by many in his native New Hampshire.

92. A nickname for New Hampshire.

93. Probably *The Scholar's Arithmetic* by Daniel Adams (1773–1864), first published in 1801 in Leominster, Mass.

94. Probably Oliver Beale Pierce (b. 1808), the author of *Abridgment of the Grammar of the English Language*, published at Boston in 1840.

95. One who analyzes words and sentences grammatically.

96. Cf. "Hardyknute" in Thomas Percy, *Reliques of Ancient English Poetry*, 3 vols. (1765; reprint, ed. Henry B. Wheatley, New York: Dover Publications, 1966), 2:120, line 313: "Now loud and chill blew th' westlin wind."

97. Probably the Wolfeborough and Tuftonborough Academy founded in 1820, which continues today as the Brewster Free Academy in Wolfeboro, N.H.

98. Since ancient times, women had done spinning while walking. "To spin street yarn" became a colloquialism meaning to rove about gossiping.

99. A female teacher, instructor, or tutor.

100. Good-bye, farewell.

101. The Temperance Movement advocated abstinence from alcoholic beverages. The movement gained in strength and numbers as the nineteenth century progressed.

102. Probably the Presbyterian catechism prepared by the Westminster Assembly (1643–52) and published as *Assembly's Catechism*. The American Spelling Book by Noah Webster, the second edition of which was published at Boston in 1790.

103. Probably *The Village Harmony; or, Youth's Assistant to Sacred Musick*, first published at Exeter, N.H., in 1795; *The Coquette; or, The History of Eliza Wharton* (1797) by Hannah Webster Foster; *Charlotte. A Tale of Truth* by Susanna H. Rowson, first published in 1790 and reprinted many times as *Charlotte Temple*; *Female Quixotism: Exhibited in the Romantic Opinions and Extravagant Adventures of Dorcasina Sheldon* (1801) by Tabitha Gilman Tenney; probably *Louisa; or, the Cottage on the Moor* (1789) by Elizabeth Helme.

104. *Thomas's New England Almanac*, published by Isaiah Thomas.

105. *Arabian Nights Entertainments: Consisting of One Thousand and One Stories*, told by the Sultaness of the Indies (first American edition, Philadelphia and Baltimore: H. and P. Rice and J. Rice, 1794); *The Asylum; or, Alonzo and Melissa* (1811) by Isaac Mitchell.

106. Nathaniel Cotton (1705–88), "An Epistle to the Reader" (1791): " 'Tis true my little purse grows light; / But then I sleep so sweet at night!" (lines 113–14).

107. From *Mother Goose's Quarto* (1825).

108. Cinderella.

109. Probably Brookfield, N.H.

110. A shop where wooden vessels, such as barrels, buckets, and casks, are made.

111. Transformed, often by enchantment or other supernatural means.

112. George Fox (1624–91) was an English religious leader and the founder of the Society of Friends, known as the Quakers.

113. John Bassett of Wolfeboro, N.H.

114. Ebenezer Allen, town minister of Wolfeboro, N.H., from 1792 to 1806.

115. The parsonage or minister's lot was a parcel of Wolfeboro land set aside for the town minister's residence. See Parker, *History of the Town of Wolfeborough*, 294–303. Parker's account of events differs somewhat from Chamberlain's.

116. Wolfeboro, N.H.

117. At designated intervals during Protestant Christian church services, each church member extends the right hand of fellowship to the person on his or her right and left.

118. See Matt. 6:7: "But when ye pray, use not vain repetitions, as the heathen *do*: for they think that they shall be heard for their much speaking."

119. Probably Newmarket, N.H.

120. Scotland.

121. The meaning is unclear in this context. "Cote" may mean either a laborers' cottage or a stall or shed for sheltering small animals, such as sheep.

122. An English folk song, "The Lass of Richmond Hill" was composed by James Hook (1746–1827) and published about 1787. Leonard McNally (1752–1820) wrote the lyrics. The song was also popular in the United States during the 1790s.

123. These lines form the first two eight-line stanzas of a thirty-two-line Christmas poem, "Shepherds, Rejoice!" composed by Isaac Watts (1674–1748). The tune "Boston" by William Billings (1746–1800) was written as a setting for Watts's poem.

124. Luke 2:14.

125. The "Messiah" and the "Prince of Peace" are epithets for Jesus Christ.

126. The Boston Tea Party, 1773, a colonists' protest against the British tea tax.

127. Chamberlain's great-grandmother, Abigail Dame (born circa 1716, Newington, N.H.), who married Solomon Loud (1713–62) of Portsmouth, N.H.

128. Domicile, home.

129. A mercantile marine ship.

130. An inexpensive black tea popular in the eighteenth century.

131. *Bason* is a variant spelling of *basin*. A gill is one-fourth of a pint of liquid.

132. An emetic is a medicine that produces vomiting. An outbuilding is an outhouse or outdoor toilet.

133. John Wentworth (1737–1820) served from 1767 to 1775 as New Hampshire's last colonial governor. He built a lavish country estate on Lake Wentworth in Wolfeboro, N.H., which he often occupied during his tenure as governor.

134. Possibly Jonathan Lary, who was "evidently of Irish origin" (see Parker, *History of the Town of Wolfborough,* 111).

135. Younkers are children, youngsters. The whortleberry is a species of blueberry.

136. A epithet denoting Lake Winnipesaukee.

137. James Gate Percival (1795–1856), "The Land of the Blest": "The sunset is calm on the face of the deep, / And bright is the last look of day in the west, / And broadly the beams of its parting glance sweep, / Like the path that conducts to the land of the blest" (lines 1–4).

138. Matt. 19:6 and Mark 10:9: "What therefore God hath joined together, let not man put asunder." In this account of the wedding of Clifford and his bride, Chamberlain has apparently blended two weddings famous in Wolfeboro history. The first is the circa 1766 wedding of Reuben and Sarah Libby, reputedly celebrated on Lake Winnipesaukee's shore under a large oak tree (see Parker, *History of the Town of Wolfeborough,* 107, and Libby, *The Libby Family in America,* 128). The second wedding was that of Lemuel Clifford and Betsy Fullerton, performed by Governor Wentworth at his Wolfeboro estate. As in Chamberlain's sketch, the ceremony was followed by a gala feast lasting far into the night (Parker, *History of the Town of Wolfeborough,* 90).

139. Lady Frances Deering Wentworth (ca. 1745–1813), the wife of Governor John Wentworth.

140. "The Friar of Orders Gray" and "Gilderoy" were published in Thomas Percy, *Reliques of Ancient English Poetry,* 1765, 1: 242–46, 318–23. "Jemmy and Nancy" was a ballad popular in nineteenth-century America. On "The Lass of Richmond Hill," see note 122.

141. John Greenleaf Whittier, "The Times": "Farewell the pleasant husking match, its merry after scenes, / When Indian pudding smoked beside the giant pot of beans" (lines 9–10).

142. During the autumn in early New England, rural people would gather in groups to help one another shuck (husk) their harvested ears of colorful Indian corn. On these festive occasions, any man discovering a red ear of corn would kiss all the women present. Such a husking is described in Canto 3 of Joel Barlow's *The Hasty-Pudding* (1793).

143. Members of the Religious Society of Friends, known as the Quakers.

144. Variant spelling of "banns."

145. A small grove of trees or undergrowth.

146. The harvest spirit is probably derived from the headless horseman of Washington

Irving's "The Legend of Sleepy Hollow" (1820) and from ancient European and Native American spirits of the harvest.

147. Washing.

148. A hearty and popular early New England dish of probable Native American derivation. Ingredients include milk, cornmeal, molasses or maple syrup, cinnamon, and ginger, boiled and then baked.

149. Probably South Wolfeboro, N.H.

150. Eighteenth-century French currency.

151. Marseille (sometimes anglicized as "Marseilles") is France's second largest city and a major port.

152. An order of Roman Catholic friars.

153. A street in Paris, France, usually spelled "Rue St. Denis."

154. A town in the western suburbs of Paris.

155. A Roman Catholic religious order; its members subsisted by begging.

156. A superior in a religious house or order.

157. Located in Groton, Conn., Fort Griswold was the site of a Revolutionary War battle on 6 September 1781. Chamberlain's account accords with other American versions of the event. Under the command of Colonel William Ledyard, the American forces were soon overcome by the British. After Ledyard surrendered his sword, the British killed him with it and proceeded to massacre, wound, and mutilate the American troops.

158. Wolfeboro.

159. John Trumbull, "M'Fingal: Canto First" (1776), *The Satiric Poems of John Trumbull*, ed. Edwin T. Bowen (Austin: University of Texas Press, 1962): "Nor less avail'd his optic sleight, / And Scottish gift of second-sight" (lines 57–58).

160. Damaged, made defective.

161. The notion that Governor Wentworth was much older than his bride was not accurate, perhaps an element of the mythology that later developed around the governor's life. When John Wentworth married Frances Wentworth Atkinson in 1769, he was thirty-two and she twenty-three (Paul W. Wilderson, *Governor John Wentworth and the American Revolution* [Hanover, N.H.: University Press of New England, 1994], 171, 173).

162. Parker, *History of the Town of Wolfeborough*, 89: "A large pine tree of Mount Delight was also a chosen spot for afternoon entertainments [at the Wentworth Farm]."

163. During the Revolution, Governor John Wentworth was actually a British loyalist.

164. Chamberlain's account adheres fairly closely to the history as currently known and published by the Friends of the Governor Wentworth State Historic Site. In 1805, the Wentworth farm was bought by Daniel and Margaret Whitten Raynard. Mrs. Raynard was indeed a native of Yorkshire, England. When Daniel Raynard died in 1815, Margaret inherited the property. On 8 August 1820, Deeren Stoddard married Margaret Raynard. The Wentworth house completely burned on 12 September 1820, when the roof caught fire from the chimney (see "Wentworth House Plantation, 1767–1820: A Brief History" [Wolfeboro, N.H.: Friends of the Governor Wentworth State Historic Site, 199?]).

165. The English author Mary Russell Mitford (1786–1855) published a popular collection of village sketches, *Our Village* (1824–32).

166. *Quirl* is a variant spelling of *querl*, a curl or twist. "The pond" is probably Lake Winnipesaukee.

167. An enginehouse was probably a place where firefighting vehicles and equipment

were kept. Connected with a church, a vestry is a meeting place where church business is conducted.

168. Gen. 6.

169. A fence made of rails crossed to support one another, forming a zigzag pattern.

170. Lake Winnipesaukee.

171. Perhaps the northern lights.

172. Deut. 32:10: "He found him in a desert land, and in the waste howling wilderness." The phrase "howling wilderness" was used by some seventeenth-century Puritans, such as Richard Mather, to describe the New England area as first encountered by English settlers.

173. Timon is a misanthropic character from Shakespeare's *Timon of Athens.*

174. An excuse meant to quiet the conscience.

175. Jokers, mischievous persons.

176. Footstools.

177. A chair with a seat made from woven reeds.

178. *Trunnel* is a variant spelling of *treenail,* a cylindrical piece of wood.

179. Cf. Luke 14:10–11: "But when thou art bidden, go and sit down in the lowest room; that when he that bade thee cometh, he may say unto thee, Friend, go up higher. . . . For whosoever exalteth himself shall be abased; and he that humbleth himself shall be exalted." Luke 20:45–47: "Beware of the scribes, which desire . . . the highest seats in the synagogues, and the chief rooms at feasts; . . . the same shall receive greater damnation."

180. George Whitefield (1714–70) was an English evangelistic preacher, the leader of the Calvinistic Methodist Church. He made seven trips to America. The Methodists were known for greater social egalitarianism than was found in other Protestant sects, such as Congregationalism.

181. The singing of psalms or of sacred music generally, especially in public worship.

182. The Guelphs and the Ghibellines were two great feuding parties in Germany and Italy from the twelfth through the fourteenth centuries. The Montagues and Capulets are the feuding families of Shakespeare's *Romeo and Juliet.*

183. Tubes, pipes.

184. A small wooden or stone platform to facilitate mounting a horse.

185. A soldier, often one of the tallest and most excellent in the regiment.

186. A leghorn bonnet was made from bleached and plaited wheat straw imported from Leghorn (Livorno) in Tuscany. Broadcloth was plain, fine woven cloth.

187. *Posie* is an obsolete spelling of *posy,* a bunch of flowers or bouquet. Pinks are sweet-smelling garden flowers.

188. Treating as of small value; despising, disdaining.

189. Ishmael was the son of Abraham and an Egyptian servant, Hagar. According to Gen. 16:12, "his hand *will be* against every man, and every man's hand against him."

190. Saul, who became Paul the Apostle, was born about A.D. 10 in the city of Tarsus (Acts 21:39, 22:3). After a vision of the Lord and the risen Christ, he converted to Christianity and assumed the name Paul (see Gal. 1:11–17; 1 Cor. 15:8).

191. Heterodoxy.

192. 1 Sam. 3:18: "It *is* the Lord: let him do what seemeth him good."

193. A cord with wire running through it.

194. Japanned or varnished.

195. 2 Cor. 1:3: "Blessed *be* God, . . . the Father of mercies." James 1:17: "Every good gift and every perfect gift is from above, and cometh down from the Father of lights."

196. Possibly the Capt. James Nute mentioned in Parker, *History of the Town of Wolfeborough*, 302.

197. Heb. 4:16: "Let us therefore come boldly unto the throne of grace."

198. Ezek. 33:4: "his blood shall be upon his own head."

199. Josephine (1763–1814), was the empress of France from 1804 to 1809 as the consort of Napoleon I.

200. Mica.

201. The mallow is a common wild or garden plant.

202. In discussing "old time customs" of Wolfeboro, N.H., Parker observes that "[b]lue was a color greatly in vogue [for clothing], and an indigo dye-pot was found in almost every chimney corner" (*History of the Town of Wolfeborough*, 534).

203. Possibly an old game, Spin the Plate.

204. "King Lab" may be an English fairy tale, "Story of King Lud." The others are old English fairy tales.

205. A perpetual traveler, the Wandering Jew is a legendary figure originating in the time of Christ and said to be Pilate's porter. The Man Friday, an aborigine, is a character in Daniel Defoe's *Robinson Crusoe* (1719).

206. A rod, cane, or flat piece of wood, often used in school discipline.

207. To courtesy is to make a curtsy. According to Brigden's history of North Wolfeboro, N.H., boys and girls sat on opposite sides of the antebellum schoolroom. A teachers' "favorite punishment was for a boy to go and sit with the girls, and for a girl to sit with the boys" (Theodore H. Brigden, *Around Dimon's Corner; A History of North Wolfeboro, New Hampshire* [Wolfeboro, N.H.: North Wolfeboro Area Association, 1985], 61–62).

208. These punishments were common in early New Hampshire schools. As described in "School Customs in Epping," "His [the student's] punishment might be a whipping, but more likely something worse like sitting on nothing for fifteen or even thirty minutes; [or] standing still, toeing a crack in the floor with a finger touching another crack" (Eva A. Speare, comp., *More New Hampshire Folk Tales* [Brattleboro, Vt.: Stephen Daye Press, 1936], 217).

209. The Leaning Tower of Pisa, Italy.

210. The Syracusians Damon and Pythias were inseparable, deeply loyal friends. "Money will make the mare to go" is a line from an old song published in *The London Collection of Glees, Duets & Catches* (18?).

211. David Everett (1770–1813), "Lines Written for a School Declamation," lines 1–2.

212. William Cowper, "Verses Supposed to Be Written by Alexander Selkirk" (1782), lines 1–4.

213. Thomas Moss, "The Beggar's Petition" (1766), lines 9–10.

214. "Friend H." was Tobias Hanson (1771–1845), a Quaker who settled in Brookfield, N.H., in the early 1790s, and married Hannah Meader (1780–1846) (Chase, Bowker, and Pinkham, *Our Yesterdays*, 39, 50, 414). Moose Mountain is a 1,700-foot mountain in Brookfield. A lowery day is one on which the sky is overcast, cloudy. Whortleberries are a species of blueberries.

215. Wakefield Corner is a village just east of Brookfield, N.H.

216. Copplecrown is a 1,860-foot mountain on the border of Brookfield and New Dur-

ham, N.H. Merrymeeting Lake is located in New Durham. Benjamin Randall (1749–1808), a New Hampshire native, was a Freewill Baptist preacher who traveled throughout the Northeast, baptizing and marrying people, preaching, and founding churches. After 1780 he made his home in New Durham.

217. Tumbledown Dick Mountain is located in Brookfield, N.H.

218. Plentiful.

219. Tobias Hanson was known as "Bear" or "B'ar Hanson." When he first settled in Brookfield, N.H., he lived alone in a cave fronted by a wooden lean-to (Chase, Bowker, and Pinkham, *Our Yesterdays*, 39).

220. Wooden floors were covered with a thin layer of sand to keep them clean and absorb spills.

221. Cf. "The Lass of Richmond Hill," by Leonard McNally (ca. 1787): "On Richmond Hill there lives a lass / More bright than May-day morn / Whose charms all other maids' surpass / A rose without a thorn" (lines 1–4).

222. A family cemetery.

223. Prov. 31:10: "Who can find a virtuous woman? for her price *is* far above rubies."

224. Stagecoach.

225. "Friend H." was Tobias Hanson.

226. A tool used by carpenters for boring holes in wood.

227. One of Tobias and Hannah Hanson's daughters was named Abigail (Chase, Bowker, and Pinkham, *Our Yesterdays*, 414). *Rundlet* is a variant spelling of *roundlet* or *runlet*, a small cask.

228. This name denotes Chamberlain herself, since she signed this piece "Jemima."

229. A shallow ladle or strainer.

230. A portable oven for baking.

231. Rough planks of wood.

232. Covered with a lining of woodwork or plaster.

233. An ox, cow, or other such animal.

234. The hoop-handle.

235. A wooden bucket with a handle and cover.

236. Cloth and related articles.

237. I.e., not unlike slaves.

238. The moon.

239. From Mother Goose, "Girls and Boys, Come Out to Play": "Girls and boys, come out to play, / The moon is shining as bright as day. . . . Come with a whoop, come with a call, / Come with a good will or not at all" (lines 1–2, 5–6).

240. Probably Jesse Whitton (see Parker, *History of the Town of Wolfeborough*, 229–30).

241. Without ceremony or fuss.

Selected Bibliography

Addison, Daniel D. *Lucy Larcom: Life, Letters, and Diary*. Boston: Houghton, Mifflin, 1895.

Anderson, Rufus B., ed. *Memoir of Catharine Brown, A Christian Indian of the Cherokee Nation*. Philadelphia: American Sunday School Union, 1832.

Apess, William (Pequot). *On Our Own Ground: The Complete Writings of William Apess, a Pequot*. Edited and with an introduction by Barry O'Connell. Amherst: University of Massachusetts Press, 1992.

Banks, Marjorie G. H. *Through the Open Doors of the First Congregational Church, Wakefield, New Hampshire*. Wakefield, N.H.: M. G. H. Banks, 1985.

Bartlett, Alice P. "Portsmouth [N.H.] Families." Unpublished typescript microfilmed by the Genealogical Society, Salt Lake City, Utah, 1952.

Bataille, Gretchen M., and Kathleen Mullins Sands. *American Indian Women: A Guide to Research*. New York: Garland, 1991.

———. *American Indian Women: Telling Their Lives*. Lincoln: University of Nebraska Press, 1984.

Baym, Nina. "Reinventing Lydia Sigourney." *American Literature* 62 (1990): 385–404.

Beidler, Peter G. "Native American Writing: Fiction." In *Oxford Companion to Women's Writing in the United States*. Edited by Cathy N. Davidson and Linda Wagner-Martin. New York: Oxford University Press, 1995, 616–18.

Belknap, Jeremy. *The History of New-Hampshire*. 3 vols. 1784. Reprint, Dover, N.H.: Printed for O. Crosby and J. Varney by J. Mann and J. K. Remick, 1812.

Bennett, L. G., E. A. Lyons, and H. Brooks, comps. "Map of Du Page County, Illinois." 1862. Reprint, Wheaton: Du Page County Historical Society, 19?.

Blanchard, Rufus. *History of Du Page County, Illinois*. Chicago: O. L. Baskin, 1882.

Blatchford, Tannisse T. *An Honorable Heritage: A Biography of Wayne Township, Illinois, 1834–1984*. Wayne, Ill.: Wayne Community Association, 1984.

Bodge, George M. *Soldiers in King Philip's War*. 1906. Reprint, Baltimore: Genealogical Publishing Company, 1967.

"Bond of Administration of Estate of Joshua Guppy Late of Beverly [Mass.] Deceased" (15 April 1740): No. 11984.

Bowers, Q. David. *History of Wolfeboro, N.H., 1770–1994*. 2 vols. Wolfeboro, N.H.: Wolfeboro Historical Society, 1996.

Bowman, Walter P. *Lake Wentworth*. Wolfeboro, N.H.: Lake Wentworth Association, 1956.

Brigden, Theodore H. *Around Dimon's Corner: A History of North Wolfeboro, New Hampshire*. Wolfeboro, N.H.: North Wolfeboro Area Association, 1985.

Brookfield (N.H.) Town Records. Unpublished. New Hampshire State Library, Concord.

Brown, Charles Brockden. *Edgar Huntly.* 1799. Reprint, edited by David Stine-back, New Haven, Conn.: New College and University Press, 1973.

Bruchac, Joseph. *The Faithful Hunter: Abenaki Stories.* Greenfield Center, N.Y.: Greenfield Review Press, 1988.

———. *Lasting Echoes: An Oral History of Native American People.* New York: Avon Books, 1997.

———. *The Wind Eagle and Other Abenaki Stories.* Greenfield Center, N.Y.: Bow-man Books, 1985.

Bryent, Walter. "Walter Bryent's Winnipesaukee Journal, 1747." *The New-England Historical and Genealogical Register* 32 (1878): 297–302.

Burleigh, Charles. *The Genealogy and History of the Ingalls Family in America.* Mal-den, Mass.: Geo. E. Dunbar, 1903.

———. *The Genealogy of the Burley or Burleigh Family of America.* Portland, Maine: B. Thurston & Co., 1880.

Bushman, Claudia L. *"A Good Poor Man's Wife": Being a Chronicle of Harriet Hanson Robinson and Her Family in Nineteenth-Century New England.* Hanover, N.H.: University Press of New England, 1981.

Buzzell, John. *The Life of Elder Benjamin Randal.* Limerick, Maine: Hobbs, Wood-man & Co., 1827.

Calloway, Colin G., ed. *After King Philip's War: Presence and Persistence in Indian New England.* Hanover, N.H.: University Press of New England, 1997.

———. *Dawnland Encounters: Indians and Europeans in Northern New England.* Hanover, N.H.: University Press of New England, 1991.

———. *North Country Captives: Selected Narratives of Indian Captivity from Vermont and New Hampshire.* Hanover, N.H.: University Press of New England, 1992.

Cane, Aleta Feinsod, and Susan Alves, eds. *"The Only Efficient Instrument": American Women Writers and the Periodical, 1837–1916.* Iowa City: University of Iowa Press, 2001.

Canney, Robert S. *The Early Marriages of Strafford County, New Hampshire, 1630–1850.* 2 vols. Bowie, Md.: Heritage Books, 1995.

Carpenter, Cecelia Svinth. *How to Research American Indian Blood Lines.* Bountiful, Utah: Heritage Quest, 1999.

Case, Eliphalet. "A Sketch of Lowell." *Star of Bethlehem* (Lowell, Mass., and Man-chester, N.H.), 13 March 1841.

Cemetery Readings [containing lists of cemeteries in Du Page County, Ill., and also some lists from Kane, Will, and Cook counties] (2 vols., loose-leaf). N.p., 19?. Held by Wheaton (Ill.) Public Library.

Chase, Carolyn D., John E. Bowker, and Ann Bailey Pinkham. *Our Yesterdays: The Story of Brookfield, New Hampshire.* Brookfield, N.H.: Queen's Bay Publish-ing, 1999.

Child, Lydia Maria. "Adventure in the Woods." 1826. In *Nineteenth-Century American Women Writers: An Anthology.* Edited by Karen L. Kilcup. Oxford: Black-well Publishers, 1997, 65–68.

————. *The First Settlers of New-England: or, Conquest of the Pequods, Narragansets and Pokanokets. As Related by a Mother to Her Children.* By a Lady of Massachusetts. Boston: Munroe and Francis, 1829.

————. *Hobomok; A Tale of Early Times.* 1824. In *Hobomok, and Other Writings on Indians.* Edited by Carolyn L. Karcher. New Brunswick: Rutgers University Press, 1986, 3–150.

Church of Jesus Christ of Latter-Day Saints. *Family Search International Genealogical Index.* Online. Internet. Available: http://www.familysearch.org (20 July 2002).

Cole, Emily E. "The Early Meserves." Unpublished typescript microfilmed by the Genealogical Society, Salt Lake City, Utah, 1952.

Coleman, Emma Lewis. *New England Captives Carried to Canada between 1677 and 1760.* 2 vols. Portland, Maine: Southworth Press, 1925.

Cornelius, Elias. *The Little Osage Captive, an Authentic Narrative.* Boston: Samuel T. Armstrong and Crocker & Brewster; New York: John P. Haven, 1822.

Cutter, William Richard, comp. *New England Families, Genealogical and Memorial.* 4 vols. Baltimore: Clearfield, 1994.

D. "Female Education." *The Lady's Pearl* (Lowell, Mass.) 1 (1840): 154–55.

"Dam, Moses." Portsmouth Family Records, microfilm held by New Hampshire State Library (Concord, N.H.), A–H.

Dame, Clarence E. "Descendants of Dea. John Dam of Dover, N.H." *New England Historical and Genealogical Register* 111 (1957): 45–55.

Davidson, Cathy N. *Revolution and the Word: The Rise of the Novel in America.* New York: Oxford University Press, 1986.

Davidson, Cathy N., and Linda Wagner-Martin, eds. *Oxford Companion to Women's Writing in the United States.* New York: Oxford University Press, 1995.

Day, Gordon M. *In Search of New England's Native Past: Selected Essays by Gordon M. Day.* Edited by Michael K. Foster and William Cowan. Amherst: University of Massachusetts Press, 1998.

Day, Gordon M., and Michael K. Foster. "Oral Literature of the Northeastern Algonquians and the Northern Iroquoians." In *Dictionary of Native American Literature.* Edited by Andrew Wiget. New York: Garland Publishing, 1994, 73–82.

"The Death-List of a Day. An Eminent New York Journalist Is Dead." *New York Times*, 10 March 1881, 5.

Donovan, Josephine. *New England Local Color Literature: A Women's Tradition.* New York: Frederick Ungar, 1983.

Douglas, Ann. *The Feminization of American Culture.* New York: Knopf, 1977.

Drake, Samuel G. *Biography and History of the Indians of North America.* 7th ed., rev. and enl. Boston: Antiquarian Institute, 1837.

————. *History of the Early Discovery of America and Landing of the Pilgrims. With a Biography of the Indians of North America.* 2 vols. Boston: Higgins and Bradley, 1854.

————. *Indian Captivities; or, Life in the Wigwam.* 1851. Reprint, New York: AMS Press, 1975.

Dublin, Thomas. *Women at Work: The Transformation of Work and Community in Lowell, Massachusetts, 1826–1860.* 2d ed. New York: Columbia University Press, 1979.

Editors. "The Garland of the Mills." *Lowell Offering* Ser. 1, no 4 (March 1841): 64.

————. "A social meeting . . ." *Lowell Offering* Ser. 1, no. 2 (December 1840): 19.

————. "To Readers and Correspondents." *Lowell Offering* Ser. 1, no. 3 (February 1841).

————. "We have many excellent articles . . ." *Lowell Offering* Ser. 1, no. 4 (March 1841): 64.

Eisler, Benita, ed. *The Lowell Offering: Writings by New England Mill Women (1840–1845).* 1977. Reprint, New York: W. W. Norton, 1997.

Erlenkotter, Donald. "Boutell-Boutelle-Boutwell: Descendants of James Bowtell of Salem and Lynn." Unpublished typescript, 1999.

Evans, Helen F., ed. *Abstracts of the Probate Records of Strafford County, N.H., 1771–1799.* Bedford, N.H.: H. F. Evans, 1983.

F., H. [Farley, Harriet]. "Editorial." *Lowell Offering* 3, no. 2 (November 1842): 47–48.

————. "Editorial." *Lowell Offering* 3, no. 9 (June 1843): 213–16.

————. "Editorial: The Factory Girls and Their Magazine." *Lowell Offering* 5, no. 11 (November 1845): 263–64.

————. "Our Introductory." *The New England Offering* 7, no. 1 (January 1849): 1.

————. *Shells from the Strand of the Sea of Genius.* Boston: James Munroe, 1847.

"Factory Life—Romance and Reality." *The Voice of Industry* 3.21 (3 December 1847).

Featherston, James S. "Samuel S. Chamberlain (25 Sept 1851–25 January 1916)." In *American Newspaper Journalists, 1901–1925.* Edited by Perry J. Ashley. Detroit: Gale Research Co., 1984, 38–42.

Feister, Lois M., and Bonnie Pulis. "Molly Brant: Her Domestic and Political Roles in Eighteenth-Century New York." In *Northeastern Indian Lives, 1632–1816.* Edited by Robert S. Grumet. Amherst: University of Massachusetts Press, 1996, 295–320.

Fetterley, Judith, and Marjorie Pryse. Introduction to *American Women Regionalists, 1850–1910.* New York: W. W. Norton, 1992, xi–xx.

Fipphen, John S. *Cemetery Inscriptions, Wolfeboro, New Hampshire.* Bowie, Md.: Heritage Books, 1993.

————. *1798 Direct Tax, New Hampshire District No. 13.* Bowie, Md.: Heritage Books, 1989.

First Church (Wakefield, N.H.). *Memorial of the One Hundredth Anniversary of the*

Organization of the First Church, and Ordination of the First Settled Town Minister of Wakefield, N.H. Wakefield, N.H.: Printed for the parish, 1886.

Foner, Philip S., ed. *The Factory Girls: A Collection of Writings on Life and Struggles in the New England Factories of the 1840s by the Factory Girls Themselves.* Urbana: University of Illinois Press, 1977.

Franklin, Benjamin. *The Complete Poor Richard Almanacks.* 2 vols. 1733–1758. Reprint, Barre, Mass.: Imprint Society, 1970.

Fuller, Margaret. "The Great Lawsuit. Man versus Men. Woman versus Women." July 1843. In *The Feminist Papers: From Adams to de Beauvoir.* Edited by Alice S. Rossi. 1973. Reprint, Boston: Northeastern University Press, 1988, 158–82.

———. *Woman in the Nineteenth Century.* 1845. Reprint, New York: W. W. Norton, 1971.

Garvin, Donna-Belle, and James L. Garvin. *On the Road North of Boston: New Hampshire Taverns and Turnpikes, 1700–1900.* Concord: New Hampshire Historical Society, 1988.

George, Nellie Palmer. *Old Newmarket, New Hampshire: Historical Sketches.* Exeter, N.H.: News-Letter Press, 1932.

Getchell, Sylvia Fitts. *The Tide Turns on the Lamprey: Vignettes in the Life of a River: A History of Newmarket, N.H.* Newmarket, N.H.: S. F. Getchell, 1984.

Gilmore, William J. *Reading Becomes a Necessity of Life: Material and Cultural Life in Rural New England, 1780–1835.* Knoxville: University of Tennessee Press, 1989.

Glazier, Prentiss. "Chamberlain Families of Early New England." *The American Genealogist* 51.3 (July 1975): 151–53.

Glos, Hattie G., and Frederick S. Weiser. *Wayne Community and Township History.* Rev. and enl. ed. [Glen Ellyn?], Ill.: Priv. print., 1953.

Gollin, Rita K. *Nathaniel Hawthorne and the Truth of Dreams.* Baton Rouge: Louisiana State University Press, 1979.

Goss, Winifred L., comp. *Colonial Gravestone Inscriptions in the State of New Hampshire.* Baltimore: Genealogical Pub. Co., 1974.

Green, Rayna. *American Indian Women: A Contextual Bibliography.* Bloomington: Indiana University Press, 1979.

Green, Rayna, and Frank W. Porter III. *Women in American Indian Society.* New York: Chelsea House, 1992.

Grumet, Robert S., ed. *Northeastern Indian Lives, 1632–1816.* Amherst: University of Massachusetts Press, 1996.

Guppy family papers, unpublished documents in the possession of Jill Cresey-Gross, Westford, Mass.

Guppy, Nicholas. "Genealogy of the Guppy Family." 1990. Unpublished typescript held by the Dover (N.H.) Public Library.

"Guppy Note. From North Church Records, Portsmouth, N.H." *Genealogical Bulletin* 1.15 (26 March 1904): 111.

H., L. T. "A Letter to Cousin Lucy." *Lowell Offering* 5, no. 5 (May 1845): 109–12.

Hale, Sarah Josepha Buell. *Northwood: A Tale of New England*. Boston: Bowles & Dearborn, 1827.
––––––. "An Old Maid." In *Traits of American Life*. Philadelphia: E. L. Carey & A. Hart, 1835, 247–58.
Ham, John R. *Dover, New Hampshire Marriages, 1623–1823*. Dover, N.H.: n.p., 1904.
––––––. "Ham Family in Dover, N.H." *New England Historical and Genealogical Register* 26 (1872): 388–94.
Ham, Thomas C. *Genealogy of the Ham Family and of the Young Family*. Arlington, Mass.: n.p., 1949.
Hamilton, Kristie. *America's Sketchbook: The Cultural Life of a Nineteenth-Century Literary Genre*. Athens: Ohio University Press, 1998.
Hammond, Otis G. *Notices from the New Hampshire Gazette, 1765–1800*. Lambertville, N.J.: Hunterdon House, 1970.
––––––, ed. *Probate Records of the Province of New Hampshire. Vol. 7 (1760–1763)*. Concord: State of New Hampshire, 1939.
Hand-Book for the Visiter to Lowell. Lowell, Mass.: D. Bixby and Co., 1848.
Handbook of North American Indians. Vol. 15, Northeast. Washington, D.C.: Smithsonian Institution Press, 1978.
Hayley, John W. *Tuftonboro, New Hampshire: An Historical Sketch*. Concord, N.H.: Rumford Press, 1923.
Hazen-Hammond, Susan. *Spider Woman's Web: Traditional Native American Tales about Women's Power*. New York: Berkley, 1999.
Hazlett, Charles A. *History of Rockingham County, New Hampshire, and Representative Citizens*. Chicago: Richmond-Arnold, 1915.
Henry, Lorraine Rainwaters. *Native American Directory: Vital Records of Maine, Massachusetts, Rhode Island, Connecticut, New York and Wisconsin*. Bowie, Md.: Heritage Books, 1998.
Herzog, Kristin. "Native American Oral Traditions." In *Oxford Companion to Women's Writing in the United States*. Edited by Cathy N. Davidson and Linda Wagner-Martin. New York: Oxford University Press, 1995, 607–9.
"Highlights of Historic Newmarket." Newmarket, N.H.: Published by the Town, 1998.
Hobbs, Michael. "Native American Literature." In *Reader's Guide to Literature in English*. Edited by Mark Hawkins-Dady. London, Chicago: Fitzroy Dearborn, 1996. 512–14.
Holbrook, Jay Mack. *New Hampshire 1732 Census*. Oxford, Mass.: Holbrook Research Institute, 1981.
Hurd, D. Hamilton. *History of Rockingham and Strafford Counties, New Hampshire, with Biographical Sketches of Many of Its Pioneers and Prominent Men*. Philadelphia: J. W. Lewis & Co., 1882.
Irving, Washington. *The Sketch Book of Geoffrey Crayon, Gent*. 1819–20. Reprint, New York: Penguin Books, 1988.
Irving, Washington, William Irving, and James Kirke Paulding. *Salmagundi; or,*

The Whim-Whams and Opinions of Launcelot Langstaff, Esq. & Others. 1807–08. In *History, Tales and Sketches.* New York: Library of America, 1983, 45–361.

Izard, Holly V. "Hepsibeth Hemenway's Portrait: A Native American Story." *Old-Time New England* 77.267 (Fall/Winter 1999): 49–85.

Jaskoski, Helen, ed. *Early Native American Writing: New Critical Essays.* Cambridge: Cambridge University Press, 1996.

Johnson, Steven F. *Ninnuock (the People): The Algonkian People of New England.* Marlborough, Mass.: Bliss Publishing, 1995.

Josephson, Hannah. *The Golden Threads: New England's Mill Girls and Magnates.* New York: Duell, Sloan and Pearce, 1949.

Kilcup, Karen L. "Writing 'The Red Woman's America': An Introduction to Writing by Earlier Native American Women." In *Native American Women's Writing, 1800–1924: An Anthology.* Edited by Karen L. Kilcup. Oxford: Blackwell Publishers, 2000. 1–12.

Kirkland, Caroline M. *A New Home—Who'll Follow? or, Glimpses of Western Life.* 1839. Excerpted in *The Meridian Anthology of Early American Women Writers.* Edited by Katharine M. Rogers. New York: Penguin, 1991, 318–42.

Knight, Charles, and Harriet Martineau, eds. *Mind amongst the Spindles: A Selection from the Lowell Offering, a Miscellany Wholly Composed by the Factory Girls of an American City.* London: Charles Knight, 1844.

Krupat, Arnold, ed. *Native American Autobiography: An Anthology.* Madison: University of Wisconsin Press, 1994.

Kulik, Gary, Roger Parks, and Theodore Z. Penn, eds. *The New England Mill Village, 1790–1860.* Cambridge, Mass.: MIT Press, 1982.

Larcom, Lucy. "Among Lowell Mill-Girls: A Reminiscence." *Atlantic Monthly,* November 1881: 593–612.

———. *A New England Girlhood: Outlined from Memory.* 1889. Reprint, Boston: Northeastern University Press, 1986.

———. *The Poetical Works of Lucy Larcom.* Boston: Houghton, Mifflin, 1884.

"The Late Mr. Chamberlain." *Harper's Weekly,* 26 March 1881, 204.

Libby, Charles T. *The Libby Family in America: 1602–1881.* 1882. Reprint, Salem, Mass.: Higginson Books, 1991.

"Lines for Newmarket." *The Gleaner* (Manchester, N.H.), 8 February 1845.

"A List of Deaths in Beverly, Made by Col. Robert Hale." *Essex Institute Historical Collections* 5 (1863): 16–24.

Littlefield, Daniel F., Jr., and James W. Parins. *American Indian and Alaska Native Newspapers and Periodicals, 1826–1924.* Westport, Conn.: Greenwood Press, 1984.

———. *A Biobibliography of Native American Writers, 1772–1924.* Metuchen, N.J.: Scarecrow Press, 1981.

———. *A Biobibliography of Native American Writers, 1772–1924: A Supplement.* Metuchen, N.J.: Scarecrow Press, 1985.

Lowell, Massachusetts. City Library. *Catalogue of the City School Library* and *1st Suppl. (January 1855).* Lowell: S. J. Varney, 1853.

————. *Catalogue of the City School Library, Lowell, Mass., Established May 20, 1844*. Lowell: Courier Steam Press, 1858.

Lowell, Massachusetts, First Unitarian Society. *Catalogue of Books of the Parish Library*. Lowell: S. J. Varney, 1854.

Lowell Circulating Library. *Catalogue of Books Contained in the Lowell Circulating Library, Connected with the Lowell Bookstore*. Lowell, Mass.: Stevens and Co., 1834.

Lowell Directory. Lowell, Mass.: various publishers, 1832–65.

"'The Lowell Offering.'" *North American Review* 52, no. 2 (1841): 538.

Marchalonis, Shirley. *The Worlds of Lucy Larcom, 1824–1893*. Athens: University of Georgia Press, 1989.

"Marriages." *Columbian Centinel* (Boston), 18 April 1834.

"Marriages and Deaths: Wakefield, N.H., 1784–1834." Unpublished typescript microfilmed by the Genealogical Society, Salt Lake City, Utah, 1952.

"Married." *Lowell Mercury* (Lowell, Mass.), 18 April 1834.

Massachusetts. Commissioners to Examine into the Condition of the Indians in the Commonwealth. *Report of the Commissioners Relating to the Condition of the Indians in Massachusetts*. Boston: n.p., 1849.

Masta, Henry Lorne *Abenaki Indian Legends, Grammar and Place Names*. Victoriaville, P.Q.: La Voix des boisfrancs, 1932.

Mather, Cotton. *Magnalia Christi Americana: or, The Ecclesiastical History of New-England*. 2 vols. 1702. Reprint, Hartford: Silas Andrus, 1820.

McBride, Bunny. *Women of the Dawn*. Lincoln: University of Nebraska Press, 1999.

McBride, Bunny, and Harald L. Prins. "Walking the Medicine Line: Molly Ockett, a Pigwacket Doctor." In *Northeastern Indian Lives, 1632–1816*. Edited by Robert S. Grumet. Amherst: University of Massachusetts Press, 1996, 321–47.

McCallum, James D., ed. *The Letters of Eleazar Wheelock's Indians*. Hanover, N.H.: Dartmouth College Publications, 1932.

McCauley, Elfrieda B. "The New England Mill Girls: Feminine Influence in the Development of Public Libraries in New England, 1820–1860." Ph.D. diss., Columbia University, 1971.

McDuffee, Franklin. *History of the Town of Rochester, New Hampshire, from 1722 to 1890*. Manchester, N.H.: J. B. Clarke Co., 1892.

Meader, Robert F. W. *The Saga of a Palace: The Story of Wentworth House at Wolfeboro, New Hampshire*. Wolfeboro, N.H.: Wolfeboro Historical Society, 1962.

Merrill, Georgia Drew, ed. *History of Carroll County, New Hampshire*. Boston: W. A. Fergusson & Co., 1889.

Meserve Family Association. "The Meserve Family: The First Four Generations, with Ancestry of Clement-1 Meserve of Portsmouth, N.H." Unpublished typescript. Edited by Michael J. Denis. Oakland, Maine: Danbury House, 1982.

Metcalf, Henry H., ed. *Probate Records of the Province of New Hampshire. Vol. 3 (1741–1749)*. Concord, N.H.: Rumford Press, 1916.

Middlesex Mechanic Association (Lowell, Mass.). *A Catalogue of the Library of the Middlesex Mechanic Association, at Lowell, Mass*. Lowell, Mass.: Leonard Huntress, 1840.

"Miss Esther M. Meserve. 40392." *Lineage Book*. Washington, D.C.: National Society of the Daughters of the American Revolution, 1915. 41:149–50.

Mitford, Mary Russell. *Our Village*. 1824–32. Reprint, London: Macmillan, 1910.

Minority Military Service, New Hampshire, Vermont, 1775–1783. Washington, D.C.: National Society of the Daughters of the American Revolution, 1991.

Moody, Richard, ed. *Dramas from the American Theatre, 1762–1909*. Cleveland: World Publishing, 1966.

Moore, Howard Parker. *A Genealogy of the First Five Generations in America of the Lang Family*. Rutland, Vt.: Tuttle Co., 1935.

Mullin, Molly H. "Native American Writing: Overview." In *Oxford Companion to Women's Writing in the United States*. Edited by Cathy N. Davidson and Linda Wagner-Martin. New York: Oxford University Press, 1995, 611–15.

National Society of the Daughters of the American Revolution. *Lineage Book*. Vol. 35. Compiled by Sarah Hall Johnston. Washington, D.C., 1912.

"Native American Genealogy," State Historical Society of Missouri. Online. Internet. Available: http://www.system.missouri.edu/shs/nativeam.html (28 July 2002).

"Ne-Do-Ba (Friends)." Online. Internet. Available: http://avcnet.bates.edu/ne-do-ba/ (28 July 2002).

New Hampshire. *Provincial and State Papers*. 40 vols. Concord, N.H.: Published by authority of the legislature of New Hampshire, 1867–1942.

The New Hampshire Genealogical Record. 1.1 (July 1903)–7.2 (April 1910). Reprint, Bowie, Md.: Heritage Books, 1988.

North Church (Portsmouth, N.H.). *Records of North Church, Portsmouth, N.H.* Compiled by Louise H. Rainey. New York: n.p., 1931.

"Notices." *Lowell Offering* 3, no. 4 (January 1843): inside back cover.

Obituary. Harriet (Guppy) Kelley. "New England Items: New Hampshire." *Boston Morning Journal*, 18 December 1877, 4.

"Obituary. Ivory Chamberlain." *New-York Daily Tribune*, 10 March 1881.

"Obituary. Ivory Chamberlain, Journalist." *New York Herald*, 10 March 1881.

O'Brien, Jean M. "'Divorced' from the Land: Resistance and Survival of Indian Women in Eighteenth-Century New England." In *After King Philip's War*. Edited by Colin G. Calloway. Hanover, N.H.: University Press of New England, 1997, 144–61.

O'Meara, Kathy. *Remember When: A Collection of Old Photographs of Wolfeboro, N.H.* Wolfeboro, N.H.: Wolfeboro Chamber of Commerce, 1976.

"Our New York Letter. The Late Ivory Chamberlain." *Concord {N.H.} Daily Monitor*, 16 March 1881.

Owens, Louis. *Mixedblood Messages: Literature, Film, Family, Place.* Norman: University of Oklahoma Press, 1998.

Parker, Benjamin F. *History of the Town of Wolfeborough, New Hampshire.* 1901. Reprint, Wolfeboro, N.H.: Wolfeboro Historical Society, 1988.

Parker, Trudy Ann (Abenaki). *Aunt Sarah, Woman of the Dawnland: The 108 Winters of an Abenaki Healing Woman.* Lancaster, N.H.: Dawnland Publications, 1994.

Percy, Thomas. *Reliques of Ancient English Poetry.* 3 vols. 1765. Reprint, edited by Henry B. Wheatley, New York: Dover Publications, 1966.

Perdue, Theda, ed. *Cherokee Editor: The Writings of Elias Boudinot.* Knoxville: University of Tennessee Press, 1983.

Peters, Marjorie Herlache, ed. *Du Page County, Illinois Churches and Their Records, 1833–1920.* Lombard, Ill.: Lombard Suburban Genealogical Society, 1981.

—————. *Landowners of Du Page County, Illinois, 1835–1904: An Index to Plat Maps and Related Sources.* Lombard, Ill.: Du Page County Genealogical Society, 1984.

Peyer, Bernd C. *The Tutor'd Mind: Indian Missionary-Writers in Antebellum America.* Amherst: University of Massachusetts Press, 1997.

—————, ed. *The Elders Wrote: An Anthology of Early Prose by North American Indians, 1768–1931.* Berlin: Dietrich Reimer, 1982.

Plato, Ann. *Essays including Biographies and Miscellaneous Pieces, in Prose and Poetry.* 1841. Reprint, New York: Oxford University Press, 1988.

Poor Sarah; or, The Indian Woman. 1820. Reprint, New York: American Tract Society, [between 1827 and 1833].

Potter, Chandler E. *The Military History of the State of New Hampshire, 1623–1861.* 2 vols. in 1. Baltimore: Genealogical Publishing Company, 1972.

Pritchard, Evan (Micmac). *No Word for Time: The Way of the Algonquin People.* Tulsa, Okla.: Council Oak Books, 1997.

Prude, Jonathan. *The Coming of Industrial Order: Town and Factory Life in Rural Massachusetts, 1810–1860.* Cambridge, Eng.: Cambridge University Press, 1983.

Ranta, Judith A. *Women and Children of the Mills: An Annotated Guide to Nineteenth-Century American Textile Factory Literature.* Westport, Conn.: Greenwood Press, 1999.

"Recent Deaths: Ivory Chamberlain." *Boston Evening Transcript*, 11 March 1881, 8.

Reynolds, David S. *Beneath the American Renaissance: The Subversive Imagination in the Age of Emerson and Melville.* New York: Knopf, 1988.

Richmond, C. W. *A History of the County of Du Page, Illinois.* 1857. Reprint, Naperville, Ill.: Naperville Sun, 1974.

Robb, Ruth Flesher. *Du Page County, Illinois, Probate Records 1839 to 1900 Inclusive.* Du Page County, Ill., 199?.

—————. "1850 Du Page County, Illinois, Federal Census." Unpublished typescript. November, 1976.

Robertson, Susanne M. *Programme—Lowell Musicale (1825–1900): A Musical Portrait of the Spindle City*. N.p.: Euterpe Press, 1984.

Robinson, Harriet Hanson. "The Life of the Early Mill-Girls." *Journal of Social Science* 16 (December 1882): 127–40.

———. *Loom and Spindle; or, Life among the Early Mill Girls*. Rev. ed. 1898. Reprint, Kaulua, Hawaii: Press Pacifica, 1976.

———. *Massachusetts in the Woman Suffrage Movement*. Boston: Roberts Brothers, 1881.

Robinson, Harriet Hanson, and Harriette Lucy Robinson Shattuck. Papers, 1833–1937. Schlesinger Library, Radcliffe College.

Roemer, Kenneth M., ed. *Native American Writers of the United States*. Detroit: Gale, 1997.

Ruoff, A. LaVonne Brown. *American Indian Literatures*. New York: Modern Language Association, 1990.

———. *Literatures of the American Indian*. New York: Chelsea House, 1991.

Rust, Albert D. *Record of the Rust Family*. Waco, Tex.: A. Rust, 1891.

Salmon, Marylynn. *Women and the Law of Property in Early America*. Chapel Hill: University of North Carolina Press, 1986.

Sanborn, Frank B. *New Hampshire: An Epitome of Popular Government*. Boston: Houghton, Mifflin, 1904.

Savage, James. *A Genealogical Dictionary of the First Settlers of New England*. 4 vols. 1860–62. Reprint, Baltimore: Genealogical Publishing Co., 1990.

Scales, John. *Colonial Era History of Dover, New Hampshire*. 1923. Reprint, Bowie, Md.: Heritage Books, 1977.

———, ed. "Some Descendants of Deacon John Dam of Dover, N.H., 1633." *New England Historical and Genealogical Register* 65 (1911): 212–19, 310–14.

Schoolcraft, Henry Rowe. *The Literary Voyager; or, Muzzeniegun*. 1826–27. Reprint, Westport, Conn.: Greenwood Press, 1974.

Schouler, William. "Report of the Committee on the Ten Hour System." *Lowell Courier*, 19 April 1845.

Sedgwick, Catharine Maria. *Hope Leslie; or Early Times in the Massachusetts*. 1827. Reprint, New York: Garrett Press, 1969.

———. "Old Maids." In *Tales and Sketches*. Philadelphia: Carey, Lea, and Blanchard, 1835, 97–116.

Selden, Bernice. *The Mill Girls: Lucy Larcom, Harriet Hanson Robinson, Sarah G. Bagley*. New York: Atheneum, 1983.

Sigourney, Lydia H. *Traits of the Aborigines of America: A Poem*. Cambridge, Mass.: University Press, 1822.

Simmons, William. *Spirit of the New England Tribes: Indian History and Folklore, 1620–1984*. Hanover, N.H.: University Press of New England, 1986.

Sinnett, Charles N. *The Ham Family in New Hampshire and Maine*. Fertile, Minn., 1924.

South Church, Portsmouth, N.H. "Church Records." Unpublished typescript microfilmed by the Genealogical Society, Salt Lake City, Utah, 1952.

Speare, Eva A., comp. *More New Hampshire Folk Tales*. Brattleboro, Vt.: Stephen Daye Press, 1936.

————. *New Hampshire Folk Tales*. Rev. 1964. Reprint, Charlestown, N.H.: Old Fort No. 4 Associates, 1993.

Stackpole, Everett S., Lucien Thompson, and Winthrop S. Meserve. *History of the Town of Durham, New Hampshire (Oyster River Plantation) with Genealogical Notes*. 2 vols. Durham, N.H.: Pub. by vote of the town, 1913.

Stearns, Bertha Monica. "Early Factory Magazines in New England: The *Lowell Offering* and Its Contemporaries." *Journal of Economic and Business History* 2.4 (August 1930): 685–705.

Stearns, Ezra S., ed. *Genealogical and Family History of the State of New Hampshire*. 4 vols. 1908. Reprint, West Jordan, Utah: Stemmons Publishing, 1990.

Stone, John Augustus. *Metamora; or, The Last of the Wampanoags*. 1829. In *Dramas from the American Theatre, 1762–1909*. Edited by Richard Moody. Cleveland: World Publishing, 1966, 205–27.

Swann, Brian, and Arnold Krupat, eds. *I Tell You Now: Autobiographical Essays by Native American Writers*. Lincoln: University of Nebraska Press, 1987.

Taylor, Catherine. "Native American Writing: Nonfiction." In *Oxford Companion to Women's Writing in the United States*. Edited by Cathy N. Davidson and Linda Wagner-Martin. New York: Oxford University Press, 1995, 618–20.

Tenney, Tabitha G. *Female Quixotism: Exhibited in the Romantic Opinions and Extravagant Adventures of Dorcasina Sheldon*. 1801. Reprint, New York: Oxford University Press, 1992.

Thatcher, Benjamin B. *Indian Biography*. 2 vols. New York: Harper & Brothers, 1836.

Thomas, Abel Charles. *Autobiography of Rev. Abel C. Thomas*. Boston: J. M. Usher, 1852.

————. "Editorial." *Lowell Ofering* 1, no. 6 (August 1841): inside back cover.

————. "Editorial Corner." *Lowell Offering* Ser. 1, no. 1 (October 1840): 16.

————. "Editor's Valedictory." *Lowell Offering* 2, no. 11–12 (August 1842): 379–80.

————. "Permanency of the Offering." *Lowell Offering* Ser. 1, no. 4 (March 1841).

————. "Things Needful." *Star of Bethlehem* (Lowell, Mass., and Manchester, N.H.), 27 May 1843.

Thompson, Mary P. *Landmarks in Ancient Dover, New Hampshire*. Complete ed. 1892. Reprint, Durham, N.H.: Durham Historic Association, 1965.

Thompson Brothers & Burr. "Map of Wayne Township." In *Combination Atlas Map of Du Page County, Illinois*. 1874. Reprint, Wheaton, Ill.: Du Page County Historical Society, 1975, 98–99. Internet, available: http://users. anet.com/~jeffb/dupagewb/atlas.htm (28 July 2002).

————. "Wayne." In *Combination Atlas Map of Du Page County, Illinois*. 1874. Reprint, Wheaton, Ill.: Du Page County Historical Society, 1975, 7–8.

Ulrich, Laurel Thatcher. *The Age of Homespun: Objects and Stories in the Creation of an American Myth.* New York: Knopf, 2001.

Velie, Alan R., ed. *American Indian Literature: An Anthology.* Rev. ed. Norman: University of Oklahoma Press, 1991.

Vital Records of Dover, New Hampshire, 1686–1850. 1894. Reprint, Bowie, Md.: Heritage Books, 1977.

Vital Records of Lowell, Massachusetts, to the End of the Year 1849. 4 vols. Salem, Mass.: Essex Institute, 1930.

W., J. S. [Jane S. Welch]. "The Mother and Daughter." *Lowell Offering* 4, no. 6 (April 1844): 126–28.

Walker, Nancy A. *A Very Serious Thing: Women's Humor and American Culture.* Minneapolis: University of Minnesota Press, 1988.

Walker, Nancy A., and Zita Dresner, eds. *Redressing the Balance: American Women's Literary Humor from Colonial Times to the 1980s.* Jackson: University Press of Mississippi, 1988.

"Wayne." *Wheaton Illinoian,* 1 October 1886, 8.

Weiser, Frederick S., ed. *Genealogical and Historical Records of Wayne Township:* Vol. 1, *Genealogical.* Wayne, Ill.: Wayne Township, 1953.

"Wentworth House Plantation, 1767–1820: A Brief History." Wolfeboro, N.H.: Friends of the Governor Wentworth State Historic Site, 199?.

Whipple, Frances H. (m. Green, m. McDougall). *Memoirs of Elleanor Eldridge.* 2nd ed. 1843. Reprint, Salem, N.H.: Ayer, 1971.

Whittier, John Greenleaf. *Legends of New England.* 1831. Reprint, Baltimore: Clearfield, 1992.

———. *Supernaturalism of New England.* 1847. Reprint, Baltimore: Clearfield, 1993.

———. "To the National Era." 1853. In *The Letters of John Greenleaf Whittier.* Edited by John B. Pickard. Cambridge, Mass.: Belknap Press of Harvard University, 1975. Vol. 2 (1846–60): 227–33.

Wiget, Andrew, ed. *Critical Essays on Native American Literature.* Boston: G. K. Hall, 1985.

———. *Native American Literature.* Boston: Twayne Publishers, 1985.

Wilbur, C. Keith. *The New England Indians.* 2nd ed. Old Saybrook, Conn.: Globe Pequot Press, 1996.

Wilderson, Paul W. *Governor John Wentworth and the American Revolution.* Hanover, N.H.: University Press of New England, 1994.

Williams, Roger. *A Key into the Language of America.* 1643. Excerpted in *The Heath Anthology of American Literature.* 3d ed. Paul Lauter, general editor. Boston: Houghton Mifflin, 1998, 269–87.

Wilson, Emily S. *Inhabitants of New Hampshire, 1776.* Lambertville, N.J.: Hunterdon House, 1983.

Winnetka Public Library. Genealogy Projects Committee. *An Index to the Names of Persons Appearing in "History of Du Page County, Illinois."* Thomson, Ill.: Heritage House, 1973.

Wiseman, Frederick Matthew. *The Voice of the Dawn: An Autohistory of the Abenaki Nation*. Hanover, N.H.: University Press of New England, 2001.

"Witchcraft in New-Hampshire, 1656." *Collections of the New-Hampshire Historical Society, for the Year 1824* 1:255–57.

"Witchcraft in New Hampshire and the Witchtrot Road." *Meetings in Print: Wakefield-Brookfield Historical Society* 2.2 (Summer 1947).

Wolfboro (N.H.) Town Records. Unpublished. New Hampshire State Library, Concord, N.H.

"Yeaton. Mary Yeaton." *Boston Transcript Genealogical Columns*, 7719 (10 October 1928).

Index

Abenaki, 8, 9, 15, 18. *See also* Algonkian Confederacy; New England Native Americans; Penobscot

Addison, Daniel D., 54, 85

"Adventure in the Woods" (Child), 13, 64, 91

African Americans, 204, 209–10

After King Philip's War (Calloway), 8

"Afternoon Ramble, An" (S. T.), 101

Age of Homespun, The (Ulrich), 8, 114

Algic Researches (Schoolcraft), 72, 75

Algonkian Confederacy, 7, 63, 86, 87, 90. *See also* Abenaki; Narragansett; New England Native Americans; Penobscot

"Allegory, An" (N. S. L.), 100

Allen, Ebenezer, 17, 179–81, 254*n*114

Alves, Susan, 80

American Indian Women (Bataille and Sands), 106, 108

American Indians. *See* Native Americans

American Lady, An, *The Hapless Orphan*, 38

American Revolution. *See* Revolutionary War

American Women Regionalists, 1850–1910 (Fetterley and Pryse), 110

"Among Lowell Mill-Girls" (Larcom), 77

Anderson, Rufus B., 13, 66, 74

Apess, Mary, 67

Apess, William (Pequot), 12, 13, 90; *Eulogy on King Philip*, 95–96; *The Experiences of Five Christian Indians of the Pequot Tribe*, 67, 99; *A Son of the Forest*, 99

Arabian Nights' Entertainments, 70, 72

Arthur, T. S., "Ten Nights in a Barroom," 61

As You Like It (Shakespeare), 251*n*29

Asylum; or, Alonzo and Melissa, The (Mitchell), 70

"Aunt 'Dear Soul,'" 120–21

Aunt Sarah, Woman of the Dawnland (Parker), 4

Autobiography, 13–14, 106, 108

Autobiography of Rev. Abel C. Thomas (Thomas), 78, 84

Awashonks (Sakonnet), 113

Bagley, Sarah, 5

Bame-wa-wa-ge-zhik-a-quay. *See* Schoolcraft, Jane Johnston

Barlow, Joel, *The Hasty-Pudding*, 255*n*142

Barnum, Austin (BGC's son-in-law), 51, 60, 242–43*n*105

Barnum, Comfort Chamberlain (BGC's daughter), 28, 51, 58, 59–60, 242–43*n*105

Bassett, Hannah, 17

Bassett, John, 17, 254*n*113

Bataille, Gretchen M.,106, 109

Battle of Fallen Timbers, 95, 249–50*n*1

Belknap, Jeremy, *The History of New-Hampshire*, 87

Beneath the American Renaissance (Reynolds), 13

Bible, 34, 64, 100

Biography and History of the Indians of North America (Drake), 72, 88

"Black Glove, The," 17, 106

Blanchard, Amos, 47

Blueberry picking, 216–20

Bodge, George M., 18

Boston Morning Journal, 48

Boudinot, Elias (Cherokee), 66–67, 243*n*115

Boutwell, Betsey. *See* Chamberlain, Betsey Guppy

Boutwell, Charles (BGC's third husband), 52–57, 60, 62, 241–42*n*89

Boutwell, Charles M. (BGC's stepson), 56

Boutwell, George (BGC's stepson), 56

Boutwell, Lafayette (BGC's stepson), 56

Bowers, Q. David., 18

Bowker, John E., 42

Brant, Molly (Mohawk), 113

"Bridemaid, The" (Gould), 251*n*43

Brookfield, N.H.: Betsey and Josiah Chamberlain's home in, xi, 37–39, 41–42; as BGC's birthplace, 21; BGC teaching school in, 35–37; as Joshua and Sarah Guppy's home, 24; vital records of, 51; William Guppy in, 28, 29, 31; witchcraft in, 118, 254*n*109

Brown, Catharine (Cherokee), 65–66

Brown, Charles Brockden, *Edgar Huntly*, 119

Bruchac, Joseph (Abenaki), 88

Bryant, William Cullen, "An Indian at the Burial-Place of His Fathers," 97